China's Opening Society

Since the instigation of the reform and open-door policy almost three decades ago, China has been experiencing rapid economic growth. An increasingly open economy has created the sound infrastructure necessary for an open society. Communist regimes in the Soviet Union and Eastern Europe were not able to survive reform, and the fall of these regimes led to democratisation. Despite an open economy and an opening society, China's political system remains authoritarian. Yet, the regime has found it increasingly difficult to govern its increasingly open and complicated society. Will China be able to establish good governance?

This book answers this key question by focusing on the dynamics of the development of the non-state sector and its impact on governance in China. It examines international experiences of the development of civil society and sustainable development, ranging from international NGOs and global civil society to newly rising civil organisations in Russia. It then explores the major issues facing the development of the non-state sector and of governance in China, covering important areas such as corporate social responsibility, the Internet and deliberative institutions. Special attention is paid to development in Zhejiang province, which has a developed private sector. This book also discusses the experiences of international NGOs in China and how they have promoted democratic governance in rural China.

Zheng Yongnian is Professor and Director of Research, China Policy Institute, School of Contemporary Chinese Studies, University of Nottingham. He researches on China's domestic transformation and its external impact. He has written numerous books, including *Discovering Chinese Nationalism in China*, *Globalization and State Transformation in China*, *Will China Become Democratic?* and *Technological Empowerment: The Internet, State and Society in China*. **Joseph Fewsmith** is Director of East Asian Studies Program and Professor of International Relations and Political Science at Boston University. He is also a research associate of the John King Fairbank Center for East Asian Studies at Harvard University. His books include *China Since Tiananmen: The Politics of Transition*; a second edition of *China since Tiaanmen: From Deng Xiaoping to Hu Jintao* is to be published in 2008.

China policy series
Edited by Zheng Yongnian
University of Nottingham, UK

China's Opening Society

The non-state sector and governance

**Edited by Zheng Yongnian and
Joseph Fewsmith**

Routledge
Taylor & Francis Group

LONDON AND NEW YORK

First published 2008
by Routledge
2 Park Square, Milton Park, Abingdon, Oxon OX14 4RN

Simultaneously published in the USA and Canada
by Routledge
270 Madison Ave, New York, NY 10016

Routledge is an imprint of the Taylor & Francis Group, an informa business

Transferred to Digital Printing 2009

© 2008 Selection and editorial matter, Zheng Yongnian and Joseph
Fewsmith; individual contributors, the contributors

Typeset in Times by Wearset Ltd, Boldon, Tyne and Wear

British Library Cataloguing in Publication Data
A catalogue record for this book is available from the British Library

Library of Congress Cataloging in Publication Data
China's opening society: the non-state sector and governance/edited by
Zheng Yongnian and Joseph Fewsmith.
p. cm. – (China policy series)
Includes index.
1. Non-governmental organizations–China. 2. Civil society–China. I.
Zheng, Yongnian. II. Fewsmith, Joseph, 1949–

JQ1516.C45275 2008
320.951-dc22   2007034243

ISBN10: 0-415-45176-0 (hbk)
ISBN10: 0-415-54639-7 (pbk)
ISBN10: 0-203-93092-4 (ebk)

ISBN13: 978-0-415-45176-5 (hbk)
ISBN13: 978-0-415-54639-3 (pbk)
ISBN13: 978-0-203-93092-2 (ebk)

Contents

Tables

Editors and contributors

Baogang He, Professor and Chair in International Studies, the School of Politics and International Studies, Deakin University, Australia.

Catherine Goetze, Lecturer, School of Politics and International Relations, The University of Nottingham, UK.

Gary D. Rawnsley, Professor of International Communications, Institute of Communication Studies, University of Leeds, UK.

Grigory A. Kliucharev, Professor of Comparative Education, Institute of Sociology, Russian Academy of Sciences, Russia.

Jean-Philippe Béja, Senior Research Fellow CNRS/CERI, Paris, France.

Joseph Fewsmith, Professor of Political Science, Department of International Relations and Political Science, Boston University, USA.

Qingshan Tan, Professor, Department of Political Science, Cleveland State University, USA.

Vanessa Pupavac, Lecturer, School of Politics and International Relations, The University of Nottingham, UK.

W. John Morgan, UNESCO Chair of the Political Economy of Education, Centre for Comparative Education Research, University of Nottingham, UK.

Yang Zhong, Professor of Political Science, The University of Tennessee, USA.

Yiyi Lu, Research Fellow, China Policy Institute, School of Contemporary Chinese Studies, University of Nottingham, and Research Associate, the Chatham House, UK.

Youxing Lang, Professor, the School of Government and Public Administration, Zhejiang University, China.

Zengke He, Senior Fellow, China Centre for Comparative Politics and Economics, Beijing, China.

Zheng Yongnian, Professor and Director of Research, China Policy Institute, School of Contemporary Chinese Studies, The University of Nottingham, UK.

Acknowledgements

The chapters in this volume were initially presented at the International Conference on The Development of the Non-State Sector, Local Governance and Sustainable Development in China held at Zhejiang University, Hangzhou, China, 24–25 June 2006. The conference was co-sponsored by the China Policy Institute (CPI), School of Contemporary Chinese Studies, University of Nottingham and the Department of Political Science and Public Administration, Zhejiang University. Thanks go to Elizabeth Wright, Richard Pascoe, Chen Shengyong, Youxing Lang and many others who provided valuable support for the conference. Mr Peter Sowden and Mr Tom Bates at Routledge provided useful guides from the very beginning of the project to the end of production.

Zheng Yongnian
Joseph Fewsmith

Introduction

Zheng Yongnian and Joseph Fewsmith

China's transition and uncertainties

Since the instigation of the reform and open-door policy of 1978, China has been undergoing rapid socio-economic transformation, and its economy is growing at an annual rate of more than 9 per cent. China's per capita gross domestic product (GDP) reached US$1,200 in 2004, a figure approaching that of middle income countries. An increasingly open economy has created the sound infrastructure necessary for an open society. By 2003, China had overtaken the USA to become the world's largest telephone market, and today, China's registered Internet users number over 1,300 million and form the world's second largest 'Web population' after the USA.

Communist regimes in the Soviet Union and Eastern Europe were not able to survive reform, and the fall of these regimes led to democratisation. Despite an open economy and an opening society, China's political system remains authoritarian. Yet, the regime has found it increasingly difficult to govern its increasingly open and complicated society. Will China be able to develop the good governance needed to cope with drastic socio-economic transformation? This question, the key concern among proponents of 'China uncertainties' which have developed within and outside China recently, is not easily answered. Some would argue that the futures of India, Russia and even Indonesia can be charted with more certainty, since all of these countries have an established democratic political framework. The Chinese Communist Party (CCP) has remained the only ruling organisation in the country since 1949, and there are no alternatives available for the people to choose.

All transformations bring about uncertainties. China's current transformation is unprecedented in the history of modern states, and its associated uncertainties are understandable. The question is, Can China overcome all of them?

To cope with all of the challenges resulting from socio-economic transformation, political transition is the key. Political transition can be understood as transformation from authoritarianism towards an uncertain 'something else', as Guillermo O'Donnell and Philippe Schmitter pointed out a long time ago.[1] That 'something else' can be the instauration of a political democracy, or even perhaps the restoration of a possibly more severe, form of authoritarian rule. It can be reasonably argued that a meaningful political transition in China must involve the former scenario, that is, a transition from the existing authoritarian structure to the one with a higher degree of political democracy. It is also safe to believe that after almost three decades of economic reforms, China is unlikely to return to either Maoist or other types of totalitarianism.

Will China be able to establish good governance? There are some positive signs that the economic development of recent decades has led to the rise of a non-state sector in which a private economy, non-governmental organisations (NGOs) and different forms of social forces are playing an increasingly power-ful role in facilitating political change and promoting good governance. The ongoing social reforms under the Hu Jintao/Wen Jiabo leadership are generating new momentum for the development of the non-state sector, especially for civil society.

From economic reform to social reform

Social reforms can be regarded as responses to all kinds of negative con-sequences resulting from economic reform. In the 1980s, the Chinese leadership under the late Deng Xiaoping operated under the principle of 'get rich first'. In the aftermath of the Cultural Revolution, Chinese socialism faced serious chal-lenges. Deng initiated China's economic reform and believed that the highest priority for economic reform was to increase productivity; only by so doing would Chinese socialism be able to provide the people with a comfortable life (*xiaokang*). The collapse of the former Soviet Union and Eastern European communism reinforced the 'get rich first' mindset among Chinese leaders. For the leadership, the sustainability of the CCP itself now depended on the need to promote rapid economic development and deliver economic welfare to the people. Under Jiang Zemin (1989–2002), the CCP leadership pushed Deng's directives to an extreme. It was under Jiang that GDP growth became the single most important performance indicator for local government officials. Capitalists were invited to attain CCP membership, and private properties were granted constitutional protection.

China has been successful in promoting economic development and reducing the scale of poverty in the country. Wang, Li and Ren note that '[b]ased on the World Bank's $1/day income measure, the number of poor dropped from about 490 million in 1981 to 88 million in 2002, a decline in poverty incidence from 29% to 6.9% of the population'.[2] China's achievements have contributed greatly to the cause of poverty reduction in the world, and China has been regarded by the World Bank, the UN and other international organisations (IGOs) as a 'para-digm' for other countries.

Despite its impressive achievements, high economic growth has also brought China tremendous challenges, such as widening income disparities, declining state capacity in achieving fair income redistribution and lack of social institu-tions in delivering public services, let alone other negative consequences such as environmental degradation. The new leadership found that although economic development has to be given high priority, development alone cannot solve the mounting problems that the country faces today. After more than a decade of the ruthless, single-minded pursuit of GDP growth, the leadership feels it necessary to step back from its previous mode of economic development. All kinds of undesirable consequences are today affecting not only economic growth itself, but also social stability.

Facing a new wave of social protests (*qunti shijian*) in recent years, the Hu/Wen leadership continues to be hardline on the political front, since it fears that any political liberalisation would possibly light a nationwide 'prairie fire' of protest. However, on the economic front, the leadership has begun to turn the wheels of China's economic growth in a different direction.

Evidence of this change is the subtle replacement of Jiang's timetable for 'building a well-off society' (*xiaokang shehui*) with Hu's aim to 'build a harmonious society' (*hexie shehui*). The present aim of the so-called 'scientific development' approach is, in essence, to 'strike a balance' among Beijing's various policies. More specifically, it raises the importance of social justice in the pursuit of China's long-term development, in terms of more even distribution of economic, legal and political rights between different regions and different social groups.

To achieve sustainable development, the leadership has now given priority to social reforms, in areas such as welfare, medical care, education and public transportation. The government is making efforts to transform itself from a 'developmental state' to a public service provider. Social reforms are aimed at building a set of social institutions which will not only enable the government to provide public services to its people, but also provide more institutionalised mechanisms for wider social groups to participate in both political and economic processes and share the benefits of China's growth.

Social reform can not only create a favourable political environment for civil society to grow, but also empower society. The development of civil society and NGOs has become a major theme of the social reform process. Chinese NGOs have increased steadily in number over the years; their significance varies, depending on their nature and function. In the economic sphere, the government has attempted to reduce its direct management role by establishing intermediary organisations such as trade associations and Chambers of Commerce to perform sectoral coordination and regulatory functions. In the social welfare sphere, the government wants to foster NGOs onto which it can offload some of the burden of service provision. In the social development sphere, the government wants NGOs to mobilise societal resources to supplement its own spending. These NGOs will have to perform their role in line with the government's wishes; that is, they will be 'helping hands', rather than autonomous organisations.

Due to a lack of autonomy, the political influences of China's NGOs vary widely across different areas, as well as between different NGOs. In some areas such as poverty reduction, charity and environmental issues, NGOs are being encouraged to play a greater role, but in other areas such as religious issues, ethnicity and human rights, the influence of NGOs is virtually absent, although some NGOs are more powerful than others. Most commercial organisations are, however, extremely powerful in influencing the government's policy-making process. It is not unusual to find business people sitting in the People's Congress and the Chinese People's Political Consultative Conference at different levels of government, two main formal political institutions to reflect public opinions. But workers and farmers are not allowed to organise themselves and thus do not have any effective mechanisms to articulate and aggregate their interests.

When powerful social groups can organise themselves, they become even more powerful. There is no way for weak social groups such as workers and farmers to promote their own causes. This is so partly because China is in an early stage of economic development and development is generally given higher priority than political participation. Workers and farmers might be able to play a more important role with further economic progress: take trade unions as an example. The government's attitude towards workers' rights is under change. Today, even the hidebound, government-dominated All-China Federation of Trade Unions (ACFTU) has recognised the need to take a more activist approach to workers' rights. China is now facing a rising tide of labour disputes, which could destabilise Chinese society and thus undermine the political legitimacy of the CCP. Therefore, there is a need for employers to better understand and honour their obligations under China's labour laws. In an apparent reflection of this new attitude, at the 2003 annual ACFTU Congress, the federation made a direct appeal to multinational retail corporation Wal-Mart Stores, Inc., to allow its workers to establish trade unions.

This volume examines the dynamics of the development of the non-state sector and its impact on governance in China in the context of international experience. In this introduction, consisting of three main sections, we attempt to summarise major arguments and findings in individual chapters. Section 1 demonstrates international experiences of the development of civil society and sustainable development, ranging from international NGOs and global civil society to newly rising civil society in Russia. Section 2 examines major issues facing the development of the non-state sector and of governance in China, covering different areas such as corporate social responsibility (CSR), the Internet and deliberative institutions. Special attention is paid to development in Zhejiang province, which has a developed private sector within China; the manner in which civil society has emerged, there is strongly indicative of China's future development. Section 3 discusses the experiences of international NGOs in China, focusing on how they have promoted democratic development in rural areas.

International experiences

The ongoing social reform in China is aimed at changing the existing inefficient development model and thus achieving sustainable development; this scheme fits with the bigger picture of sustainable development in the world. In other words, international discourse on sustainable development has a deep impact on the Chinese government. However, this does not mean that the Chinese government would accept any international discourse without hesitation; as a matter of fact, the government has selectively accepted international development ideas to fit its own development agenda.

In her chapter on international NGOs and sustainable development, Vanessa Pupavac examines the complicated relationship between these discourses. Sustainable development philosophy has become axiomatic in international development thinking today, and NGOs are an integral part of this discourse. Pupavac traces the rise of NGOs in international development in the context of the shift from early modernisation theories to sustainable development theories. However, the role of NGOs in advocating sustainable development is complicated. NGOs in the West more often then not embody low expectations of material improvement; to sustain development, most NGOs tend to adopt an anti-modernisation and anti-materialist stance. Whilst the development of such an ideological stance reflects the general trend of development policies in the West, this ideology often faces challenges when it comes to developing countries. As Pupavac points out, developing countries have long found themselves caught between the contradictions of the market and international development policies, and they often find it difficult to accept an anti-materialist development approach, as advocated by NGOs in the West.

Such a background is helpful in understanding the behaviour of the Chinese government towards international NGOs. In past years, the Chinese government has encouraged major IGOs, such as the United Nations Development Programme (UNDP), the World Bank and the International Monetary Fund (IMF), to participate in China's development. These IGOs have played a major role in introducing new ideas of economic reform into China, experimenting with different reform models, and engaging in poverty reduction, but in other areas, especially in fields such as political reform, human rights and religion, the Chinese government has been very suspicious of international NGOs. Only a few of them, such as the Ford Foundation, have met with any success in helping the Chinese to develop rural democracy. The stance of the Chinese government towards international NGOs exactly reflects its development philosophy, namely economic development first, political participation later. In recent years, this stance seems to be in direct conflict with that of international NGOs, which tend to focus more and more on social and political development.

Nowadays, in academic and policy circles, civil society has become widely regarded as playing an important role in leading human emancipation and freedom. Civil society is increasingly used as synonymous for 'democratic participation', in order to correct the effects of neo-liberal economic globalisation on the one hand and of an overly intrusive state apparatus on the other. This is also the case in the context of Chinese politics. Scholars often regard the emergence of civil society as a sign of progress towards a more democratic, and assumingly more participative, system. However, the role of NGOs is questioned by Catherine Goetze, who argues that even before the question can be asked as to who in China can or should be considered a civil society actor, the concept of civil society itself needs closer scrutiny. According to her, before one analyses the nature of the emerging associational sector in China, one has to answer some general theoretical questions, including how is the sector consti-tuted, how does it relate to the other two sectors/spheres of the state and the market and what are the politics that are produced within the sector?

Despite its wide use, the concept of civil society has been extremely vague and open to numerous interpretations. Goetze distinguishes three models of civil society: namely the republican–liberal–democratic model, the hegemony model and the model based on Bourdieu's works. The 'republican–liberal–democratic model' has been formulated in its most elaborate way by theorists who aimed at capturing the new social movements of the post-1968 era with post-Marxist con-cepts of society and politics.

The hegemony model is usually related to Antonio Gramsci's ideas on hege-mony and civil society. These two approaches make diametrically opposed assumptions about the social and political nature of civil society. According to Goetze, the republican–liberal–democratic model considers civil society as a critical counterforce to the state and the market, whereas the hegemony model conceives of the global civil society as an extension of the hegemonic liberal thought and as supportive of liberal-democratic states and market economy. Goetze attempts to develop a third model, which she believes will integrate both the republican–liberal–democratic model and the hegemony model, in order to establish criteria which will allow the distinguishing of the critical and the sup-portive features of global civil society. This third model is based on the soci-ology of Pierre Bourdieu and his concepts of 'fields', 'capital', 'discourse', 'practice' and 'symbolic power'.

Goetze believes that such a conceptual/theoretical construction is useful when one engages in empirical research on civil society in China. After review of some key works in the area of Chinese civil society, Goetze found that many aspects of these studies are closely relevant to this third model. Goetze draws four significant implications for China studies. First, the social group which con-stitutes the leading social class at this time has to be analysed with respect to its participation and the formation of an independent public sphere. Second, the same sociological analysis applies to an analysis of those social groups which had specific political and social power in communist mass organisations. Third, the importance of kinship ties and familism has to be taken into account. And the fourth is the internationalisation of Chinese activities of social self-organisation, associational life and large parts of the 'public sphere'. While China experts have paid attention to these aspects of civil society in China, as discussed briefly by Goetze, her arguments should also be able to remind China scholars how it will be fruitful to bring the studies on Chinese civil society into the mainstream of social science literature.

In recent years, during which the Chinese government has focused on social reform, more space has become available for civil society to develop, but as dis-cussed earlier, the government has been very suspicious of civil society, so how will its growth affect Chinese politics? The government has watched the development of civil society elsewhere closely and has tried to draw lessons, and gain experience, from these countries, in particular Russia. Indeed, after the collapse of the former Soviet Union, China has observed every development in Russia with great interest, which is understandable since the Chinese leadership does not want what happened to the Soviet Communist Party to happen to the CCP. The Russian leadership has tightened its control over civil society and NGOs, in order to prevent a 'Color Revolution' such as has been seen in other former Soviet Republics in Central Asia. A similar hardline policy has been adopted in China. As mentioned earlier, whilst the Chinese leadership encourages a greater role for NGOs in economic and social areas, it is reluctant to provide more space for NGOs in the political realm and other areas which are regarded as sensitive.

But the Chinese government could be wrong. NGOs will not necessarily present a threat to the regime even in the areas which are regarded as sensitive, such as education. In their chapter on civil society in the Russian Federation, Grigory Kliucharev and John Morgan present us with such a picture. They argue that the development of civil society provides a framework for citizenship participation and action autonomous of state authority and control and creates the conditions in which individual citizens, associations, societies and other group interests may achieve a voluntary, legal and hopefully harmonious (but not subservient) relationship with the state. Kliucharev and Morgan's chapter examines the growth of a nascent civil society in the Russian Federation since the end of the Soviet Union by focusing on contemporary Russia. They look at the specific example of non-formal (and informal) education provided by clubs, societies and other voluntary associations. Drawing upon data derived from an empirical survey conducted in Russia in 2005–2006, Kliucharev and Morgan show that non-formal education, separate from that provided by the state, provides a source for the grass-roots development of civil society in contemporary Russia and also contributes to sustaining its growth. As the two authors suggest, such experiences are relevant to China. Needless to say, if China wants to learn from Russia in a constructive way, what China should look at is not how the Russian government control civil society and NGOs, but how civil society and NGOs have been constructed there and how they have contributed to democratic political development.

The Chinese experience

More often than not, the scholarly community links the development of NGOs to political changes, especially democratisation, which they believe that NGOs could become main actors in promoting democracy. Given the fact that NGOs played an important role in political transition in Eastern Europe, a similar situation could happen in China. In his chapter, Jean-Philippe Béja tells us that such an intellectual supposition could be false. Whilst China has experienced a quite rapid development of NGOs, it is always important to look at the nature of these entities.

When China scholars use the concept of civil society, they often refer to an informally structured network of NGOs which have a loose relationship with the party-state. However, Béja points out that such a concept is quite different from the combative structure which had developed in Poland in the 1970s, in Czecho-slovakia in the 1980s and, to a certain degree, in China during the first decade of the reforms. Furthermore, the associations which are developing in China today do not play the same roles as the ones which emerged in Eastern Europe and China in the 1980s. In other words, the development of such a 'civil society' does not mean that the Chinese regime is democratising, nor does it mean that the evolution of China will follow a pattern similar to that of Eastern Europe.

Béja shows the changes that have taken place in terms of the development of civil society in China, which, whilst it struggled for political reform in the 1980s, was virtually co-opted by the party-state. When one examines the role of civil society, it is important to look at the interaction between civil society and the state, simply because under China's one-party state, the development of civil society is seriously constrained by the party-state. This confirms our observation that the party-state decides the nature of NGOs. What role NGOs can play in China depends on their relations with the party-state.

It is not so difficult to observe that civil society or NGOs are most active in well-developed democratic states. The state and society can often form a partnership, and both the state and society can be strong and mutually reinforce one another. Civil society can take part in policy-making processes on the one hand and help the state implement relevant policies on the other, but this is not the case in China. While China remains an authoritarian system, the capacity of the state is becoming increasingly problematic. A seemingly strong state often lacks capability to enforce its policies. The state does not provide effective means for civil society to participate in politics, and the latter is not able to help the former in policy enforcement. How the state and civil society can build a partnership is a serious challenge for China.

In her chapter, Yiyi Lu also explores the nature of NGOs in China. She notes that China watchers have often attached importance to NGOs for their widely per-ceived potential for bringing about democratic political changes or for the vital functions that they are supposed to be able to perform, such as providing social services, promoting community development, protecting vulnerable and margin-alised social groups and generating debate on public policies, but in reality, NGOs in China might not be able to live up to such high expectations. Based on her field research over several years, Lu discusses in detail some major problems that have negatively affected the ability of Chinese NGOs to perform the benevolent func-tions which are generally expected of them. She points out that the effectiveness of NGOs either as service providers or as advocates for the interest of their con-stituencies cannot be automatically assumed but must be empirically proved. In China, NGOs have encountered enormous difficulties in their struggle for China's development. Difficulties arise not only from the political side, such as the control of the government, and their relations to the government, but also from NGOs themselves, such as the quality of their leadership and organisations, and the resources available to them. Also important is Chinese political culture, which Lu believes significantly affects the functioning of NGOs.

Furthermore, Lu also points out that all of these problems, faced by Chinese NGOs, have no quick or easy solutions; those afflicting NGOs cannot simply be removed by, say, teaching them some modern management techniques, or the importance of working together with other NGOs. Most of the problems stem from the political and institutional arrangements that currently exist in China. Organisational capacity-building for Chinese NGOs is an enterprise which cannot be achieved in a short period of time; political culture also changes slowly. Lu thus argues that to help Chinese NGOs to better fulfil their potential, interested parties need to look beyond the NGOs themselves and to direct more efforts at improving the general environment for the development of these organisations.

In his chapter, Zheng Yongnian looks at the state–society relations in the case of corporate social responsibility. CSR is a concept that suggests that while firms are responsible for maximising their profits and their shareholders' interests, they also have a duty of responsibility towards their employees, customers, and the environment and communities where they operate their business. CSR covers areas such as business ethics, operational safety, occupational health, protection of workers' legal rights and interests, environmental protection, engagement with charities, donations to public welfare and aid to weak social groups. Whichever way one looks at it, CSR in China is in a seriously poor state. Zheng places China's CSR in the context of the relationships between the state, firms and society and analyses why China's CSR lacks a good regulatory framework. He argues that the Chinese state does not have a strong capacity to regulate market players effectively. Lacking a good legal foundation, the leadership faces the daunting task of ensuring the future success of its new CSR policy. Furthermore, civil society in China has yet to develop an effective mechanism for voicing grievances and regulating corporate behaviour. Apparently, to improve its CSR, the Chinese state needs to continue to transform itself into a regulatory state while allowing more space for civil society to develop. Only after civil society becomes strong will it become capable of helping the state to enforce CSR.

The tension between the state and society is also reflected in Internet governance. The development of information and communication technologies (ICT) has been an integral part of China's economic development, and indeed ICT development has become a main driving force for its continued economic growth. Rapid economic development has created a condition for an open society; however, the regime remains a closed one. To reconcile an increasingly open society and a continuously closed regime is becoming a difficult task in China.

In his chapter on Internet and governance, Gary Rawnsley elaborates the contradiction between Internet development and the authoritarian regime in China. Rawnsley argues that China's economic miracle in the past few decades is based on market forces which are dependent on the free flow of ideas. The Chinese government has censored the Internet while enjoying its fruits. According to Rawnsley, while the Chinese leadership is unlikely to tolerate the development of a critical public sphere that will challenge one-party rule, it may grow to realise that the freedom of publication is crucial for good governance and its continuing success. With the proliferation of new media and a print industry with a growing tendency to challenge the government, he concludes that a centrally created and disseminated propaganda message is proving unable to compensate a society ever more willing to protest and express its grievances in public. It is reasonable to argue that Internet governance in China has been characterised by trial and error. On the one hand, as Rawnsley points out, the party-government attempts to censor it in order to maintain its rule, and on the other hand, the government has to employ the Internet to improve its governance. Indeed, the government has come to realise that the state and society can be mutually empowering over the space that the Internet has provided.

When coming to the issue of governance, one cannot ignore waves of social protests since the mid-1990s. Undoubtedly, most social protests take place in rural China where the governance system has been under a great transformation since the mid-1990s. Is growing social protests related to changes in the system of governance? One can draw some implications from Yang Zhong's chapter on institutional changes in county government. Zhong examines the issue of governance by focusing on county governmental institutions and relationships between the county on the one hand and higher governmental authorities and township/town government on the other. Since the reform and open-door policy, county authorities have been increasingly placed under the authority of municipal government; they have thus steadily lost power and authority over personnel and economic decisions. With this centralisation, most money-making and fee-collecting agencies have also been 'verticalised', or made subject to the jurisdiction of higher authorities, so the fiscal problems encountered by county governments have seriously increased and they have thus had to find alternative resources of funds.

From here, it is not difficult to find the origin of the peasants' burden, which in turn is a major source of social protests in rural China. In recent years, to ease the tension between the state and society in rural areas, the Chinese government has carried out, on an experimental basis, a reform project which places county authorities directly under the jurisdiction of the provincial government. However, the project has met with enormous difficulties, resulting in problems including the extreme reluctance on the part of municipal governments to relinquish their power and the inability of provincial governments to exercise authority over county governments, while county governments are not trusted to use their newly gained power properly.

In his chapter, Zengke He focuses on some key institutional barriers of the development of civil society in China. He believes that there are three major barriers, including the dual approval system designed for the registration of civil organisations, the annual review of the regulations and the reporting system, and that these institutional barriers have created many dilemmas for civil organisations throughout the whole process of their development. These institutional barriers affect the role that civil organisations can play, the financial resources that are available to them, their access to skills and knowledge, their access to skilled and talented people and their ability to gain the trust of society. Zengke He frankly points out that these institutional requirements for civil society were designed on the part of the Chinese government to control and restrict civil organisations, so that the political regime and political stability can be maintained. Zengke He also points to a highly institutionalised ideational factor which is unfavourable for the development of civil society in China, that is, the 'civil society versus the state' mindset amongst party cadres and officials, and even to be found in the opinions of many ordinary citizens. Under the influence of this mindset, civil society is viewed as the anti-thesis of the state. So, apparently, the development of civil society in China depends on not only changes to the existing institutional arrangements for civil society, but also on the formation of a new mindset which views the relationship between civil society and the state as a partnership.

Are there any chances for China to develop a better system of governance? This is the key question. It is important not only to identify the main problems which China faces in building good governance, but also to look at what alternatives are available to China in looking to the future. In the following two chapters, Joseph Fewsmith and Baogang He, respectively, look at the case of Zhejiang to show how new institutions could be built and what challenges China faces in sustaining these new institutions. The case of Zhejiang is particularly meaningful when one thinks about the future of China from various perspectives. Zhejiang is famous for its thriving private economy; the non-state sector has become dominant after almost three decades of reform, and the development of the non-state sector economy has had a major impact on society. In Zhejiang, the development of civil society and/or NGOs has gained a momentum, something which is especially true in the economic and environmental areas. The province has been known for its rapid development of Chambers of Commerce and other types of trade associations and, in recent years, has also experienced an environmental movement, in which local citizens began to resist pollutant industries. Zhejiang has been regarded as an experimental base for China's new development policy which aims to build an environmental friendly society; all such new developments make the province an attractive study for the scholarly community, and for policy circles as well, when they try to look to China's future.

In his chapter, Fewsmith discusses the growth of chambers of commerce and other trade associations in Wenzhou. By looking at the development of chambers of commerce, one can understand changing relations between the state and society, at least in the sector of commerce. With a booming private sector, chambers of commerce have gained development momentum in the area. These organisations are changing the structure by which China is governed and policy is made. Chambers of commerce have done much to promote standards within industry and maintain Wenzhou's competitiveness and they have brought about new forms of state–society accommodation. However, as Fewsmith observed, chambers of commerce so far have not challenged party rule. On the contrary, they are one more expression of the emergence of a new political-economic elite that see issues in similar turns.

Over years, the CCP has learned how to accommodate capitalistic institutions like chambers of commerce and use them to promote the local economy and bring order to an unruly sector. This reflects an increasing accommodation between the political system and the interests of an increasingly diverse society. Although chambers of commerce can exercise their influence over decision making on the part of the government, their autonomy becomes limited in doing so. In this sense, the impact of the growth of commercial organisations on China's democratisation will be limited.

Baogang He discusses the development and key challenges of newly established consultative and deliberative institutions. He observed that deliberations are being practiced at the national level. An increasing number of public hearings have provided people with opportunities to express their opinions on a wide range of issues such as the price of water and electricity, park entry fees, the relocation of farmers, the conservation of historical landmarks and even the relocation of the famous Beijing Zoo, to name but a few. Baogang He argues that deliberative institutions can be seen as a deliberative way of democratising China, since they are helping to develop deliberative Chinese citizens, who will be the basis of a participatory democracy. However, Baogang He also questions the sustainability of such newly established institutions, given the fact that deliberative institutions do, more often than not, result from political initiatives on the part of individual local political leaders.

Although Baogang He presents us with a local story in Zhejiang, it is not difficult to draw some wider implications. It seems to him that although political deliberation is now given tremendous attention in China, it has not become highly institutionalised. Individual leaders play an important role in establishing these institutions and their sustainability is thus highly dependent on these leaders, and once there is a leadership change, deliberative institutions are often affected badly. As a matter of fact, such a situation is not only limited to different levels of local government, but also takes place frequently at the national level. China is still in a process of building the rule of law, and many new practices are not susceptible to being institutionalised by law. Therefore, they often appear as policy practices, which are subject to change alongside major personnel changes. However, Baogang He also reminds us that there is no need to be pessimistic. The reason is simply that, although the leadership initiative is important in establishing deliberative institutions, the demands from the people are even more important. The leadership takes such initiatives in order to meet such demands. Therefore, as long as there are demands, deliberative institutions will find their own space in which to survive and develop.

International NGOs in China

Another important source of facilitation of good governance in China is external. Given the fact that China and the world are becoming increasingly interdependent, the international community now has more and more means to influence China's domestic development. In other words, external forces will play an important role in facilitating the transformation of China. In Zheng's discussion on CSR, described earlier, it was observed that multinational corporations (MNCs) have played an important role in improving CSR in China. MNCs have been an integral part of China's economic development, and they bring new business ideas and practices to China. Moreover, external influence is not limited to the business side, playing an important role in other areas. In their chapters, Tan Qingshan and Lang Youxing, respectively, focus on how international NGOs have made great efforts in promoting rural democracy in China, an area which is regarded as more politically sensitive than that of CSR.

Village elections and self-government in rural China have made substantial progress since their coming into existence in the late 1980s. Tan believes that international NGOs have played an important role in publicising and contributing to this process, making funds available to sponsor the publication of foreign books and training materials on elections, and international conferences on village elections. They have also provided training for electoral officials and conducted training courses for elected members of villagers' committees from all over the country. Tan focuses on three major US NGOs which have been involved in developing rural elections in China, namely the Ford Foundation, the International Republican Institute and the Carter Center China Program. Tan explores how the interaction between central and local election officials and various foreign individuals and groups affects policy implementation and innovation and the development of the village electoral institution. He concludes that international NGOs' involvement in village elections and governance has had an important and positive impact on the process of village elections and has contributed to building and improving the village electoral institution.

Lang also examines the role of external actors in the development process of village elections in China, mainly that of the Carter Center and the International Republican Institution (IRI), with a focus on the strategies that these NGOs have adopted in their interaction with China. Like Tan, Lang also believes that foreign NGOs have unquestionably played an important role in promoting village elections in China. However, Lang observes that an effective strategy is needed if these NGOs want to generate influence in China. From his research, Lang found that these NGOs need good domestic partners to help them manage their projects effectively and successfully. In this regard, the establishment of networks is critical to the success of any NGO activities, and NGOs are better off cooperating with China's governmental agencies, rather than non-governmental ones. Furthermore, NGOs will have to focus on certain non-sensitive areas to promote democracy. This is a reality that most NGOs will have to accept: that only after they win the approval of the Chinese government, can they ensure a welcome for their programmes inside China. The IRI and the Carter Center have been successful in China, since the assistance that they have provided was prudently restricted to technically sound but non-controversial areas. Needless to say, the approval system also limits the role of international NGOs in China.

Lang argues that under the current political system, Chinese democracy will have to be built by internal actors. In other words, the responsibility for democratic development lies with the Chinese people. However, this does not mean that external actors are not important. Lang argues that, as shown by the IRI and the Carter Center, democratic development inside China needs now, and will continue to require, the support of external actors. This is especially true in the age of globalisation, where the distinction between the internal and the external is becoming increasingly blurred.

Notes

1 Guillermo O'Donnell and Philippe C. Schmitter, *Transitions from Authoritarian Rule: Tentative Conclusions about Uncertain Democracies* (Baltimore and London: The Johns Hopkins University Press, 1989).
2 Wang Sangui, Li Zhou and Ren Yanshun, 'The 8–7 National Poverty Reduction Program in China. The National Strategy and Its Impact', p. 7, from *Scaling Up Poverty Reduction: A Global Learning Process and Conference,* Shanghai, 25–27 May 2004. Available at http://info.worldbank.org/etools/docs/reducingpoverty/case/33/full-case/China%208–7%20Full%20Study.pdf (accessed 27 March 2007).

1 A critical review of the NGO sustainable development philosophy

Vanessa Pupavac

Sustainable development philosophy has become axiomatic in international development thinking. This chapter critically reviews the sustainable development philosophy of non-governmental organisations (NGOs). In important respects, the spectacular rise of NGOs is related to the rise of sustainable development approaches.

NGO development advocacy has enjoyed a radical reputation with the public, yet NGO sustainable development approaches embody low expectations of material improvement. Developing countries have long found themselves caught between the contradictions of the market and international development policies. Here I want to highlight influences, which have shaped NGOs' sustainable development philosophy and its anti-modernisation stance, which have encouraged an anti-materialist turn in development advocacy, before considering some implications of the divorce of material conditions from normative goals in development advocacy. The normative development goals of NGOs have become increasingly detached from material transformation.

First, this chapter traces Western cultural influences on sustainable development philosophy. Second, this chapter discusses Western ambivalence towards modernisation of developing countries and how support was conditioned by the Cold War context. This chapter explores the shift from modernisation theories to sustainable development theories. This chapter then considers the implications of NGO sustainable development policies for the goals of development. Finally, this chapter considers the implications of sustainable development for international equality between industrialised and developing countries and NGOs' evolving role as ethical gatekeepers mediating North–South relations.

Western cultural antecedents

The need for long-term development aid over short-term emergency aid has been a perennial theme of NGO advocacy, but NGO development philosophy has been wary of imposing Western development models on non-Western societies. NGO development philosophy has largely defined itself against a Western modernisation model of national development and industrialisation of developing countries along the lines of Western societies, which is seen as destructive of the environment, alienating and harmful to the interests of communities. The NGO sustainable development approach champions strategies that are respectful of local cultures and address the needs of individuals or communities and emphasise rural rather than urban development. NGO development thinking is encapsulated in the much quoted maxim: 'Feed a man a fish and you feed him for a day. Teach a man to fish and you feed him for life.' The maxim has been repeatedly invoked since it was used in 1960 by the UN Campaign against Hunger.

The anti-industrialisation position of NGO thinking has long antecedents in Western thought. The pastoral idyll as a cultural trope can be traced back to classical Greek philosophy and the philosopher's withdrawal from the affairs of the world into a life of contemplation. In the modern period, we can consider Romanticism's hostility towards industrialisation expressed in the poetic works of William Blake, George Byron, William Wordsworth and others. Major strands of modern Western culture and philosophy have defined themselves against industrialisation. The historian Thomas Carlyle raged in the nineteenth century against a culture based around the 'cash nexus' and men 'grown mechanical in head and in heart, as well as in hand'.[1] Earlier pastoral idylls were often simply rhetorical or literary conventions, but rural communities began to be considered more seriously as social models among middle-class social reformers during the nineteenth century fearful of industrial society's consequences. The American writer Henry Thoreau's mid-nineteenth-century *Walden* idealised a simple rural contemplative life.[2] Similarly, the British Victorian Arts and Crafts Movement looked nostalgically back to an idealised pre-modern Middle Ages in their revulsion against modern urban society. Victorian writers such as Thomas Carlyle, William Morris and John Ruskin wanted to promote rural labour and the handicrafts against the dominance of mechanised work.[3] Contemporary sustainable development approaches, community development, intermediate technology and micro-income generation schemes, resonate with arts and crafts thinking. Again in the twentieth century, writers like D.H. Lawrence and T.S. Elliot question the character of modern mass society and express cultural primordial ideas. The literary critics F.R. Leavis and Denys Thompson outline a modest harmonious and simple rural life, anticipating the basic needs approach of international development:

> they satisfied their human needs, in terms of the natural environment; and the things they made – cottages, barns, ricks, and wagons – together with their relations with one another constituted a human environment, and a subtlety of adjustment and adaptation, as right and inevitable.[4]

The negative aspects of rural subsistence living are not dwelt or are attributed to modernity's incursions. Romantic portrayals of organic, pre-industrial communities have been treated sceptically by social scientists in the past. Williams argued fifty years ago, 'it is foolish and dangerous to exclude from so called organic society the penury, the petty tyranny, the disease and mortality, the ignorance and frustrated intelligence which are also among its ingredients'.[5] But the pastoral idyll remains a culturally compelling ideal, although anti-industrial ideas were not taken up as viable social models by the mass twentieth-century political movements.

The anti-industrialisation position of NGO development philosophy may be traced more directly to Western anthropological perspectives, which in turn informed colonial administration. Leading twentieth-century anthropologists notably that of the Culture and Personality School associated with anthropologists such as Ruth Benedict and Margaret Mead were partly inspired by their doubts about their own societies.[6] They were concerned with the alienating consequences of modernity, and wanted to find alternative ways of life, which would support their progressive reform agenda at home by demonstrating the possibility of different ways of organising society. Anthropological thinking therefore considered it important to preserve the pluralism of cultures, because they thought traditional communities could provide insights for modern society. Their work often expressed alarm at how contact with modernity was destabilising the societies they studied. Hence, anthropologists had serious reservations about international development policy seeking to transform the developing world on the lines of the advanced industrialised societies. Concerns over modernity's destabilising impact on traditional societies were also taken up colonial administrators and shaped colonial thinking on development as it tried to deter nationalist movements.[7]

Moreover, the anti-mechanisation position of NGO sustainable development philosophy appears to outdo its romantic utopian predecessors. William Morris, for one, was not against the use of labour-saving machines where the labour was back-breaking, repetitive and uninteresting. He wanted to free people from dull routine labour so they could spend more time on creative labour. However, too often NGOs have celebrated low or medium technology as appropriate for developing countries without thinking through whether the labour in question is experienced as drudgery or not. NGOs romanticise the experience of non-mechanised labour-intensive agricultural work or petty trade as micro-enterprise. Too little consideration is given to how time-consuming routine labour-intensive work checks the aspirations of people in developing countries and prevents them engaging with more interesting creative work.

Rise and fall of modernisation theories

NGO development advocacy understands itself as radically challenging a Western modernisation orthodoxy requiring developing countries follow a Western path of national development. Yet, this self-projection is against a straw modernisation model that has long since lost favour with Western governments. The growth of Western development NGOs and their prominent role in international development has been founded on Western scepticism towards the industrialisation of the South in both official and radical circles. I now want to briefly sketch the rise and fall of modernisation theories.

International development policy came into being in the context of national independence struggles and Cold War competition between the Western and Soviet blocs for influence in the newly independent states. Core concerns of Western policy-makers were first the destabilising impact of weak pre-industrial states on an international order based on national sovereignty and state capacity and second securing the new states to the Western bloc. How could the newly independent states be developed so that they were stable self-sustaining states without becoming new security threats to the West, whether in their own right or as states loyal to the Soviet bloc?

Western thinking was torn between Cold War fears and unspoken racial fears. Western policy-makers were anxious that the international balance of power was slipping from Western nations with the ascendancy of formerly subject peoples in Asia and Africa, including demographically.[8] These fears built on fears of the masses and their new political role in the mass societies created through industrialisation, urbanisation and the erosion of tradition.[9] However, there was consciousness that developing countries enjoyed a choice internationally that the West had to address.[10] Western policy-advisors repeatedly warned of competing with the Soviets for the hearts and minds of the South and the need to outline 'what we have to offer the developing country as compared with the Communists'.[11] Indicative of the political concerns underlying economic development policy, Walt Rostow's famous treatise on *The Stages of Economic Growth* is subtitled *A Non-Communist Manifesto*.[12] As Rostow and Max Millikan of MIT stated in a report to the director of the CIA Allen Dulles in 1954: 'Where men's energies can be turned constructively and with some prospect of success to the problems of expanding standards of living in a democratic framework we believe that attractions of totalitarian forms of government will be much reduced.'[13]

Western qualms over the destabilising impact of development for the existing international order of nations were suppressed by concerns that if the West did not promote an industrial development programme, then the new states would turn communist. Its model of modernisation was to promote westernisation and secure the developing countries to the Western bloc. The problem was considered urgent in Asia where if countries were to be brought: 'more effectively into the free world alliance they must believe that the U.S. interest in Asia is not confined merely to our top priority concern – military security – but authentically extends to their top priority concern – economic development'.[14]

Having accepted the necessity of promoting economic development, Western policy-makers hoped that reducing the economic development gap between states would also reduce ideological differences and promote international consensus around the values of the advanced Western industrial states. Amitai Etzioni in his *The Hard Way to Peace* neatly encapsulates Western thinking at the time:

> Development of the 'have-not' countries will bring them closer to the 'have' countries, not only in economic terms, but also in their social, cul-

tural, and political structure, since economic development both requires and effects modernization in all these spheres. Thus differences of interest and viewpoint among countries will be reduced, and a major barrier to international consensus formation will be removed.[15]

Development thinking complimented Western postwar domestic policy, which drew political legitimacy from economic prosperity. The 'engineering of consent' was based on citizens' identification with the mass consumer products of capitalism elaborated by political advisers such as Edward Bernays, pioneer of public relations and Sigmund Freud's nephew.[16,17] Hence, the major debates of the first two decades after the Second World War accepted the necessity of supporting international economic development. International economic development goals were ambitious and meant the industrialisation of the newly independent states, designated *developing* countries. Development thinking revolved around the difficulties of generating economic take-off and urban industrial development; questioning whether it should be pursued was not acceptable internationally.

Modernisation strategies only enjoyed two decades of official support. Even then developing counties found it very difficult to secure financial investment; except if they were in areas of strategic interest such as the Asia-Pacific region. Anxieties over the destabilising impact of development continued to surface. We can see this concern in the WHO's constitution which refers to the problem of people's capacity to live harmoniously in a time of rapid social change. This subject was studied in the UN Tensions and Technology research series, later entitled Technology and Society whose authors included the anthropologist Mead.[18] Research concerned with the functionality of the non-Western culture and personality in circumstances of rapid change remained an important strand of Western thinking as an adjunct to Western security policy, particularly in relation to the strategically important areas of Asia. Publications on the Third World mind and the difficulty of nation-building and promoting a democratic political culture especially on Asian countries were a staple theme in Western area studies and political science literature. We can see these themes in Ruth Benedict's *The Chrysanthemum and the Sword*[19] or the works of the political scientist Lucian Pye[20] and others. Psychosocial risk studies sought to evaluate the risk factors for Third World revolution and could provoke international controversy, most vividly testified in the scandal over the aborted Camelot project.[21]

Western governments were far more willing to offer technical expertise than capital investment, although the efficacy of the technical advice offered was sharply criticised by Galbraith among others.[22] Indeed, Western advisors' emphasis on developing societies' attitudes and skills, Galbraith suggested, represented a rationalisation of the services being provided by the West rather than necessarily reflecting the needs of recipient countries.[23]

Infecting people with the modernisation virus?

The attitudes towards modernisation in developing countries were studied because it was contended that:

> a nation is not modern unless its people are modern.... We doubt that its economy can be highly productive, or its political and administrative institutions very effective, unless the people who work in the economy and staff the institutions have attained some degree of modernity.[24]

One reason for Western modernisation's theories' preoccupation with the cultural disposition of developing societies was the problem of capital investment. Although capital investment was championed, in practice developing countries found it difficult to secure capital investment from the West unless they were of strategic importance. The lack of external capital investment was to be countered by limiting population growth and galvanising the resources and enthusiasm of the population to create the demand for machines and investment and maximise productivity. The preference for technical expertise, increasingly targeting the subjectivity of populations, has become more pronounced over the decades.

Yet, there are distinctions in the cultural and personal traits viewed as desirable in Western development thinking of this period and today. Fifty years ago, the desirable character to be cultivated was the rational ambitious mature masculine ego, inoculating the individual against the perceived irrationalism of mass society as well as challenging the atavistic remnants of traditional society. This conception of the ideal citizen as an ambitious moderniser is in sharp contrast to the ecologically sensitive modest personality of today's sustainable development model. Strikingly earlier economic discussions sought to raise the aspirations of populations so that they actively foster economic growth. In this vein, Rostow speaks of how 'the horizon of expectations must lift; and men must become prepared for a life of change and specialized function'.[25] David McClelland's *The Achieving Society* seeks to identify the 'mental virus', which leads people to need to achieve and thereby promote economic growth, and he wants to train people to 'infect' people with the need to achieve.[26] Galbraith takes up this idea and speaks of tackling 'the equilibrium of poverty', that is, the poor's accommodation to poverty, their 'absence of aspiration' and 'the tendency to prefer acquiescence to frustration'.[27] Accordingly, Galbraith proposes literacy as a tool for raising aspirations.[28]

Industrialisation and urbanisation were treated internationally as desirable goals, not antithetical to social justice, but essential for its realisation. This view was held not just among the Bretton Wood institutions, but the international welfare organisations such as UNICEF as the leading international child agency. Indeed, UNICEF redefined itself as a development agency because of the strong link being made between industrialisation and advancing a population's welfare. Consequently, we can read in UNICEF reports of the period that government policy prioritising national economic growth was regarded as compatible with child welfare concerns.[29] It was almost regarded as an economic law then that 'the poorer the country, the greater the difference between poor and rich',[30] a presumption that today's sustainable development thinking rebuts.

In the first two decades of international development, rural poverty was seen as the great evil to be eradicated. Urban poverty however visible was regarded in the optimistic progressive outlook as a lesser evil to rural poverty and a condition whose extremes were a transitory feature of a dynamic indus-trialising economy – moreover one that also provided its own checks. Mobile urban populations had greater expectations of well-being and opportunities for political engagement, and therefore to articulate and defend their interests. However, these very advantages that the urban poor enjoyed over their rural cousins also raised the spectre of the risks of political radicalisation during industrialisation.

But even before alarm over international security and the risks of political radicalisation of the Third World became manifest, Western debates on the impact of technological advancement on their own societies cast doubt on inter-national modernisation strategies. Initially, doubts over modernisation related to the implications of new machinery for the workforce, later doubts became more fundamental as policy thinking took on board environmentalist critiques of technological progress. The next section considers how Western policy advisers were concerned with the problems of unemployment or underemployment through technical innovation in the 'affluent society'.[31]

Problems of the leisure society

Prominent economists such as John Maynard Keynes and Galbraith argued that the problem of production was one that humanity was overcoming and would not be a problem in the future.[32] Instead economists fretted over the problem of how Western societies would have to adapt to leisure in a world of technological advancement that would make the work of millions redundant. Policies main-taining employment rather than increased production were recommended for the new circumstances in which the production of goods, it was argued, was becom-ing important for employment rather than for the goods themselves. In the words of Galbraith, 'Production for the sake of the goods produced is no longer very urgent'; however, 'production does remain important and urgent for its effects on economic security'.[33] The psychological not just the financial consequences of being deprived of employment were extensively discussed.[34] Current strat-egies were questioned as storing up problems for the future, 'We cannot let labour-saving and thought-saving devices proliferate.'[35] 'Man must be brought into equilibrium with his new environment' it was argued, 'He must be adapted to leisure, and his work must become *occupational therapy*.'[36] Strategies such as the rejuvenation of the crafts were suggested as 'the best occupational therapy' although advocates could be scathing of the aesthetic merits of handicrafts pro-duced by ordinary people![37]

These debates had little impact on capital investment and technological innovation in Western domestic production but did influence how policy-makers thought about strategies for international development. Employment was put forward as the goal of development,[38] discouraging labour-saving technological investment and encouraging policies for labour retention. These arguments on the importance of employment strategies were reinforced by the conclusions of US presidential commissions on civil disorder and violence that rocked the United States in the 1960s. Both the Kerner Commission and the National Commission on Violence highlighted how too high expectations of what society could do had intensified dissatisfactions and fuelled the riots and suggested the need to focus on employment.[39] The problem of employment was taken up by international organisations, notably the International Labour Organisation (ILO). The ILO published a series of reports and launched its World Employment Programme, which prioritised employment and shifted its policy away from capital-intensive to labour-intensive activities.[40]

Initially, this policy of employment generation through retaining labour-intensive activities was still within a strategy of industrialisation, but the weight of Western policy thinking was already turning against industrialisation of the developing world as a whole by the late 1960s. Problems of insufficient capital, uneven development, mass urban poverty and widening economic disparities were becoming apparent, but these problems were no longer dismissed as temporary remediable features of the early stages of industrialisation as experienced by Western societies. Instead, these problems were discussed as dangerous unstable conditions susceptible to political radicalisation and posing risks to Western security concerns. The next section discusses the rise of sustainable development in official development thinking.

Rise of sustainable development

Modernisation strategies were effectively abandoned in international development aid policies by the late 1960s. The shift away from modernisation strategies was promoted by the fears that modernisation strategies were failing to win hearts and minds in the Third World and fostering political alienation and discontent globally.[41] Dudley Seers, director of the Institute of Development Studies in Sussex, alerted at the end of the 1960s, 'it looks as if economic growth not merely may fail to solve social and political difficulties; certain types of growth can actually cause them'.[42] The assumption that prosperity from economic growth would trickle down to all sections of society was questioned by patterns of uneven development and sharp inequalities within developing countries. Instead of urbanisation leading to urbanism, understood as civic norms of behaviour and values, as modernisation theories hoped, urban expansion was becoming associated with social problems, epitomised in the vast squatter settlements developing around cities. International development advisers began to advocate alternative goals such as sustainable livelihoods and basic needs.[43]

Alarm towards modernisation among Western policy-makers was captured in E.F. Schumacher's *Small Is Beautiful*,[44] which became the bible of the sustainable development approach and adopted by NGOs. Its publication during the 1970s oil crisis, which suggested to Western states how developing countries could challenge their access to cheap raw materials, galvanised huge interest in Schumacher's arguments. Schumacher argued that modernisation policies were damaging communities and livelihoods, and promoting greed and frustration, and were therefore counter to international peace and security. Development strategies should reject industrialisation and universal prosperity as a goal and concentrate on small-scale production and basic needs, maintaining traditional communities and livelihoods by disseminating low technological solutions.

The sustainable development model was incrementally codified from the mid-1970s in documents such as the Brandt report *North–South: A Programme for Survival*.[45] Sustainable development policy-makers challenged the idea that 'the whole world should copy the models of highly industrialized countries'.[46] International development policy discernibly shifted to small-scale rural development projects away from funding large-scale industrial development projects. Investment in low or medium technology was considered appropriate for developing countries, not industrialisation, to encourage small-scale income generation, rather than wage labour, to help the population secure basic needs. The policy implied continued reliance on self-generated income activities and subsistence farming and the retention of labour-intensive work for the vast majority of the population.

The modified international development agenda complimented the shift from Keynsian to liberal economics in Western economic policy and the idea of the state playing a smaller role as employer and welfare provider. The national development of developing countries to the level of industrialised countries has simply not been an aspiration of Western development policy, although states are subject to extensive externally imposed reforms. Rather than raising people's expectations and encouraging social mobility, sustainable development policies have sought to stabilise communities and promote local solutions.

Western governments began to provide more and more development aid through NGOs rather than bilateral aid, helping sponsor the spectacular growth of the NGO development sector in recent decades. The major Western disaster organisations such as Oxfam, which began as a famine relief organisation in the Second World War, re-oriented their activities from Europe to developing countries in the postwar period and began to incorporate development work into their activities and define themselves as primarily development organisations. Their needs-based and people-focused relief work lent itself to sustainable development thinking and as organisations they were well-placed vehicles to carry forward sustainable development ideas. Again, like their anthropological predecessors, many of those working in NGOs were often inspired to work in the developing world because of doubts over Western societies and the desire to seek alternative ways of life. NGO staff have been heavily influenced by limits to growth arguments and environmentalism. Accordingly, the NGO development philosophy has defined itself against industrial development and embodied local small-scale, technologically simple, community-based development.

If sustainable development legitimises different expectations for developing countries than industrialised countries, it has done so from a culturally relative perspective, which challenges the earlier development assumptions that developing countries should aspire to become like the advanced industrial societies. Sustainable development advocates often consciously reverse the old development and underdevelopment hierarchy by positively comparing the materially simpler lifestyle of populations in developing countries as ethically superior to the consumerism of Western societies. In this reversal, sustainable development thinking, following earlier cultural anthropological research, posits traditional societies as frugal, living harmoniously with nature and self-sustaining against the excesses of Western societies.

The next section considers the convergence of radical development thinking with official development policies. Official concern over modernisation strategies was complimented by the counter-culture critique of mass society that influenced radical politics in the 1970s as it grappled with its failures to galvanise a movement for radical political transformation. Meanwhile, Third World nationalism was on the wane and developing countries exercised declining influence on the international development agenda, likewise the Soviet Union's influence was eroding.

Counter-culture sustainable development

The early dominant theories in development studies attacking modernisation policies were underdevelopment and dependency theories, inspired by Marxism and anti-colonialism. These critical theories originally targeted capitalism and imperialism, rather than industrialisation per se as underpinning international inequalities. Dependency theories attacked foreign ownership of industries and economic exploitation in developing countries and sought autonomous development. However, autonomous industrial development appeared difficult to achieve, and dependency theorists were increasingly attracted to non-industrial sectors of developing economies.

Rethinking in radical circles over the political potential of industrial workers joined arguments concerned with foreign domination, ownership and exploitation in industrial sectors. If Western policy-makers were fearful of urbanisation promoting political radicalism, radical politics had the opposite concern. In trying to understand why the masses were not embracing radical politics, critics suggested that modern consumerism anaesthetised people and created conformists, inhibiting political radicalism.[47] Instead of the industrial proletariat as the agent of revolution assumed in earlier Marxist-inspired accounts, new works such as the critical philosopher Herbert Marcuse's *One Dimensional Man* or the liberation theologist Paulo Freire's *The Pedagogy of the Oppressed* suggested that the hope of radical politics lay with those outside industrial production. A new interest was taken in the role of peasants, particularly following the Vietnamese defeat of the United States in the Vietnam War. In the words of another Catholic priest Ivan Illich, who worked in Latin America and whose ideas were influential among radicals:

> In Vietnam a people on bicycles and armed with sharpened bamboo sticks have brought to a standstill the most advanced machinery for research and production. We must seek survival in a Third World in which human ingenuity can peacefully outwit machined might.[48]

If political radicalism would only emerge from those outside the processes of the modern industrial state, counter-culture critics concluded that they should be opposed to developing countries becoming modern industrial states like their own. Moreover, modernisation strategies were further politically discredited by Rostow's close association with US military intervention in Vietnam. Rostow was not only an important modernisation theorist, but advised on US bombing strategies in Vietnam, which caused huge suffering among the Vietnamese population. Radicals were also less and less enamoured by the communist model with the Soviet Union's suppression of dissent in Eastern Europe. State sovereignty (and national development by association) was becoming linked, not with national independence struggles but with violence, whether the two superpowers' military interventions around the globe or their support for military regimes in the developing world.

The counter-culture critique idealised an authentic life of peasant farmers and independent artisans producing traditional crafts as still existing in parts of the developing world, but being crushed by economic development. These ideas inform NGO advocacy which envisages people in developing countries not adopting consumerist Western lifestyles, but retaining more authentic, simpler ways of life within a modified market economy. In their anti-materialism, counter-culture and NGO critiques of modernisation also implicitly borrow from Christian and non-Christian theology which emphasise spiritual goods over material goods. Many NGOs obviously have a religious foundation. The writings of Freire and Illich are unsurprisingly infused with religious references given their religious training. But Schumacher's *A Guide for the Perplexed*[49] explicitly explores the spiritual dimension and his desire for society to re-emphasise the spiritual, encompassing Christian theology and Buddhist meditation as well as social psychology.

The anti-materialist aspects of counter-culture and NGO thinking was further supported by the rise of environmentalism within Western thought expressed in books such as Rachel Carson's influential *Silent Spring*, which condemned industrialisation as destroying the planet's resources. The ecological holistic vision wants to minimise humanity's imprint on the planet and return to a simpler way of life, which balance human needs against the needs of the environment. Environmentalist perspectives on the limits to growth and the impact of industrialised societies on the planet were absorbed into the anti-modernisation critique as it became codified into the concept of sustainable development. The idea of small-scale non-wage production was taken up as being less destructive of the environment and also less exploitative than large-scale production as nationalisation programmes lost favour as a way of spreading ownership of the means of production with the shift away from Keynsian economics.[50]

NGO activities took on new significance in the 1980s with the international debt crisis and the setbacks in national development. NGOs made trenchant attacks on impact of structural adjustment programmes on welfare in developing countries in the last and sought ways of limiting their effects. Their debt relief recommendations have sought conditions involving the external regulation of national budgets in developing countries to ensure basic welfare spending including health. At best, development policies prioritising basic needs have had significant success in improving survival rates such as UNICEF's GOBI (Growth Monitoring, Oral Rehydration, Breast-feeding and Immunization) infant programmes despite the worsening economic situation in many developing countries under structural adjustment programmes.[51] Yet, however, impressive these programmes are as lifelines for populations in precarious circumstances, it would be a misnomer to describe them as development. Neither official nor NGO international development goals aim that developing countries achieve Western levels of economic development. Both retain normative goals, but there is an evident scepticism in international development circles towards the need for significant material advancement.

From wealth to well-being

The sustainable development approach has defined itself against the earlier modernisation model based on industrialisation and economic growth. International development thinking originally emphasised the correlation between a state's wealth and its social progress. Development thinking in recent decades has wanted to counter the idea that a country's wealth necessarily determines a population's well-being. The idea underpins the UNDP's (United Nations Development Programme) annual human development index, which compares the welfare of populations in different countries. Predictably, human development rankings categorise many developing countries as widely failing their populations while categorising the advanced industrial countries as generally securing their populations' welfare. Yet, the human development index was inspired by the desire to demonstrate that social progress is possible without material advancement. There is an emphasis on highlighting examples where countries with lower national wealth are providing better welfare than those with higher national wealth. A broad correlation between per capita income and ranking is consciously contested in the human development literature, and cases countering this linkage emphasised, although the commonly cited examples such as Cuba suggest rather different conclusions being drawn from those in the literature! These examples are interesting to study, and aspects of their success can be used by other countries. Nevertheless, a broad correlation between a country's wealth and its population's well-being exists, although this correlation is continuously downplayed in international development circles today. The UNDP's 2005 National Human Development Report for China reports that 'In the past 26 years, GDP has grown by 9.4 percent a year on average, and the absolute poor population in rural areas has dropped from 250 million to 26.1 million.'[52] The UN Millennium Development Goals Report 2006 also highlights how 'Asia leads the decline in global poverty', yet does not mention the role of China's economic growth on the region.[53] Meanwhile, sub-Saharan Africa is one of the poorest regions of the world with some of the lowest growth rates and predictably has the some of the worst health problems.

There is a discernible non-materialist strand in official and NGO international development thinking. The World Bank's seminal *Voices of the Poor* report, officially endorsed by Britain's Department for International Development among other major donors, has adopted a holistic view of development and champions the idea that the goal of development should be not wealth but well-being.[54] Its concepts of well-being and illbeing are set out as follows:

> Wellbeing and illbeing are states of mind and being. Wellbeing has a psychological and spiritual dimension as a mental state of harmony, happiness and peace of mind. Illbeing includes mental distress, breakdown, depression and madness, often described by participants to be impacts of poverty.[55]

Repeatedly, the report downplays the significance of material prosperity by highlighting the non-material aspects of well-being.[56] The report suggests that spiritual poverty is worse than material poverty citing a Bosnian woman participant, 'You can never recover from spiritual impoverishment.'[57] Indeed, the report suggests that wealth and well-being are not necessarily compatible, 'Wealth and well-being are seen as different, and even contradictory.'[58] The study focuses on individuals at the bottom of society and their personal aspirations, experiences and relationships and sees fulfilment of their modest aspirations as international development priorities. The study highlights how 'poor people's views of wellbeing ... span wide and varied experiences and meanings', although 'Historically many development professionals have given priority to the material aspect of people's lives.'[59] It goes on to cite the words of a poor Ethiopian woman that 'A better life for me is to be healthy, peaceful, and live in love without hunger. Love is more than anything. Money has no value in the absence of love.'[60]

At first glance, re-orientating development policies around the expressed needs of the poor seems very progressive. Yet, international development advisers in the past were concerned with the poor's fatalistic acceptance of their condition and felt that they needed to raise populations' expectations. Low expectations are evident in this study, which states how its participants 'hope for moderate, not extravagant, improvements'. But orientating policies around people with low expectations leads to minimalist goals. So the report may be accused of disingenuously using the poor's low expectations to legitimise low development goals. The report's conclusions relativise material advancement and emphasise non-material aspects. The report's authors deny this charge arguing that the importance of small changes to the poor reinforces the requirement to prioritise their needs. The contemporary development approach is reconciled to the abandonment of substantial material transformation, because its holistic concept of development as well-being is regarded as distinct from material prosperity. Essentially, well-being is seen as different from wealth and not dependent on wealth for its realisation.

The importance of material improvement for other goods has been axiomatic to secular progressive thinking. 'All human progress, political, moral, or intellectual, is inseparable from material progression', wrote Auguste Comte, the founder of the discipline of sociology.[61] However, the relationship between social progress and material advancement is being broken, and normative change is becoming the substantial meaning of development. Consider the Millennium Development Goals project, which describes itself to be 'an expanded vision of development'. The project does not aspire to universal prosperity, but expects states to realise its normative agenda in 2015 including universal primary education and gender equality without industrialisation and only modest economic growth. For its vision makes changing culture and individual behaviour the primary means of social advancement in its idea of 'vigorously [promoting] human development as the key to sustaining social and economic progress'. In effect, they expect pre-industrial societies to adopt post-industrial norms, while based on enhanced tradition household production and eschewing the material comforts and welfare enjoyed by post-industrial societies. The next section considers contradictions in NGO sustainable development thinking.

Some contradictions of NGO development advocacy

NGOs are also divorcing well-being from material well-being. But official and NGO policy convergence does not mean that NGO development advocacy is irrelevant. NGO development advocacy crucially helps legitimise official development policy's rejection of transforming the material conditions of developing societies by giving this rejection a radical gloss. British anti-poverty campaigns such as Make Poverty History[62] initially appear ambitious in their demands to end poverty, but closer examination reveals that they do not aspire to prosperity for all, but have effectively redefined poverty eradication in terms of managing survival through better self-reliance. Their hopes in external regulation may be contrasted with the earlier dependency theories, which were suspicious of outside intervention in developing countries.

Sustainable development advocacy effectively compliments the erosion of the welfare state model and makes a virtue of people having to create their own employment opportunities to support themselves in the face of structural adjustment reforms cutting state welfare and public employment. Consider how Oxfam United Kingdom summarises its development approach:

> Over six decades of experience has shown us that the best people to help poor communities are community members themselves. We listen carefully

to make sure we understand their needs, then we provide expertise, training, and funding so local people can find the best possible way to improve their situation.[63]

Similarly, Christian Aid's home page declares how it 'believes in strengthening people to find their own solutions to the problems they face'. Equally, the recent Africa Commission aims to 'empower poor people to shape their own lives, including by investing in their health and education ...' and emphasises the need 'to foster small enterprises'.[64] The NGO themes of sustainable livelihoods, small-scale agriculture, microfinance and programmes empowering people with the skills and confidence to start up their own micro-enterprises chime with the dominant international development approaches. As Mark Duffield observes, 'Sustainable development shifts the responsibility for self-reproduction from states to people reconfigured as social entrepreneurs operating at the level of the household and communities.'[65] Effectively, people are being condemned to back-breaking labour-intensive subsistence farming or petty trading work under the banner of cultural relativism. Overall, the sustainable development model leaves most of the world's population in poverty relying on household production, their lives dominated by the forces of nature and very exposed without the safety nets that citizens of post-industrial states expect.

Crucially, the sustainable development model does not address the limited capacity of the developing state, which can hardly be transformed into a progressive redistributive state guaranteeing its citizens' welfare without a developed economy and infrastructure. In so far as the problem of the weak state is belatedly being recognised by official donors or NGOs, the problem of the weak state is moralised in terms of corruption or bad governance. The material conditions underlying the weak illiberal state and social inequalities are side-stepped.

Reluctance to address contradictions in their development model is not unrelated to NGO antipathy towards their own modern industrial societies, associating them with violence and injustice, together with their Romantic perceptions of non-Western populations' self-reliance, non-materialist expectations and restraint. This belief contrasts with earlier progressive politics, which while often heavily critical of Western modernisation models, nevertheless saw social progress as contingent upon material advancement. Wilde's words are apposite to describe NGO development philosophy when he writes of how 'Men ... rage against Materialism, as they call it, forgetting that there has been no material improvement that has not spiritualized the world.'[66] In their anti-materialism, NGOs echo traditional apologies for poverty.

Meanwhile, the demise of the national development drive is not returning countries to a simple holistic life in harmony with nature as NGO development philosophy hopes, but is brutal and competitive. The reality of a society organised around small-scale family producers or pastoralists and strong communal or kinship ties is likely only to be able to support a precarious state with a weak relationship to the population and characterised by a nepotistic public sphere.

At the same time, NGO sustainable development advocacy makes inequality between developing and developed countries an indefinite condition. Namely, abandoning the technological advancement of developing countries essentially means abandoning the advancement of equality between developing and developed states. The marginalised position of developing countries within the global market economy is assumed. Consider, for example, fair trade advocacy, which far from eradicating international inequalities, assumes unequal means of production between developed and developing countries with the latter engaged in low or medium technology in micro-enterprises as opposed to large-scale automated production, and trading in international markets through a paternalistic relationship with ethical Western companies or NGOs, not independently. Moreover, proposed fair trade conditions, like microcredit conditionality, presume the right to dictate extra-financial terms based on the Western advocates' vision of the ethical life. Accordingly, while the Make Poverty History coalition is demanding that developing countries decide their own economic policies and strategies and want external economic conditions on liberalisation to be removed, NGOs continue to demand alternative social conditions being put on developing states. So while NGOs are wary of developing countries following Western paths of economic development, they are not wary of Western states intervening in developing societies to change social and political norms. Again when one reflects on the Make Poverty History coalition's demands to stem the flow of industrial goods exported to developing countries, it is evident that the demands are not accompanied by policies to support the industrial sectors of developing countries. Rather they are effectively demands to protect the developing world from industrialisation and its associated higher material expectations.

There is an evident growing preference for moral advocacy over material aid in NGO projects. Accordingly, Live Aid's mission in 1985 was sending material aid to Africa; Live 8's mission in 2005 was about promoting awareness of poverty in the West. These initiatives have the feel of quasi-religious rites rather than representing practical programmes. The shift of attention from practical field programmes to moral advocacy suggests that sustainable development initiatives represent a secular form of religious observance for a post-industrial consumer age.

Ethical gatekeepers in a world of international equality

Ironically, NGOs are developing closer ties to both Western governments and industries while remaining wary of national industrial development for developing countries. Thickening relations of global governance are being created and becoming embedded in the public institutions of developing countries. On the thickening ties between NGOs and business, these are manifested in initiatives such as the Oxfam, Novib and Unilever's joint report *Exploring the Links Between International Business and Poverty Reduction: A Case Study of Unilever in Indonesia*.[67]

China's economic growth and new trade relations in Asia and Africa have the potential to shake the current international development consensus. China's new role has been greeted with some apprehension in Western official and NGO development circles because its approach challenges the sustainable development thinking and political and social conditionality they favour. As yet China has not elaborated an alternative international development philosophy to sustainable development and has confined itself to trade and charity. China has not so far sought to combine goals of material prosperity and justice into an alternative development model, although its new economic relations in the developing world are rekindling aspirations.

Sustainable development advocacy originally evaded the political consequences of effectively making inequality an indefinite feature of the international system, but NGO political advocacy since the 1990s is plainly abandoning the principle of sovereign equality. Ironically, the anti-development critique, despite its avowed antipathy towards modern industrial societies, now endorses in its political advocacy those very states having greater powers against developing countries. The assumptions of the NGO political advocacy belie the current idea in NGO circles that the 1990s offered developing countries the chance to become 'equal partners on a new, more equal and more prosperous stage'.[68]

If the sustainable development model complimented the anti-state liberal economic policies of the 1980s,[69] NGOs evolving political advocacy of the 1990s assumed the failing capacity of developing states to protect their populations and the necessity of reordering international relations to deal with this reality. The newly independent states looked forward to achieving equality with developed states in the early heady days of international development, but inequality is an indefinite condition for many states under the sustainable development approach. The normative, non-materialist agenda of international development policy-makers can only undermine the possibility of developing countries becoming equal subjects internationally or moral agents domestically securing their population's welfare. Developing countries find themselves caught between the contradictions of NGOs' anti-materialist development outlook and NGOs' idealist accounts of international relations. NGO political advocacy strategies entrust the international community of responsible states to intervene in violating states on the behalf of vulnerable populations. NGO political advocacy has essentially come to challenge developing countries' legitimacy and enhances the legitimacy of Western powers to intervene around the world, undermining the principle of sovereign equality between states.

Intervention is positively endorsed in NGO political advocacy contrary to the UN Charter. NGOs such as Oxfam are actively lobbying to rewrite the UN Charter to change the rights of national sovereignty and non-inference in favour of international enforcement rights. The Charter's prohibition on interference was based on fears of its potential abuse by powerful states. Tellingly, NGO enforcement demands have neglected the potential conflict of interest between intervening states and the population of developing states or indeed between foreign NGOs and the population of developing countries. This neglect is striking given how the NGO literature pointedly draws attention to the conflict of interests between a state and its population. Western NGOs talk of their international relations in terms of belonging to an intimate global community as if we are living in one big inclusive extended village, where people enjoy an equal voice and mutual ties of accountability, where wealth does not matter, and individuals in the South can just pop along to their neighbours in the North. In this vein, Oxfam talks of its 'interconnectedness':

> Oxfam is a world wide network. A community that's crossing continents. Linking villages, towns, countries. Connecting individuals who live thousands of miles apart. And from Bangalore to Bolton, from Tokyo to Tajikistan, this community is changing lives. People across the world are coming together with a shared goal.[70]

A direct disinterested relationship is being assumed by NGOs bypassing the developing state where NGOs place themselves as voicing the interests of people in developing countries rather than their delegitimised governments. The possibility that NGOs might be drawn to certain voices that echo their thinking is overlooked. The unequal distribution of power in this relationship is unacknowledged. In the unequal relationship, international Western-based NGOs become political gatekeepers, determining which voices in the developing world they will represent, how their problems are represented and addressed, along with their implied role as economic gatekeepers in fair trade or debt relief. NGO development advocacy continues to enjoy a radical reputation. Yet, NGO sustainable development approaches effectively condemn people in developing countries to back-breaking labour-intensive subsistence, while their normative goals have become divorced from material advancement. The Romantic imagination of NGOs has become detached from the material reality of people's lives in developing countries. Overall, three decades of sustainable development philosophy has offered spiritual nourishment to alienated Westerners rather than significant material and social transformation for people in developing countries.

Notes

1 Carlyle in Raymond Williams, *Culture and Society 1789–1950* (Harmondsworth: Penguin, 1963), p. 86.
2 Henry Thoreau, *Walden* (Princeton, NJ; Oxford: Princeton University Press, 2004).
3 Williams, *Culture and Society 1789–1950*, p. 37.
4 F.R. Leavis and Denys Thompson, *Culture and Environment: The Training of Critical Awareness* (London: Chatto & Windus, 1933), p. 91, in Williams, *Culture and Society 1789–1950*, p. 252.
5 Ibid., p. 253.
6 Ruth Benedict, *Patterns of Culture* (London: Routledge, 1961).
7 Mark Duffield, 'Getting Savages to Fight Barbarians and the Colonial Present', *Conflict, Security and Development*, 2005, Vol. 5, No. 2, pp. 142–159.
8 Frank Furedi, *Population and Development: A Critical Introduction* (Cambridge:

Polity, 1997) and *The Silent Race War: Imperialism and the Changing Perception of Race* (London: Pluto, 1998).

9 J. Dollard, L.W. Doob, Neil E. Miller, O.H. Mowrer and R.R. Sears, *Frustration and Aggression* (New Haven, CT: Yale University Press, 1939); Jose Ortega y Gasset, *The Revolt of the Masses* (London: Allen & Unwin, 1961); Gustave LeBon, *The Crowd: A Study of the Popular Mind* (New Brunswick, NJ: Transaction Publishers, 1995).

10 John Kenneth Galbraith, *Economic Development* (Cambridge, MA: Harvard University Press, 1964), p. 23.

11 Ibid., p. 24.

12 Walt W. Rostow, *The Stages of Economic Growth: A Non-Communist Manifesto* (Cambridge, MA: Cambridge University Press, 1960).

13 Max Millikan and Walt W. Rostow, 'Notes on Foreign Economic Policy', in Christopher Simpson (ed.), *Universities and Empire: Money and Politics in the Social Sciences during the Cold War* (New York: The New Press, 1998), p. 41.

14 Ibid., p. 54.

15 Amitai Etzioni, *The Hard Way to Peace: A New Strategy* (New York: Crowell-Collier Press, 1962), p. 203.

16 Edward Bernays, *Engineering of Consent* (Norman: University of Oklahoma, 1956); Benedict, *Patterns of Culture*.

17 For an excellent documentary which discusses the engineering of consent through consumerism, see Adam Curtis, *The Century of the Self*, first broadcast on BBC2, March 2003.

18 Margaret Mead (ed.), *Cultural Patterns and Technical Change* (Paris: UNESCO with the World Federation for Mental Health, 1953).

19 Ruth Benedict, *The Chrysanthemum and the Sword: Patterns of Japanese Culture* (Boston, MA: Houghton Mifflin Co., 1946).

20 Lycian Pye, *Politics, Personality and Nation Building: Burma's Search for Identity* (New Haven, CT: New York University, 1962); Lucian Pye and Sidney Verba, *Political Culture and Political Development* (Princeton, NJ: Princeton University Press, 1965).

21 Ellen Herman, *The Romance of American Psychology: Political Culture in the Age of Experts* (Berkeley: University of California Press, 1995), pp. 124–173.

22 Galbraith, *Economic Development*, p. 58.

23 Ibid., pp. 40–41.

24 Alex Ikeles and D.H. Smith, *Becoming Modern: Individual Change in Six Developing Countries* (Cambridge, MA: Harvard University Press, 1974), p. 9.

25 Walt W. Rostow, *Politics and the Stages of Growth* (London: Cambridge University Press, 1971), p. 26.

26 David C. McClelland, *The Achieving Society* (Princeton, NJ; London: Van Nostrand, 1961).

27 J.K. Galbraith, *The Nature of Poverty* (Cambridge, MA; London: Harvard University Press, 1979), pp. 61–62.

28 Galbraith, *Economic Development*, pp. 42, 46.

29 UNICEF, *Children of the Developing World* (London: William Clowes, 1964).

30 Gunnar Myrdal, *An International Economy* (New York: Harper & Bros, 1956), p. 133.

31 J.K. Galbraith, *The Affluent Society* (Harmondsworth: Penguin Books, 1962).

32 Ibid., p. 285; John Maynard Keynes, 'Economic Possibilities for Our Grandchildren', in *Essays in Persuasion* (London: Rupert Hart-Davies, 1952), p. 366.

33 Galbraith, *The Affluent Society*, p. 165.

34 Keynes, 'Economic Possibilities for Our Grandchildren'.

35 Dennis Gabor, *Inventing the Future* (Harmondsworth: Penguin, 1964), p. 105.

36 Ibid., pp. 108–109, emphasis added.

37 Ibid., p. 109.

38 Galbraith, *Economic Development*, p. 9.
39 Kerner Commission, National Advisory Commission on Civil Disorder, *Report of the National Advisory Commission on Civil Disorders* (Washington, DC: Government Printing Office, 1968); National Commission on the Causes and Prevention of Violence, *Report of the National Commission on the Causes and Prevention of Violence to Establish Justice, to Insure Domestic Tranquillity* (Washington, DC: Government Printing Office, 1969).
40 ILO, *The World Employment Programme. Report of the Director General of the ILO (part 1) to the International Labour Conference* (Geneva: ILO, 1969); ILO, *Employment Growth and Basic Needs: One World Problem. Report of the Director General of the ILO* (Geneva: ILO, 1976); G.A. Johnston, *The International Labour Organisation: Its Work for Social and Economic Progress* (London: Europa, 1970), p. 281.
41 Samuel Huntington, *Political Order in Changing Societies* (New Haven, CT: Yale University Press, 1968).
42 Dudley Seers, 'The Meaning of Development', in David Lehmann (ed.), *Development Theory: Four Critical Studies* (London: Frank Cass, 1979), p. 9.
43 Ibid.; ILO, *The World Employment Programme*; ILO, *Employment Growth and Basic Needs*.
44 E.F. Schumacher, *Small Is Beautiful: A Study of Economics as if People Matter* (London: Blond & Briggs, 1973).
45 Brandt Report: Independent Commission on International Development Issues, *North-South: A Programme for Survival* (London: Pan Books, 1980).
46 Ibid., p. 24
47 Herbert Marcuse, *One Dimensional Man: Studies in the Ideology of Advanced Industrial Society* (London: Routledge and Kegan Paul, 1964).
48 Ivan Illich, *Celebration of Awareness: A Call for Institutional Revolution* (Harmondsworth: Penguin, 1971), p. 143.
49 E.F. Schumacher, *A Guide for the Perplexed* (London: Jonathan Cape, 1977).
50 Amartya Kumar Sen, *Employment, Technology and Development: A Study Prepared for the International Labour Office within the Framework of the World Employment Programme*, with a foreword by Louis Emmerij (Oxford: Clarendon Press, 1975).
51 Maggie Black, *Children First: The Story of UNICEF, Past and Present* (New York: Oxford University Press, 1996).
52 UNDP, *The 2005 National Human Development Report for China* (2005), www.undp.org.cn/, p. 9 (accessed 10 March 2007).
53 *UN Millennium Development Goals Report 2006*, www.un.org/millenniumgoals/, p. 4 (accessed 10 March 2007).
54 D. Narayan, R. Chambers, M. Kaul Shah and P. Petesch (eds), *Voices of the Poor: Crying Out for Change* (Oxford: Oxford University Press for the World Bank, 2000).
55 Ibid., p. 21.
56 John Pender, "Empowering the Poor?" The World Bank and the "Voices of the Poor", in David Chandler (ed.) *Rethinking Human Rights: Critical Approaches to International Politics* (Basingstoke, UK: Palgave, 2002), pp. 97–114.
57 Deepa Narayan and Patti Petesch, *Voices of the Poor: From Many Lands* (Oxford: Oxford University Press for the World Bank, 2002), p. 217.
58 Narayan, Chambers, Shah and Petesch (eds), *Voices of the Poor*, p. 21.
59 Ibid., p. 264.
60 Ibid.
61 Auguste Comte, *The Positive Philosophy* (London: George Bell Republished Batoche Books Kitchner, 2000), p. 222, http://socserv2.mcmaster.ca/~econ/ugcm/3ll3/comte/Philosophy2.pdf.
62 www.makepovertyhistory.org
63 www.oxfam.org.uk/about_us/development.htm (accessed 4 November 2006).

64 Commission for Africa, *Our Common Interest: Report of the Commission for Africa* (London: Commission for Africa, 2005), p. 2.

65 Duffield, 'Getting Savages to Fight Barbarians and the Colonial Present', p. 152.

66 Wilde in Williams, *Culture and Society 1789–1950*, p. 175.

67 Jason Clay, *Exploring the Links Between International Business and Poverty Reduction: A Case Study of Unilever in Indonesia* (Eynsham: Oxfam GB, Novib and Unilever, 2005).

68 Christian Aid, *The Politics of Poverty: Aid in the New Cold War* (London: Christian Aid, 2004), p. 10, www.christianaid.org.uk/indepth/404caweek/index.htm (accessed 10 March 2007).

69 Rita Abrahamsen, *Disciplining Democracy: Development Discourse and Good Governance in Africa* (London: Zed Books, 2000).

70 Oxfam GB (2003/4) *Annual Review*, www.oxfam.org.uk/about_us/annual_review/downloads/Oxfam_review_2003–4.pdf (accessed 30 September 2005).

2 Whose civil society is it anyway?

Catherine Goetze

Introduction

Talking of civil society means to invoke the hope that non-governmental organizations (NGOs), social movements and third sector agencies make this world more humane and fair as they open up spaces for emancipation and freedom. Civil society is increasingly used as synonymous for democratic participation in order to correct the effects of neo-liberal economic globalizations and, at the same time, of overly intrusive state apparatuses. As such it has gained enormous importance in the programmes and speeches of international democratization efforts. In the context of Chinese politics, the emergence of civil society is seen as a sign of progress towards an assumingly more democratic system. Yet, before even the question can be asked who in China can or would be considered a civil society actor, the concept of civil society itself needs some closer scrutiny. This will be done in this chapter. The question to be answered is that of the very nature of civil society: how is it constituted, how does it relate to the other two sectors/spheres of the state and the market and what are the politics that are produced in it? Only if these questions are solved, the nature of the emerging associational sector in China can be analysed. Does the emerging associational sector in China foster the critical spirit and contentious potential that is normatively associated with the concept of civil society?

Indeed, despite its wide use, the concept of civil society is extremely vague and open to numerous interpretations. In this chapter, three models of civil society will be distinguished. Yet, this distinction serves an analytical purpose. The concept of civil society is so rich that clear-cut delimitations between different approaches are extremely difficult and disputed. Notably, the conceptualization that will be discussed below as the "republican-liberal model" has been formulated in its most elaborate way by theorists who aimed at capturing the new social movements of the post-1968 era with post-Marxist concepts of society and politics.[1]

This theorizing over new social movements is, however, in this chapter distinguished from another post-Marxist concept, the Gramscian hegemony model of civil society. The designation "republican-liberal" for the former approach serves first of all its distinction from the Gramscian model; yet, it also reflects the general acceptance of liberal democracy and market economy by the "new social movement" theorists – an acceptance that, from the perspective of the more critical Gramscian perspective – qualifies these approaches as republican-liberal.[2]

The two approaches make diametrically opposed assumptions on the social and political nature of civil society. The republican-liberal model considers civil society as a critical counterforce to the state and the market, whereas the hegemony model, based on the political thought of Antonio Gramsci, conceives of the global civil society as an extension of the hegemonic liberal thought and as supportive of liberal-democratic states and market economy. A third model will integrate both approaches in order to establish criteria which allow distinguishing the critical and the supportive features of civil society. This third model is based on the sociology of Pierre Bourdieu and his concepts of "fields", "capital", "discourse", "practice" and "symbolic power".

The republican–liberal–democratic model

With the triumph of the democratic-liberal ideology in Eastern and Central Europe, the notion of civil society rapidly spread to designate any kind of private-associational sphere that is considered to contribute to politics in the sense of producing and allocating collective goods. The basic definition of civil society simply defines it "as a complex and dynamic ensemble of legally pro-tected non-governmental institutions that tend to be non-violent, self-organizing, self-reflexive, and permanently in tension with each other and with the state institutions that 'frame', constrict and enable their activities".[3]

When at the end of the 1980s Eastern European dissident voices became louder and the one-party systems of Hungary, Poland and Eastern Germany col-lapsed, the Western academic community delightfully (re)discovered the concept of "civil society".[4] Essentially, the belief spread that the peaceful over-throw of the authoritarian one-party systems in Eastern and Central Europe was the result of the protest and tacit resistance of a large range of associations and informal organizations such as Solidarność in Poland or the Monday Demonstra-tions in Leipzig. The enthusiasm in the West over the virtues of civil society was also nourished by the intellectual dissident movements that had propagated the concept of "anti-politics" in the 1980s.[5] The idea of a social sphere in which people would organize their collective lives in the private realm, out of the reach of the (totalitarian) control of the state matched well Western left-liberal con-cepts of the third sector as socially organized response to state and market failure. Here, the idea was much debated that spheres exist in which politics were developed, discussed and applied beyond the institutionalized structures of the parliamentary system, party politics and "old" social movements.[6]

The enthusiasm about the political changes in Eastern and Central Europe revived republican-liberal ideas about citizen's participation and political action "from below". The republican-liberal model of civil society is by no means a coherent body of theoretical thought. On the contrary, much discussion is still going on as to its internal differentiations. Taylor, for instance, distinguishes between a Lockean and a Montesquieu thread of civil society theorizing, depending whether the stress falls on the self-regulating autonomy of the civil society (Locke) or on its complementary function in a republican separation of the public and private sphere (Montesquieu).[7] Some concepts develop more on the question of how this sphere organizes itself and how "social capital" is accumulated in it, while others focus on the contribution of civil society to democratic policy processes. Yet, all these different accounts are based on some shared basic assumptions. These basic assumptions are

a   that civil society is constituted of individual citizens;
b   which organize themselves in voluntary associations;
c   in a sphere which is not only distinct from the state and the market but which represents a critical and complementary sphere to these other two.

Only because citizens are solitary individuals, they have to associate in voluntary unions and this only because the state or the market cannot hinder them to do so. The basic unit of civil society is the citizen, that is the modern political individual as seen by the authors of Enlightenment: reasonable, rational, endowed with inalienable human rights, equal and ... solitary. For many authors of civil society, the modern individual is a particular strong personage as it is endowed with all the capacities of reasoning, critic and scepticism. Men/women are equal and free. He/she can agree or refuse the options of live that are offered to him/her. As John Hall states, civil society is about the individual being able to "escape any particular cage": "Civil society must depend upon the ability to escape any particular cage; membership of autonomous groups needs to be both voluntary and overlapping if society is to become civil."[8]

Having the choice is in fact the main characteristic of the enlightened individual. However, this freedom is constantly endangered by the overwhelming structures of social life, the state's powers and the market economy's subjugating forces.

The fact that individuals stand alone in the world makes associations necessary. Different reasons are indicated for this. Tocqueville points to the need of uniting forces in order to produce and distribute common goods as there is not one person anymore that holds the power to ordeal this task. In a more contemporary view, Michael Walzer equally ascribes this role of producing the common good to associations. As liberalism has separated the lives of human beings into different spheres of interaction, only the individual can assure the coherence of his/her life. If, however, the individual aims at continuing to live in a community, he/she is free to do so according to his/her choice. The fear of seeing the individual being absorbed by the Leviathan is the motivation of republican-liberal accounts of civil society.

The normative complexion of the notion, which is often criticized by its detractors, derives from the critical distance all authors have towards the state.

The autonomy of the individual's sphere of interaction is best preserved if the individuals take over most of the organization of their social lives. Yet, substantial differences exist concerning the question how the relationship between the individual and the state can be defined positively. In *Between Facts and Norms*, Habermas develops a vision of civil society that postulates an entire semantic cut-off of civil society from the state and the market. Civil society is supposed to be the sphere where the lifeworld is expressed without being corrupted by the semantic codes and social logics of power or money. Yet, civil society itself, e.g. its associations, is still embedded in the politics production cycle. They contribute to the input into the political system by their capacity to reflect and debate crucial issues of society and also by their capacity to raise protest and criticism towards the state's action.

Civil society is the intermediary sphere in which the life world experiences are translated into contributions to the public and political sphere. Political debate and democratic decision-making, notably the democratic process of deliberation, are based on the constant input by civil society. Associations are the institutions which produce and process this input:

> What is nowadays called the civil society explicitly does not include anymore the privately constituted economy which is regulated by labor-, capital- and commodity markets, as Marx and Marxism postulates. Its institutional core is rather formed by all those non-state and non-economic unions and associations on a voluntary basis, which root the public sphere structures of communication in the social component of the life world. Civil society is constituted of those more or less spontaneously created associations, organisations and movements, which, in the public sphere, absorb, condense, transmit and amplify the resonance that social problematiques obtain in the life world. It is a system of associations that constitutes the core of civil society; a system that institutionalizes discourses on the resolution of problems of general interest in the organized public [sphere].[9]

Habermas' and other rather republican-liberal accounts consider civil society not as an opposing force to the state, but they see the relationship as one of mutual interdependence, where the civil society represents a necessary counterweight to the state and the market. Republican-liberal theorists prioritize the complementary aspect as their basis of thought about civil society is not the oppressing dictatorial state but the institutionalized constitution of democracy. Indeed, democratic institutions and civil society go hand in hand as civil society constitutes the social facet of democracy from which the institutional facet, the parliamentary system, is nourished and sustained. The state and civil societies are therefore in continuous interaction and depend on the mutual exchange between their respective spheres. This perspective of interaction is well captured in Keane's definition of the civil society cited at the beginning of this section.

Such a relationship of interaction implies a functioning state, one that is able to frame, constrict and enable activities. Such a state will marshal effective policies, rule by efficient administrations, enforce its laws and ought to be able to rely upon the adherence of its citizens.

In sum, the concept of civil society postulates the ideal of the democratic citizen's community, which takes care of itself for all matters that do not have to be ruled by the authoritative rule of the state. The state depends on this community of citizens for its functioning as well as for its legitimacy – just in the same way as the community of citizens depends on the well-functioning of the state's democratic institutions of law-making. Associations are the intermediary link between the individual citizen and the state. They offer space for public debate and critique, and they are the realm where social belonging is reproduced and expressed in a functionally and socially differentiated society. Indeed, it is the space where politically defined citizens become socially defined members of the community. It is also the sphere where state policies are "tested", discussed, criticized and alternative visions are developed. At the same time that civil society is complementary to the state, it also offers the correctives of erroneous policies and it provides protection against the state.

The hegemony model

The ambiguity of the complementary assumption of the republican-liberal model is at the core of the critique that the hegemony model formulates. The angle of attack against the republican-liberal model is exactly the legitimacy that civil society organizations confer to the state and the market, even though they claim to be spheres of critique. The republican-liberal version of a critical civil society is accused of offering possibilities of incremental change to the state and the market that alleviate the *effects* of the political and economic structures without altering their *fundamental* oppressive and exploitative nature.

The hegemony model is largely based on the political thought of Antonio Gramsci and picks up on his assumption that civil society actually reproduces the political and economic system in its exploitative form. As Arato/Cohen summarize Gramsci's concept of civil society:

> The idea that runs through all these [Gramsci's] attempts at a definition [of civil society] is that the reproduction of the existing system outside the economic "base" occurs through a combination of two practices – hegemony and domination, consent and coercion – that in turn operate through two institutional frameworks: the social and political associations and cultural institutions of civil society, and the legal, bureaucratic, police, and military apparatus of the state and political society.[10]

The key difference between Gramsci's view of civil society and the republican-liberal model is the assumption that civil society is not separate from the state and market but that it is fundamentally shaped by it and that it reflects the power structures that emanate from the capitalist economy and the bourgeois state. Civil society *is*, indeed, hegemony as it is the cultural, mental, ideational expression of the dominating economic production structures and of the state that protects and enhances these production structures, the liberal state. Contrary to republican-liberal theory, the hegemony model of civil society assumes that civil society itself is *internally* characterized and structured by power.

The republican–liberal model is by no way ignorant of the effects of power on civil society, but it considers that the power is exercised from *without* civil society, namely by the state and the market, on the citizens and that civil society is a sphere that can protect individuals from this outside might. The hegemony model, on the other hand, postulates that civil society in itself constitutes a sphere of power, which is the specific power of hegemony.

This idea of the reproduction of hegemony has been refined in further post-Marxist accounts which are based on Gramsci's work, notably by referring to Michel Foucault's concept of power and the reproduction of power/knowledge through dominant discourses. Foucault's understanding of power differs fundamentally from that of most republican-liberal theorists, but also from most structuralist Marxist accounts.[11] According to Foucault, power is not a resource or a force that is exercised by one agent over another, neither is it a determinate characteristic of a particular social or economic structure. Power is, from his perspective, a state of social relations in which force is exercised by and through the agents one upon another. Power is therefore ubiquitous and omnipresent as there cannot be social relations without the exercise of some kind of force between the agents. At the same time, power is not an individual, intentional act. As Philp says: "Individuals are the effect of power, they are its subjects and its vehicles, not its point of origin."[12] Power is rather the form and the way by which social agents, or more precisely societies, are formed, socialized, inspired, motivated, integrated and – individually and socially – "incorporated". Power is not a "thing" but a quality of social relations. Power is the ensemble of practices[13] by which some social agents will act upon others and transform, influence and shape their ideas, their bodies, their spaces and, even, their time. Power has thus different appearances according to the different ways it shapes social relations. Foucault calls these different appearances "technologies of power" or "mechanisms of power" without necessarily indicating an intentional actor by these metaphors but rather a certain pattern of regular cause-to-effect chains in the way power becomes apparent.[14]

This conceptualization of power (the genealogy of power, in Foucauldian terms) de-institutionalizes power and makes it possible to consider power relations as existing and effecting society *outside* of established institutions. The observation focuses then on orders of power rather than on historical and discursively construed institutions. By doing so, the observation is furthermore not reduced to a simplistic functionalism that defines power (and its occurrences) by its immediate effect and, hence, conflates force and power. Functionalism neglects the overall structures and "tactics" of power; a genealogical view of power, however, retraces its properties and operating into the smallest capillaries of society.[15] This externalization of the observation process is particularly insightful if it is applied to the analysis of political rule as it overcomes the centrality of the state and its authoritative rule in favour of a broader but at the same time more sophisticated concept of "governmentality". Rather, it proposes to establish a genealogy of power in its apparitions outside the state and to conceive of this particular power not as rule, which is force by law, but as "governmentality", that is the capacity to govern minds, bodies, practices and actions of populations.

It is by defining governmentality as this capacity, which may exist besides, beyond and further than established institutions of coercion and force, that the concept has been widely applied for the analysis of civil society. In the neo-Gramscian view, civil society is considered as a sphere of "governmentality" in which power relations are deployed that are mainly shaped by the liberal discourses about capitalist production system and individual liberty. Civil society is mainly the arena in which the core elements of this order reproduced, exactly because it is the sphere in which private lives and, hence, private property and the discourse of individual freedom are protected from the coercive force of the state. Civil society reproduces this scheme as it gives legitimacy to individual and private action, independent and removed from the state, based on social relationships that are founded on the recognition of private, individual property.[16] Additionally, the reproduction of the dominant capitalist system takes place through the adoption of market mechanisms and techniques by the organizations and associations of the civil society.[17] Moreover, much of the international action of NGOs does not question the fundamental mechanisms of power generated by the capitalist system but only its effects in specific circumstances. They are, in the words of Ronnie D. Lipschutz, not concerned with the constitutive power relations that concern the very identity of social agents and society (the question of who *is* the society?), but with distributive power (the question of who gets what?).[18]

From this perspective, alternative ideas in civil society merely reflects the particularity of liberalism to be based on the dialectic of critique and integration. The very fact that critique is possible and necessary is a reproduction of the liberal order of ideas and of the central concept of the private individual. Instead being therefore a sphere where the fundamental exploitative character of capitalism is decried and contested, civil society criticism reproduces the foundations of these structures. By doing so, it successfully substitutes the lacking world state, by assuring basic public services on the one hand and by devising the dominant discourse on the state's stead.[19]

Yet, in the neo-Gramscian idea, civil society is not only a sphere of domination but also of social interaction in which potentially the resistance against the capitalist system and the repressive state can be organized.[20] In this respect, the dividing line between the republican–liberal model of civil society and the hegemony model becomes blurred. The question that arises is at what point criticism towards the state and/or the market will reproduce the existing structures and when will it lead to a fundamental change? The empirical question that follows from this is to know if the existing agglomerate of NGOs, social movements and associations correspond to the republican-liberal or the hegemony model of civil society.

The main difference between the two approaches lies in their different views of the nature of power in civil society and, consequently, on the normative judgment of the political character of civil society. Yet, neither approach is very explicit on the particular question of how power is generated and, in the case of the republican-liberal model that considers power as a resource of action, how it is distributed. The republican-liberal model tends to conflate power with forceful actors and the capacity to coerce social agents into behaviour (the famous definition of power by Max Weber). The particularity of the civil society approach is to assume, alongside Hannah Arendt, that such power can exist in low institutionalized contexts such as associations by the sheer force of shared communication and, hence, rules of arguing and normative persuasion.[21] It is this communicative power of civil society that counters the administrative power of the state or the colonizing power of the market.

The neo-Gramscian model offers a more sophisticated and wider vision of power as it is based on the Foucauldian assumptions of power relations but, in strictly Foucauldian terms, offers only a genealogy and no general framework of the loci and the actors of reproduction of these specific power "mechanisms". This implies two major limitations for political analysis: an epistemological one and an analytical. From an epistemological point of view, the Foucauldian approach is unsatisfactory as the deconstructivist turn of the genealogical approach cannot be stopped at its own deconstruction.

Moreover, the strict contingency that is assumed in the approach of genealogy[22] inhibits any assumption of regularity or pattern by which power is generated and typified. Yet, even though the real-life conditions of power might be contingent, the emergence of domination and subordination, of exploitation and change may well follow general patterns. Hence, the second major limitation of the Foucauldian conception of power is its incapacity to tell who, at what moment in time and under what conditions reproduces which type of power.[23]

This, however, would be necessary to know if we are to decide whether existing configurations of social movements, NGOs, non-state agencies and associations are better depicted by the republican-liberal model of civil society or by the neo-Gramscian interpretation. If the former is the case, the normatively formulated hope that the very existence of civil society "makes a difference" and will contribute to a better, fairer, more just, more human world is certainly justified. If, however, the latter is the case, then civil society as such does not make a difference. Only in the rather unlikely and difficult to define case that the actions of civil society alter existing *structures*, hopes for a better world are not entirely vain.

In order to devise between the two models, a more refined analytical model of civil society is needed. Notably, it has to be able to establish the link between agents of different spheres (state, market, and civil society), the power relations between these agents and the mechanisms by which these power relations are reproduced or altered. The sociology of Pierre Bourdieu offers concepts through which such an analytical grid can be developed.

Bourdieu and bridging the agent–structure gap

The different views of power in the republican-liberal model and the neo-Gramscian model can be traced back to their different conception of agency and structure. As the republican-liberal model is based on the idea of active citizenship, it naturally implies a strong concept of agency. The neo-Gramscian model, on the other hand, is mainly preoccupied by the structural constraints and limitations on agency which are attributed to the capitalist market and the "bourgeois" (rather the liberal) state. However, it is not quite appropriate to call Foucault's power notion "structural" as this implies some regular and recurring pattern of a law-like kind; Foucault sees power rather as a property that is diffused in the context of social behaviour and takes particular and contingent forms through knowledge regimes. It is neo-Gramscian analysis that has linked power to the knowledge regime of liberalism and capitalism and qualifies it accordingly as following the structural constraints of this specific political ideology and production form. Through this, neo-Gramscian analysis tries to nail down the loci of power in order to avoid the vagueness of the Foucauldian notion. Yet, the "structuralization" of the Foucauldian power notion remains agentless and omits, therefore, the possibility to distinguish between such actions in civil society that reproduce existing structures and such which fundamentally change them.

What is needed therefore is a conception of power and social reproduction of power that allows considering agency as well as the influence of economic, political and social structures which exist beyond and despite the agents. Bourdieu has developed a vision of society in which the structure–agency divide has been bridged.[24] Bourdieu's sociology is mainly preoccupied with the analysis of patterns of social domination and the question how such social domination is reproduced. The analysis of power is thus inherent to his sociology; yet, at the same time, the patterns of reproduction are studied as practice of concrete agents and not as agentless, material or essentialist structures.

According to Bourdieu's analysis, society consists of the relationships between social agents who dispose of different types of capital such as economic, cultural, social or political capital. "Capital" means not only material resources but also the reputation that are attributed to the owner of these resources. For instance, cultural capital is not only expressed in the amount of books a person has read and the knowledge he/she has accumulated but also in the title that a university has conferred to that person. The reputation is, in turn, not only defined by the capital and its "pure" recognition but by the social field in which this recognition takes place. Hence, a university title in literature studies represents less capital in a Mercedes car assembly workshop than at Cambridge University Press.

Social fields are not merely different functional spaces as this example might make think. Rather social fields are spaces of particular social practices that evolve around one given purpose. As such we can distinguish in a large sense the economic field, the political field, the cultural field, etc. and with a narrower focus the literary or the photographic field within the cultural field, the worker's or the small shop owner's field within the economic field, etc. Within these fields, social agents hold hierarchical positions according to their configuration of capital and its appropriateness for the field's purpose and "rules of the game". The rules of the game and the field's purpose are, in turn, defined by the need to reproduce the resources necessary for those configurations of capital that institute the social hierarchy inside the field. To take once again the example of a university degree, in an existing hierarchy of universities, the academic field will reproduce this hierarchy by reproducing a higher recognition for those titles and that knowledge that emanates from the universities that rank higher in the field. A PhD title from Harvard University and the specific knowledge taught at this university ranks higher than a PhD from St Nobody's College. PhD students from Harvard will have more capital than PhD students from St Nobody's and will arrive at socially higher positions. From these positions, they will aim at reproducing the content of teaching and the reputation of Harvard – not necessarily because they explicitly, voluntarily and intentionally want to reproduce social hierarchies but because they simply *think* that it is the best.

Social positions go along with specific ways of thinking about, behaving in, and interpreting the world. Bourdieu calls these "dispositions" and argues that these reflect the hierarchical positions in the social fields. They are the mental reproductions of the existing social structures. In the way they reproduce world visions, they also reproduce the rules of the game and conditions for the appropriate capital configurations as the decision of what is "right" or "wrong" is, effectively, a decision on the quality and quantity of capital that is needed in this particular social field.

The capacity to decide over and to define the essential forms of capital, their configuration and their mechanisms of reproduction in a given social field and across fields, that is what Bourdieu calls power.

Bourdieu's concepts of "practice", "habitus" and "discourse" link the analysis of agency to the analysis of structures. The social conditioning of acting, thinking and speaking contradict the idea of an autonomous individual; yet, human beings are not entirely caught in the iron cage of social structures as the enactment of practices, habitus and discourses gives large room for individuality and change. Yet, all three types of agency have to be seen, recognized and valued by the other social agents, so that the freedom of enactment is limited by the social field. But the interaction between the agents and the struggle over social hierarchies induce changes in the social fields which at the same time reflect and create changes in dominant capital configurations.

Using Bourdieu's analytical tools for the conception of civil society

Bourdieu himself did not elaborate a concept of civil society, yet his sociology offers valuable tools to analyse this sector of social activities in order to better understand the relationship between civil society actors and the sphere of the market and the state. The reason why Bourdieu has no theoretical concept of civil society is simply that he does not conceive of the state or the market as autonomous spheres or entities either. The other two approaches' tripartition of social action that falls into state, market and civil society does not exist in Bourdieu's conception of society and politics.

But it is possible to consider politics as taking place in social fields and to assume that the state and the market are actually such social fields. Bourdieu has formulated his theory of domination not only with regard to social hierarchies within fields but also among fields. With the concept of *homologie*, he argues that social fields tend to reproduce within the domination structures that reign among them, with some social fields reproducing quantitatively more and more relevant capital. The literary field for instance is subordinate to the economic field as the value of a novel is not only established by its intrinsic qualities but also by its market value. The chances of becoming a renowned novelist are higher if the novel is published by a big publisher with the necessary resources for marketing and distributing the book.

The most dominant fields are precisely the fields of the state and of the market. The state accumulates several types of capital, its mechanisms of reproduction and has the power to define what the relevant capital configurations are (for instance with its decisional power over education). Bourdieu calls this specific power to name relevant capital and to bestow it with normality *symbolic power*. The state is the social field that evolves entirely around this type of power. From Bourdieu's perspective, politics is the struggle over symbolic power, i.e. the definition of the socially relevant capital configurations.[25]

Similar to the neo-Gramscian model, Bourdieu assumes that social fields are pre-structured by the dominant fields of the state and the market. Yet, this structuring process is not solely due to the properties of capitalist material production process as Marxist would have it neither is it the result of the natural authority of the state as liberal state analysis argues. Rather the structuring is the self-reproductive process in which social agents are engaged. The processes of the political and the economic field cannot be seen as separate from other social fields.

What comes into focus, then, is exactly this process of reproduction. This is never a smooth process nor is it obvious to observe. As Wacquant says, analysts have to "reconstruct the evolving dialectic of habitus and field across the gamut of historical configurations, ranging from situations of agreement and reciprocal reinforcement at the one end of the continuum to cases of discordance and mutual undermining on the other".[26] Conflict arises when and if social agents struggle over the definition of the relevant configuration of capital. This offers an answer to the question whether civil society is really a critical corrective to the errors and failures of market and state or if they reproduce and sustain both systems. If the organizations in the civil society display, advocate and themselves reproduce a capital configuration which is strikingly different from the dominating one, then they are creating alternative discourses and are actually struggling over the symbolic power of the dominant position. If, however, their practices, habitus and discourses reflect patterns of dominant hierarchies, they are in the neo-Gramscian sense supportive of the liberal state and capitalist market system.

In this approach, the model of capital configuration can serve as template for the analysis of contemporary, real civil societies. The European and American (Western) history of democratic, parliamentary systems, the political history of statism as well as the social history of market economy sketch out the corner-stones of the dominant democratic-liberal capital configuration. As Meyer *et al.* have shown in several studies on "world culture", the model of the democratic-liberal, market economy state has become dominant over the world, outruling other types of polity organization and economic production. Jürgen Habermas' and Reinhard Kosellek's works on the emergence of civil society have pointed out that Western civil society has developed in the nineteenth century as corol-lary to the emerging industrial-bourgeois class that it reflects, the liberal separa-tion of public and private sphere and, in the end, contributed to the consolidation of the state.[27] The emergence of civil society as process went along with the functional and social differentiation of society, with rising social and geographic mobility, with urbanization and new forms of communalization that were essential to the capitalist production mode. Seligman emphasizes how the new anonymity of cities and the dissolution of traditional forms of communalization led to new forms of association, in which individuals would establish and reaffirm their modern identities:

> The rise of new forms of mediating institutions – neighbourhood associ-ations, guild and craft confraternities, vocational, kinship, and youth organi-zations, clubs of every size and devoted to every purpose (and in which, according to one contemporary observer, more than 20,000 Londoners met every night) – was predicated on the ability to move between, to negotiate and identify with more than one set of role identities and status positions.[28]

At the same time, parliamentarism was in the process of emerging and con-solidating as device of the new bourgeois classes to be protected against the (still) dynastic state rulers. As Teschke pointed out, the need of protection against dispossession by the King was, since the seventeenth century, one of the driving forces in the establishment of parliaments and their control of the King's budget and means of violence, and hence, of the creation of public law. The freedom to own property and the right to craft law meant the freedom from dis-possession. The change from absolutist feudality to individualized private ownership translated into a change of the social groups who defined, crafted and applied law.[29] Bourdieu himself has elaborated how this same process of shifting political power to the new emerging landlord and bourgeois classes in France had the side effect of creating bureaucratic and administrative elites who, in turn, crafted the state institutions which were to be their domains of expertise and influence.[30] By the nineteenth century, the separation of the public and private sphere was established as such but still in need of consolidation and affirmation. The "public", that is the agglomerate of clubs, associations, unions but also media and public arenas, resulted from the drive of these rising social groups to reaffirm their symbolic power.

The democratic nuance of civil society concept clearly derives from this part of the Western history, nicely summarized in Tocqueville's reading of American civil society in his *Democracy in America*. Yet, as the short overview above makes clear, this type of civil society reflects a particular configuration of capital. Put in a nutshell, this configuration is constituted as follows: an economic production system that is based on individual property rights and surplus production; a social system that is based on the ideal individuality and corresponding entitlements, codified in human rights and civic liberties; a political system that is constituted by state institutions, based on territorially defined sovereignty and, importantly, of the parliamentary monopoly of law-making and finally a political culture that gives expression to the ideas of individuality, of creativity, of productivity and which is closely knitted to the economic and political capital, that is to the capitalist production mode and the law-based government. The social group that disposes of property and is able to participate in the surplus production system will live in its daily practices and its habitus the cultural values which form the basis of a specific way of thinking of rights, law and political matters; in the case of civil society, this would be the values of charity, solidarity, tolerance, altruism, voluntary engagement, etc. These practices will reproduce the very conditions of the capital configuration which founds the social and political position of this group. The often depicted and commented practice of upper class wives who are deeply engaged in neighbourhood charity work is probably the most illustrative case of how the values of liberal capitalism are reproduced through cultural practices, the aim of charitable work being exactly not to alter the economic structures that have led to the pauperization of urban populations but only to remedy its effects in search of legitimizing exactly these economic structures.

Tensions arise if the reproduction of the social position implies the contestation of the dominant capital configuration as Schmidt has shown in the case of early worker movements' associations.[31] The liberal normative content of the civil society risks to be jeopardized if social associations which intentionally do not reproduce the above-mentioned values of charity, civility, etc.

These tensions materialize as real social conflicts when the legitimacy of liberal values is rejected in practice. Through alternative practices and direct confrontation, agents contest the capital configuration symbolized through these values by proposing and advocating alternative configurations of capital. These acts of denial constitute exactly the Gramscian advocated process of transforming civil society from within into a critical force towards liberalism and liberal state forms.

Analysing non-Western associational spheres with this model can reveal in how far these spheres constitute a critical counterforce to the existing dominance of market liberalism and a space of freedom for emancipatory citizenship. The analysis has to take a double perspective, first by analysing the locally dominant capital configuration and its resemblance to the Western, liberal civil society model and, second, by enquiring about alternatives to the local *and* the Western liberal form. The double bind of local and Western comparison is necessary as the liberal, Western model is incontestably the globally dominating model. In order to know in how far the associational sphere constitutes a critical force, proposing credible alternatives to social and political dominance, this has to be tested with respect to the local circumstances and the globalized "world culture".[32]

With respect to the Chinese case, four significant questions have to be asked. First, the social group which constitutes the leading social class at this time has to be analysed with respect to their participation and formation of an independent public sphere. Such an analysis has to pay particular attention to the duality of Chinese elites, that is the double career path of party cadres on the one hand and professionals on the other. Whereas some studies show that these career paths are very distinct,[33] others rather point out the interlinkage between political office and entrepreneurship.[34] If the first finding is correct, this can be read as the establishment of two very distinct capital configurations. This could, in turn, sketch out the space of potential conflict over symbolic power and, consequently, the establishment of a "private public sphere" which is distinct from the state party dominated public sphere. If, however, the second analysis proves to be true, then a high degree of homology between the political and economic field could be expected with an accordingly low level of conflict as the politically dominant social class is basically congruent with the economically social class. Neither one finding has sufficient overall empirical support so that further research is needed as to how the social stratification of China will develop with the economic transitions under way.[35] Special attention has to be given to regional differences in the patterns of social stratification and to distinct developments in rural and urban settings.

Second, the same caveat to carefully analyse the sociological evolution applies to the analysis of those social groups which had specific political and social power in communist mass organizations. Worker's unions, peasant associations and similar organizations have gone through tremendous changes in the last two decades, partly because they lost their political importance, partly because the issues they have to deal with nowadays have fundamentally changed since the end of the Mao era. Although these organizations have lost influence and symbolic power generally, they still dispose over a huge potential of collective action and representation. In the struggle over political decisions and influence, these organizations might well continue to play an important role, and as they are continuously marginalized in the process of market liberalization, they might even play an increasingly contentious and oppositional role.

Third, the importance of kinship ties and familism has to be taken into account. Familism is generally at odds with the concept of civil society. Civil society has been seen as a response to the Western phenomenon of individualized and socially differentiated modern societies. Some authors have therefore concluded that familism and civil society are mutually exclusive forms of social structures. Yet, this conclusion seems to be premature and incomplete as it does not clearly demonstrate why familism has negative effects on the development of civil society. In such societies where kinship ties still play a primary role of social structuring, it is necessary to consider it in the light of social capital, patronage and inequality.[36] In a Bourdieusan analysis of capital configurations in China, this type of social capital is of particular importance as it seems to be intimately linked with the distribution and configuration of economic and political capital. The study of Walder and Zhao for instance indicates that in rural settings kinship is actually the link between the political sphere of party cadres and the economic sphere of entrepreneurship and other sources of extra-agricultural income.[37] It needs to be established in more detail what types of capital configuration emerge out of this combination of family social capital, political administrative capital and economic capital and how much space they allow for a contentious, critical and emancipatory civil sphere.

The fourth factor to be considered in the Chinese context is the internationalization of Chinese activities of social self-organization, associational life and large parts of the "public sphere". This internationalization takes on different facets from the influence of the Chinese diaspora to the pressure of international donor agencies and trade partners. The influence and importance of diaspora and migrant communities in the economic transformation of China can be analysed under the angle of familism but also from the perspective of introducing new and different forms of social and cultural capital into the social stratification of Mainland China. This international embeddedness of China's transformation process is, however, to be distinguished from the international influence exercised through transnationally operating NGOs, through international donor programs (World Bank, IMF, UN agencies and others) and international pressure on the Chinese government for more human rights and democracy. Yet, both processes heavily shape the capital configuration of the local actors and they set out the cornerstones of the political struggle over symbolic power on the *global* level. Party cadres, entrepreneurs, NGO leaders or unionists do not only position themselves with respect to their local context but also with respect to the international and transnational resources they can mobilize, the legitimacy they can gain from global actors and with respect to the dominating social stratification on the global level.

Conclusion

This chapter sets out to establish a model of civil society that would allow to better analyse in how far the so-called global civil society justifies the normative hope that its existence will "make a difference" to the existing world political structure. With the opposition of the republican-liberal and the neo-Gramscian model of civil society, it became clear that both suffer from analytical weaknesses that preclude an empirical answer to the question. A third model, based on the sociology of Pierre Bourdieu and taking up central ideas of both approaches, was outlined. On the basis of this approach, an empirical research agenda can be established through with global civil society can be analysed in order to establish if it supports the existing order of liberalism and market economy or the degree to which it offers fundamentally different alternatives to it. Such a research agenda has to consider the sociology of the emerging class of entrepreneurs, their capital configuration and their relationship to existing patterns of political power.[38] Moreover, it has to take into account the role of "old social movements", of familism and of the international embeddedness of China's economic transformation process. Based on this analysis, a broader picture of capital distribution and configurations in Chinese society can be drawn. The resulting map of social spaces will then indicate the conflictual and critical potential inside Chinese society.

Notes

1 See for instance, A. Arato and J. Cohen, *Civil Society and Political Theory* (New Baskerville, MIT Press 1992).
2 See in more detail, G. Baker, *Civil Society and Democratic Theory: Alternative Voices* (London, New York, Routledge 2002).
3 J. Keane, *Civil Society: Old Images, New Visions* (Cambridge/Oxford, Polity Press 1988), p. 6.
4 J. Keane (ed.), *Civil Society and the State: New European Perspectives* (London, Verso 1988); J. Keane (ed.), *Europa und die Civil Society. Castelgondolfo Gespräche 1989* (Stuttgart, Klett 1991).
5 G. Konrad, *L'antipolitique* (Paris, La Découverte 1987); V. Tismaneanu, *Reinventing Politics: Eastern Europe from Stalin to Havel* (New York, Free Press 1992).
6 J. Habermas, *Theorie des Kommunikativen Handelns* (Frankfurt, Suhrkamp 1981); Arato and Cohen, *Civil Society and Political Theory*; J. Habermas, *Faktizität und Geltung* (Frankfurt a.M., Suhrkamp 1998).
7 C. Taylor, "Die Beschwörung der Civil Society", in K. Michalski (ed.), *Europe und die Civil Society. Castelgondolfo Gespräche 1989* (Stuttgart, Klett 1991), pp. 52–84; A. Thomas, "Liberal Republicanism and the Role of Civil Society", *Democratization*, Vol. 4, No. 3 (1997), pp. 26–44.
8 J.A. Hall, "In Search of Civil Society", in J.A. Hall (ed.), *Civil Society: Theory, History, Comparison* (Cambridge, Blackwell 1995), pp. 15–17.
9 English, see J. Habermas, *Between Facts and Norms: Contributions to a Discourse Theory of Law and Democracy* (Cambridge, MIT Press 1996); German, see Habermas, *Faktizität und Geltung*, p. 443; translation Catherine Goetze.
10 Arato and Cohen, *Civil Society and Political Theory*, p. 145.
11 M. Philp, "Foucault on Power: A Problem in Radical Translation?" *Political Theory*, Vol. 11, No. 1 (1983), p. 34.
12 Ibid., p. 36.
13 Although "practice" is not a very Foucauldian term.
14 M. Foucault, *Sécurité, Territoire, Population. Cours au Collège de France, 1977–1978* (Paris, Gallimard, Seuil 2004), pp. 10–11.
15 Ibid., p. 119–123
16 R.D. Lipschutz, "Power, Politics and Global Civil Society", *Millennium: Journal of International Studies*, Vol. 33, No. 3 (2005), pp. 747–769.
17 See for instance, J.M. Beier, "'Emailed Applications Are Preferred': Ethical Practices in Mine Action and the Idea of Global Civil Society", *Third World Quarterly*, Vol. 24, No. 5 (2003), pp. 795–808.

18 Lipschutz, "Power, Politics and Global Civil Society", pp. 763–764.
19 O.J. Sending and I.B. Neumann, "Governance to Governmentality: Analyzing NGOs, States, and Power", *International Studies Quarterly*, Vol. 50, No. 3 (2006), pp. 651–672.
20 J.A. Buttigieg, "Gramscis Zivilgesellschaft und die Civil Society Debatte", *Das Argument*, Vol. 306 (1994), p. 539.
21 Habermas, *Faktizität und Geltung*, p. 182ff.
22 And for this matter in the approach of "archaeology", the other Foucauldian methodology.
23 Obviously, from the point of view of Foucault's approach this limitation is not one as any definition of the who, where, what questions is again in itself a reflection of a power order and cannot claim to be explaining society. Yet, Foucault himself concedes the possibility of altering and changing orders of power, even of some form of emancipation, and his very existence as scholar, historian and philosopher indicates some hope for escaping the *perpetuum mobile* of dominant power/knowledge regimes.
24 The following very rough and abridged presentation of Bourdieu's sociology does not draw on one specific text of his but rather on the accumulated reading of P. Bourdieu, *Esquisse d'une théorie de la pratique, précédé de trois études d'ethnologie kabyle* (Paris, Editions du Seuil 1979); P. Bourdieu, *La Distinction. Critique sociale du jugement* (Paris, Les éditions de minuit 1972/2000); P. Bourdieu, *Sozialer Raum und Klassen. Leçon sur la Leçon* (Frankfurt a.M., Suhrkamp 1985); P. Bourdieu, *La Noblesse d'Etat. Grandes écoles et esprit de corps* (Paris, Les éditions de minuit 1989); L. Wacquant and P. Bourdieu, *Réponses* (Paris, Editions du Seuil 1992); P. Bourdieu, *In Other Words, Essays towards a réflexive sociology* (Cambridge, Polity 1994); P. Bourdieu, *Propos sur le champ politique* (Lyon, Presses Universitaires de Lyon 2000); P. Bourdieu, "From the King's House to the Reason of State: A Model of the Genesis of the Bureaucratic Field", *Constellations*, Vol. 11, No. 1 (2004), pp. 16–36; L. Pinto, G. Sapiro and P. Champagne (eds), *Pierre Bourdieu, Sociologue* (Paris, Fayard 2004).
25 Bourdieu, *Propos sur le Champ Politique*.
26 Wacquant and Bourdieu, *Réponses*, p. 3.
27 J. Habermas, *Strukturwandel der Öffentlichkeit; Untersuchungen zu einer Kategorie der bürgerlichen Gesellschaft* ([Neuwied], Luchterhand 1974).
28 A.B. Seligman, *Problem of Trust* (Ewing, NJ, Princeton University Press 1997), p. 71.
29 B. Teschke, "Theorizing the Westphalian System of States: International Relations from Absolutism to Capitalism", *European Journal of International Relations*, Vol. 8, No. 1 (2002), p. 252.
30 Bourdieu, "From the King's House to the Reason of State."
31 J. Schmidt, *Zivilgesellschaft und nicht-bürgerliche Trägerschichten* (Berlin, Wissenschaftszentrum Berlin 2004).
32 J.W. Meyer, J. Boli, G.M. Thomas and F. Ramirez, "World Society and the Nation-State", *American Journal of Sociology*, Vol. 103, No. 1 (1997), pp. 144–181.
33 See A.G. Walder, B. Li and D. Treiman, "Politics and Life Chances in a State Socialist Regime: Dual Career Paths into the Urban Chinese Elite, 1949 to 1996", *American Sociological Review*, Vol. 65, No. 2 (2000), pp. 191–209.
34 See for more detail, A. Walder and L.T. Zhao, "Political Office and Household Wealth: Rural China in the Deng Era", *China Quarterly*, Vol. 186 (2006), pp. 360–362.
35 Ibid.
36 See for a helpful discussion, E.P. Reis, "Banfield's Amoral Familism Revisited: Implications of High Inequality Structures for Civil Society", in J.C. Alexander (ed.), *Real Civil Societies: Dilemmas of Institutionalization* (London, Sage 1998), pp. 21–39.

37 Walder and Zhao, "Political Office and Household Wealth."
38 Mind that this does not imply that this group has to perceive itself as coherent "class" in the sense that is disposes of a commonly shared identity. Rather Bourdieu's sociology suggests that the individual's cognition, perception, world vision as well as practices and discourses will be independently similar if they dispose of the same configurations of capital. There is hence no need for a common identity, contrary to the analysis of Tsai for instance K.S. Tsai, "Capitalists without a Class – Political Diversity among Private Entrepreneurs in China", *Comparative Political Studies*, Vol. 38, No. 9 (2005), pp. 1130–1158.

3 Non-governmental organizations, non-formal education and civil society in contemporary Russia

Grigory A. Kliucharev and W. John Morgan

> The Government could not accept that a half of the population is educated not by the state, but is self-educated or as the result of a charity set up by somebody else.[1]

Introduction

The concept of civil society is fundamental to the achievement of an authentic democracy. It provides a framework for citizenship participation and action autonomous of State authority and control. It creates the conditions in which individual citizens, associations, societies and other group interests may achieve a voluntary, legal and hopefully harmonious but not subservient relationship with the State. The countries that comprised the former Soviet Union have emerged in recent decades from the control of a political system that regarded civil society as a challenge to its authority.

This chapter examines the growth of a nascent civil society in the Russian Federation since the end of the Soviet Union. It does so first by considering the concept of civil society theoretically and historically. It then examines contemporary Russia, focusing on the specific example of non-formal (and informal) education provided by clubs, societies and other voluntary associations. Does such an educative opportunity and experience, separate from that provided by the State provide a source for the grass-roots development of civil society in contemporary Russia? Some case studies are considered in answer to this question, drawing upon data derived from an empirical survey conducted by the Institute of Sociology, the Russian Academy of Sciences, in 2005–2006. This chapter concludes with an assessment of the condition of civil society in contemporary Russia, the continuing potential of non-formal education to contribute to sustain its growth and the relevance of the Russian experience for the People's Republic of China.

Civil society, voluntary associations and non-formal education

The concept of civil society is one used by many political theorists from the seventeenth century onwards, originally by the Scotsman Adam Ferguson[2] and by the Englishmen, Thomas Hobbes and John Locke. Civil society was seen as being the sphere in which ordinary citizens, without political authority, live their lives. In *The Philosophy of History*, first published in 1837, G.W.F. Hegel identified this as intermediate between the private citizen and family on the one hand and the political authority of the State on the other.[3] This social sphere is made up of a flexible and changing pattern of associations, some based on the family, such as kinship structures, and others based on voluntary membership and active participation such as religious organizations, economic relationships such as traders and craft guilds and other common interest groups. This Hegelian account was developed by Marx and Engels, notably in *The German Ideology* written in 1845.[4] It was further developed from a Marxist perspective by Antonio Gramsci in his analysis of the development of hegemonic power through the coercive authority of the State, the economic relations of production and civil society or social life, where the individual citizen appears to have some private autonomy and the opportunity to exercise consent.[5] In a paper given in 1989, Morgan suggests the idea of civil society as a 'shock-absorber' between the coercive authority of the State. State-socialist societies attempt to 'swallow up' both the individual and society through their simultaneous bureaucratic control over the economic relations of production, and the private realm of the citizen.[6] Single-party states, such as the former Soviet Union, regard civil society as a challenge to their ideological and hegemonic authority. Such a State seeks to incorporate or even eliminate what it sees an ideological rival. The *appearance* of a civil society may be maintained, but its *essential* autonomy and voluntary nature will be denied.

As Morgan has pointed out elsewhere, there have been many examples of the relationship between non-formal education and civil society on the one hand, and the practice of citizenship on the other, notably in Britain.[7] The concept of non-formal education is an important one, and a brief explanation of its form and significance is necessary. All States have formal education systems, albeit different in structure and form, and these are identified as significant characteristics of economic and social modernization. Such formal education systems are crucial agencies through which States and those in political authority achieve their ideological and hegemonic goals. It is true however that, in some societies, formal education may be provided privately i.e. separately from the State, but usually regulated and licensed by it. Such formal education is characterized also by institutional instruction, approved curricula, length of course and the award of credentials. However, there are other ways in which an individual may acquire knowledge and skills and that is through taking advantage of non-formal and informal opportunities to learn. Such opportunities do not depend on formal structures and characteristically do not lead to an award or credential. This is not to say that structure does not exist and there may be an agreed program for learning. However, this will be voluntary and determined by the learning needs of the individual or group participating. This is a distinction often drawn between non-formal education and informal or, as it is sometimes known, incidental education. Even with informal education, it may be possible to identify a pattern e.g. regularity of learning for instance.[8] The voluntary association, such as the mutual interest club, is a classic location for non-formal and informal education. The family is, of course, a classic location for informal and incidental learning. There are many other examples, the key point being that they are located within the framework of civil society which is in a condition of negotiated autonomy with political and State authority. The implications for single-party systems or ideologies are clear, and the revival of interest in the concept of civil society during the past thirty years has much to do with the collapse of State-socialism in the Soviet Union and in its satellite states in eastern and central Europe.

Voluntary associations and civil society in Russia

The first club in Russia of a recognizably modern type and named interestingly enough *Angliiski* (English) was established in 1770 in St Petersburg. Its membership was comprised of representatives of the social and political élites. It later attracted intellectual and cultural figures, including famous poets and writers such as Alexander Pushkin, Ivan Krylov and Vasili Zhukovsky. On the eve of the nineteenth century, a number of clubs were opened in other Russian cities for noble local citizens to provide joint *bali* (balls), *maskaradi* (fancy-dress balls), *blagotvoritel'nie obedi* (charity meals). In 1853, the *Shahmatny* (Chess) club was established in St Petersburg by members of the liberally oriented intelligentsia. This was the first informal establishment of its kind where members shared progressive and democratic ideas of social improvement. The well-known radical writer Nikolai Chernyshevsky, who later had an influence on the communist movement in Russia, was among its leading members.

The first cultural establishments for the general public were opened in the same period. The facilities of the so-called *Narodnie Doma*[9] (People's Houses) consisted usually of a library with a reading room and small bookshop, a performance hall, classes for the Sunday School (of the Orthodox Church) and a tea room. People's Houses were provided by the local councils or by charitable organizations. An example of its activities in the field of non-formal education is provided by the *Obszhestvo Gramotnosty* (Society for Literacy). Its members were active in developing reading and writing among workers and artisans. Such examples of non-formal education were accompanied by a growing interest in late imperial Russia in the possibilities of a civil society contribution to the governance of the country.[10] It has been pointed out that during the period of the Russian constitutional monarchy, 1907 and 1917, the traditional Russian bureaucracy's monopoly of state business was challenged by autonomous public organizations, especially following the outbreak of World War I in 1914, which placed the Russian State under great strain.[11] The opportunity to establish a democratic relationship between a constitutional State and an authentic Russian civil society was lost with the Bol'shevik Revolution of October 1917 which established the dictatorship of the Communist Party.

The Bol'sheviks, the most authoritarian wing of the Russian communist movement, had long been engaged in the organization of political education and propaganda among the proletariat through workers' clubs. They were especially effective in the period between the Russian Revolutions of 1905 and 1917. Their activities were quite similar to the forms of political education carried out by socialist and communist groups in Western Europe at that time.[12] When the Bol'sheviks came to power, they paid special attention to political education, developing a Communist Party controlled network of workers' and peasants' clubs. A separate department for out-of-school work (*vneshkol'ny otdel*) in *Narkompros* was responsible for arranging the programs of these clubs throughout the Soviet Union. *Agit-concerts*, meetings, political *information*, lectures, evenings for questions and answers were provided for the Soviet working population on a regular basis and on a vast scale.

In the late 1920s, first Houses of Culture were opened, followed in the early 1930s by the more elaborate Palaces of Culture. These were usually under the control of local soviets or of Communist Party controlled trade unions. In rural areas, in almost every middle-sized settlement (over a 1,000 in population) a club and a library were provided by the local collective agricultural commune (*kolhoz* and *sovhoz*). In smaller settlements, the role of clubs was delegated to *izba-chital'nya* (originally one–two rooms for public use in a peasant's house). The *Glavpolitprosvet*[13] or Commissariat of Enlightenment (responsible for both formal and non-formal education) launched innovative forms of political education – mobile libraries, cinemas, exhibitions to reach peoples in remote villages.[14] A special and very effective method, considering the vast territory of the Soviet Union, was the use of agit-trains and agit-ships. A fundamental aim was to break the hegemonic influences of the former Tsarist society, such as that of the Orthodox Church. There was accordingly a determined campaign promoting atheistic ideology.[15] The purpose and form of these campaigns of 'enlightenment' was the subject of intense internal debate within the Communist Party, especially in the 1920s.[16] However, with the consolidation of Stalin's control, everything came rigidly under the ideological control of the Party and its cadres. The human cost of the Stalinist period has been well documented,[17] but the 'hidden damage' inflicted by on Russian society, its culture and intelligentsia is still being explored.[18]

In later years, such clubs and cultural establishments remained the basis of the political work of the Communist Party with the general population. However, in addition to *politicheskye kruzhki* (political study circles) and *Universities of Marxism–Leninism* linked directly to the Communist Party,[19] there were other forms of people's non-formal education and self-activity such as the *Narodnie Universitety* (People's Universities). These should be considered as among the most effective forms of club activity in the USSR. It is worth noting

Table 3.1 The development of clubs in Russia (in 1,000s)

Year	Total number of clubs	Urban areas	Rural areas
1913	0.2	0.1	0.1
1922	12.2	3.6	8.6
1940	118.0	10.0	108.0
1945	94.4	6.5	87.9
1950	125.4	9.3	116.1
1960	128.6	14.1	114.5
1975	135.1	20.2	114.9

that by 1976 there were more than 35,000 people's universities. They attracted and united people interested in music (*hudozhestvennaja samodejatel'nost'*), handicrafts, art and performance and literature.[20] The dynamics of the growth of club establishments in the USSR is depicted in Table 3.1.[21]

In practically all cases, however, during the Soviet period clubs were providers of Communist Party and State ideology, rather than authentic examples of civil society. A further example is that of the Communist Party controlled trade unions which, together with the State, managed 'palaces of culture' that housed workers' clubs and leisure time activities. These focused on developing vocational skills, honoring the leaders of socialist competition among employees and workers and promoting communist ideological leadership. By 1975, there were 99,226 club establishments functioning under the Ministry of Culture and 21,107 – under the trade unions. The most famous palaces of culture were based on heavy industry which had large concentrations of workers e.g. of the car industry plant named after Likhachev in Moscow, of the textile industry in Ivanovo, of the *Kyznetsks* steel industries in Siberia, of *Energetik* (power producer), of the *Angarsk* oil processing plant and of the *Dzherzhinsk* chemical industries. It is worth saying that club personnel were trained and given opportunities for professional development. Some 132 tertiary colleges throughout the country and sixteen universities (institutions) prepared the young school graduates and re-trained employees to be effective and innovative in managing club establishments and their particular programs. An example during the Soviet period was the influential Higher Trade Union School based in Moscow and with regional branches.

The end of the Soviet Union

Even before the final collapse of the Soviet Union, there was a significant interest in the possibilities of a nascent civil society in Russia. The question was whether the policies of *glasnost* (openness) and of *perestroika* (re-construction) introduced by Mikhail S. Gorbachev, then General Secretary of the Communist Party, could permit the maintenance of a State-socialist system in harmony with greater freedom and autonomy for citizens and their private spheres of action?[22] This proved to be impossible and the Soviet Union gave way to a Confederation of Independent States, including Russia, and a lengthy and uncertain period of political and economic transition.

The economic and political implications have been analyzed at some length, sometimes in comparison with economic change in the People's Republic of China.[23] There have also been attempts to consider the implications of the transition for educational policy and practice.[24] The present authors have contributed to this debate, notably through providing analyses of Russian adult and non-formal education that focus on the implications for ordinary Russians as they were required to make the ideological transition from 'comrades to citizens'.[25]

There has also been a significant revival of interest in the general concept of civil society and its practical reality, first in post-Soviet Russia and, most recently in the Russia that seems to be consolidating under the so-called 'managed democracy' of Vladimir Putin. These include a well-informed and comprehensive critical assessment of the present state of civil society in Russia, with the weakness that it is essentially a 'view from a distance', in that its authorship is exclusively non-Russian.[26] There are also very useful collections of essays, produced collaboratively by Russian and foreign scholars, that focus on civil society and the search for justice in Russia[27] and on the crucial relationship between Russian Orthodox Christianity and the construction of civil society and democracy in Russia.[28] As Gvosdev points out in his contribution to the 2004 volume, the Orthodox Church is 'the single largest national non-governmental actor in the Russian Federation with over ten million active members, far outstripping any political party or other voluntary association'.[29] Such studies, including those of the relationship between civil society and religious groups, will again be of comparative value to those interested in the People's Republic of China, given the political and economic conditions pertaining there.[30]

The law on non-governmental organizations (NGOs)

We turn now to an analysis of the present status of non-governmental organizations (NGOs) and voluntary associations in Russia and of the opportunities they provide for the non-formal education of citizens. How is an NGO defined in contemporary Russia? In practice, these include such varied groupings as:

- Non-profit partnerships, establishments, endowments, foundations, funds, associations and unions. Trade unions are also to be considered and treated as NGOs since there is no special legislation for them.
- They range from small clubs such as *allotment* or agricultural clubs – *sadovoogorodnoe tovarishestvo*) to huge organizations (considering the size of the membership and the total budget of the organization) such as the *Russian Soyuz Promyshlennikov I Predprinimateley* (*The Alliance of Employers and Entrepreneurs*).

Legally, these are all regulated according to the *Federal Law on Public Organizations* (adopted originally by the State Duma or Lower Chamber of the

Parliament on 14 April 1995). The key articles of this legislation are summarized below:

Article 3: the right of citizens to establish a civil society organization

This means:

- The legal right to establish voluntary public organizations in order to protect common interests and to achieve common goals.
- The legal right to join existing public organizations; or not to join them and to resign from membership at any time. (This is an important right of citizenship in contrast with the effective compulsion of the Soviet period.)
- The legal right to establish a public voluntary organization without the preliminary permission of the State authorities (This is now replaced by obligatory registration with the State authorities.).

Article 5: the notion of a public organization

- A voluntary, self-governed, non-profit organization, established on the initiative of citizens, motivated by common interests for the realization of goals stated in the statutes of their organization.
- Public organizations are conceived as helping to realize the rights and interests of citizens autonomously from the State.
- Citizens may establish public organizations either by direct cooperation of individuals or through juridical organizations.

Recent developments

In the late autumn of 2005, the State *Duma* (Lower Chamber of Parliament) initiated new legislation to regulate NGOs. The motives for changing the federal legislation are rooted both in the juridical and in the political domains. The political opposition to the new Law was provided chiefly by the NGOs themselves which by then numbered thousands throughout Russia and registered at federal and local level. As their representatives pointed out, the opinion of these organizations and their members was not considered by the Russian Government when preparing the legislative proposals.

However, the legislation is not necessarily sinister in intention. The main purpose of the new law was to make the activity and financing of the NGOs transparent. It is worth mentioning that dozens of NGOs, especially sporting and religious ones, had been allowed special tax reduction guarantees. As a result, the state budget lost a great deal of potential income as some of these organizations were, in practice, engaged in commercial activities far away from their stated social purposes. It should also be noted that the *Basic Law* on NGOs dates from as early as 1995. For a country in such rapid social transition, a decade is a very long period. In the early and middle 1990s, there was a period of economic and political instability in the country, which some economists have compared with the historical development of the 'Wild West' in the early nineteenth century United States. In short, the real activities and incomes of many NGOs are very hard to regulate and to control; they are often hidden in a very complicated system of bankruptcy, charity and corruption. For the financial activities of an NGO to be made transparent and subject to legal requirements should not be seen as State control, but as bringing Russian practice in line with that of other democratic states such as the United Kingdom which, for instance, regulates such matters through the Charities' Commission.

Most Russian NGOs are engaged in social, humanitarian and even political activity. In this context, the new requirement of their formal registration with the State is interpreted by some observers as an attempt to establish a system of controlling their activity centrally. This is emphasized by the fact that political NGOs greatly affected the outcome of the recent political revolutions in the Ukraine and in Georgia. However, there is another important reason to make the activity of NGOs more transparent. Extremist and terrorist organizations supported by international religious radicals can and do make use of NGOs for their activity. According to the new registration procedure, organizations of this type would be identified and placed outside the law. It should also be noted that in recent years legislation generally relating to economics, social affairs and politics has been greatly updated, taking into account the changing circumstances since the end of the Soviet Union. Thus, the new law on political parties was adopted in 2004.[31] Again, there is the legislation regulating the activity of private enterprises such as the *OOO* (Commercial Community Open for Stakeholders), the *OAO* (Autonomous Commercial Community) and the *ZAO* (Commercial Community Closed to New Stakeholders). Now, it is the turn of the NGOs and voluntary associations for legislative modernization.

Non-governmental organizations in practice

What does an NGO or voluntary association do in practice and why? Obviously, because of their very great diversity, it is difficult to provide a simple system of classification. In contemporary Russia, the following organizations are considered to be NGOs: non-profit partnerships, clubs, endowments, foundations, funds, associations and unions. Trade unions are also now considered and treated as NGOs, since there is no special legislation for them. The same is true for both small membership clubs, such as the *allotment* or agricultural clubs – *sadovoogorodnoe tovarishestvo*) and huge organizations such as the *Soyuz Promyshlennikov I Predprinimateley* (*The Alliance of Employers and Entrepreneurs*), which comprises the country's business elite. The next substantial group of public communities (clubs) consists of public organizations (obzhestvennie organizatzii), public movements (obzhestvennie dvizhenja), public foundations (obzhestvennie fondy), public offices (obzhestvennie uchrezhdenja) and bodies for public self-activity (organy obzhestvennoi samostojatel'nosti).

In Russia, they are usually relatively new, immature political and social movements. Many engage in political or social issues, but with a specific way, as pressure groups rather than as political parties seeking election to the legislature or to government. For example, Human Rights Watch, Greenpeace and similar organizations come into this category. At the other end of a very wide spectrum are those voluntary associations which have come into being to serve the common interest of the membership. Sporting, leisure time, cultural and intellectual pursuits, and religious organizations are the most numerous examples. Such common interest groups also tend to form according to social factor such as age, sex, ethnic background, religious affiliation and so on. However, the main characteristic of an NGO or voluntary association of citizens is acceptance of the principle of the non-profit purpose of its mission. This should be stated clearly in the foundation statute of the organization. If any profit or income is made as the result of the organization's activity, the entire should be used to promote further activity, rather than be divided among the membership. They are stakeholders who usually pay a membership fee and have voting rights determining the objectives and conduct of the organization, but they are not shareholders in commercial profit-making organizations.

Three case studies

There are many possible examples. We have restricted ourselves to three significant ones, chosen because they illustrate different aspects of the contribution of voluntary NGOs to the development of democratic citizenship and civil society. The first is an example of an NGO as a significant pressure group affecting urgent public policy. The second shows how a voluntary association can contribute to the non-formal intellectual development of the citizen.

The third, based on recent survey data, illustrates the contribution of voluntary clubs to the development of social capital and community cohesion, especially in remote rural areas, of which there are many in Russia.

The Union of the Committees of Soldiers' Mothers

One of the most active NGOs is *Soyuz Komitetov Soldatskih Materei or* the Union of the Committees of Soldiers' Mothers.[32] Its purpose is to help over one million Russian families whose sons are to join the Army. Normally, it provides consultations informing women how to protect the rights of their sons in military service; there have been many cases when the Union won civil actions in the courts. Most importantly perhaps, the Union has established a political party of soldiers' mothers – which participates in elections for various bodies. Although only women may be members, it is not intended as a gender NGO, since whole families are involved with cases.

The non-formal education activity of the organization includes a number of courses, trainings for mothers, parents and even those who are to join the Army. They attend seminars where all the legislative background of military service is studied. In short, the NGO creates the conditions for *informed participation*.[33] It

Table 3.2 The main activities of the Union of the Committees of Soldiers' Mothers

---

The reform of the military according to the needs of Russian society.
The implications of the continuing war in Chechnya.
Redressing violations of conscripts' legal rights.
The question of the militarization of the school curriculum.
The need to provide adequate legal representation and protection for soldiers.
The need to provide personal identification of fatal casualties.

---

is both non-formal and informal or incidental learning that combats bureaucracy; in this case that of the Army. It is a learning experience that builds the self-confidence and competence of individual citizens and establishes democracy and civic society. The current activities of the NGO are shown in Table 3.2.

The Union of Committees of Soldiers' Mothers (UCSM) has also addressed important statements to the President, the Government and the Federal legislative authorities on the necessity to reform the budget process and classification concerning military expenditure. In addition, it has addressed important statements to the Secretary-General of the United Nations, to the Council of Europe and to other human rights and international women's NGOs and to other international organizations supporting the principle of gender equality in the maintenance of peace and security. At a practical level, UCSM members visit military commanders, military units and military hospitals on a regular basis. Visits are also made to military prosecutors' offices in Moscow and elsewhere. Members often participate actively in the meetings of the main Military Prosecution Board. The main reasons for these visits are to achieve common understanding of the problems of human rights protection of soldiers and their parents, to establish working contacts with the State's military authorities and to resolve successfully the most serious individual complaints about the violations of human rights.

The Russian Philosophical Society[34]

The *Rossiiskoe Filosofskoe Obzhestvo* or Russian Philosophical Society (RPhS) is a successor (since 1992) of the Society of Philosophers of the USSR, founded in 1971. It is a non-commercial, scientific organization, that unites philosophers occupied in the field of philosophical research and teaching philosophy. Every member of the Society pays a membership fee for every current year. Today, it has over 4,000 members, including foreign philosophers (for example, eight American philosophers are members of the RPhS).

Its goals are the dissemination of philosophical knowledge and wisdom. In less than a decade, it has arranged dozens of seminars, conferences and congresses. It publishes on a regular basis a very informative *Quarterly* and aims also at dialogue with academic and other public education authorities. Recently, the Society became open not only to professional academics, but to any citizen. Consequently, among its current membership are those without advanced formal

Table 3.3 Non-formal education provided by the Russian Philosophical Society

Bioethics: contemporary problems
Critical thinking and decision making
Daily life in Russia and social change
The fate of Marxism in Russia
Gender studies: Problems and perspectives
Philosophical problems of free thinking
Philosophical problems of regional cultural development
Philosophy and methodology of social and ecological politics
Social philosophy and the nation
Technology, culture and the environment in the contemporary world
Violence and non-violence in the modern world
World religions and their dialogue

education, but who are interested in philosophical issues and in learning non-formally. These include miners, industrial and agricultural workers and military service men and women.[35] The Society has a considerable range of non-formal and informal courses and study circles, decided upon by the membership and provided by volunteer tutors. A selection demonstrating the relevance of the Society's program to the development of citizenship awareness, civil society and democracy, is given in Table 3.3.

Clubs in rural Russia

The rural club is a very typical form of communication and social engagement for people in remote areas. Sometimes they are located in well-built houses with libraries, organized classes, a gym-hall and even a swimming-pool. But usually, when speaking of small clubs situated two to three hours drive from the local regional center; they are the sole place for communal activities for locals, providing very basic amenities, from simple opportunities for company and conversation to a reading and television, public heating in the cold winters and folk singing on public holidays. Nevertheless, they remain isles of culture, learning and local knowledge, providing what Morgan has described elsewhere as contributing to the maintenance of local knowledge and an 'ecology of culture'.[36] Such clubs should be considered as fruitful results of cooperation between the public and the local State authorities; the buildings themselves, their maintenance and the salaries of club leaders are provided by the local authorities.[37] Quite recently, a new form of club has emerged, established by small business entrepreneurs. This is the so-called *Klubok* (small club). They are run by small NGOs or on a personal initiative and provide a variety of non-formal education, skills training and other activities for a limited number of learners and are inexpensive to operate.[38] The main activities of the clubs showing their contribution to non-formal learning, citizenship development and the growth of civil society are shown in Table 3.4. Table 3.5 shows the emergence of relatively new forms of clubs in the Moscow region, some of them reminiscent of Soviet days.

Table 3.4 Clubs and learning circles (by % of respondents' participation)

Performance clubs	65.3
General learning circles	54.2
Folk art clubs	47.5
Sports clubs	41.5
Ecological/Environment movements	19.5
Patriotic/Historical	10.7
Political learning	7.6
Religious groups	4.2

Table 3.5 Clubs in the Moscow region (by % of respondents' participation)

Competitions and parades	41.5
Children's festivals	91.5
Sports and fitness clubs	50.0
Learning circles	21.2
Libraries and e-libraries	2.5
Out-door festivals	63.9
Senior citizens' self-help	22.0

The portrait of a club leader

According to the survey, by the Russian Institute of Sociology,[39] nine out of ten club leaders in rural areas are females, while in the cities one in three is a man. The average age is forty-five years in the rural areas and forty-three in the cities). Those under thirty years of age in the rural clubs are fewer than 9.3 percent, while in the cities they represent 15 percent. This indicates that the prestige of such a job is not high among rural youth and the study recommended local authorities to provide credits for individual house-building and to arrange direct links with colleges where club leaders are trained. The majority of club leaders are bright and self-fulfilled individuals. They enjoy their work, have reliable friends and relatives. They lived all their life honestly and are very optimistic for the future. We explain this by the fact that everyday they are in contact with the people and understand their important social function. In the meantime, many club leaders do not consider their job as a prestige one and do not think that they are very successful in making a career. Some 46.4 percent consider that they 'are not living any worse than others'. But it should be noticed that in the urban clubs only 28 percent meet this indicator. As for the opportunity to visit other countries in the world, only 10.9 percent have already realized this (in the cities, it is 16 percent), while 35 percent consider that they will never manage to travel abroad.

The club leaders also have a great diversity of former professions, although 41.5 percent have a basic education (trained specially for working in the club), 19.5 percent – former teachers and educators; we noticed among our respondents book-keepers, animal-care workers, bus drivers, military service women,

Table 3.6 How do club leaders estimate the quality of their lives (% of respondents' answers)

Category	Good	Satisfactory	Bad	No response
1 Wealth (welfare)	8.2	85.5	5.5	0.9
2 Meals	36.4	60.0	0.9	2.7
3 Clothing	17.3	75.5	4.5	2.7
4 Condition of health	20.9	65.5	7.3	6.4
5 Living standards	41.8	40.9	15.5	1.8
6 Family relations	70.9	17.3	1.8	10.0
7 Leisure time	40.0	48.2	4.5	7.3
8 Situation at work place	57.3	34.5	1.8	6.4
9 Chances for interesting holidays	36.4	39.1	13.6	10.9
10 Social connections	66.4	26.4	2.7	4.5
11 Chances for further learning	26.4	40.9	9.1	23.6
12 Social status	49.1	37.3	0.9	12.7
13 Life goes well on the whole	55.5	40.0	1.8	2.7

hairdressers, cheese makers, builders and even a parachute jumping instructor. This means that if club leaders are specially trained – the easier it is for them to obtain an official license. 85.8 percent of the respondents regularly improve their professional skills, follow the professional literature and attend information and activity seminars. This indicator is approximately ten times larger than the similar average indicators of the rural population generally. The main source of professional update information is the magazine *Club* with a circulation of some 6,000 copies. This well-illustrated monthly is published by the National Union of NGOs in Culture, Tourism and Sport.[40] There are also other relevant periodicals such as *Supplementary Education, Folk Art* and *Houses of Culture.* However, it is worth noting that there is not, as yet, any literature that focuses on working with the 'third age' or with 'self-help groups', while the number of club participants over fifty-six years of age is equal to that of youth under eighteen.

It is worth mentioning that club leaders are, probably, the most happy and optimistic persons compared with other groups of employees in rural Russia (Table 3.6). Despite the difficulties of the rural life style and the permanent shortage of resources, these people maintain strongly a positive, constructive mood. As one of the respondents remarked, 'Club leaders everyday get confirmation of the importance and significance of their work from other people. This is, as I assume, the key-stone value of their life.'

Conclusion

Data gathered recently through national surveys conducted by the Institute of Sociology[41] suggest that the Russian population is ready to improve its understanding of citizenship issues through civil society movements such as NGOs, voluntary associations, trade unions and clubs. The most recent (2007) nationwide survey conducted by the Institute of Sociology shows that the majority of

Table 3.7 If you agree that the bureaucracy is the main actor for what happens in the country, why is this so (%)?

	Type of settlement			
	Megapolis (Moscow, St Petersburg)	Big regional center (more than 300.000 inhabitants)	Small regional center (fewer than 300.000)	Rural settlement
It is the engrained national cultural tradition	24.9	16.5	11.2	10.6
The huge territories and the diverse level of regional economic development	28.1	22.8	21.0	15.8
The power is concentrated in Moscow – the capital	28.5	48.0	39.6	39.9
The weakness of local authorities	22.6	26.3	26.7	27.2
Dislike of people to accept responsibility	22.2	19.8	17.5	16.8
The central bureaucracy does not want to allow self-government in the regions	40.3	26.3	31.5	25.4

respondents are of the opinion that bureaucracy continues to be the key factor in the governance of contemporary Russian society. The bureaucracy is seen as having the opportunity to set the 'rules of the game in society'. In this sense, official citizenship formation is influenced by a strong bureaucracy, at least, in the minds of the public. See Table 3.7 for the responses.

These responses are very close to an analytical report presented on 9 February 2007 to the Public Chamber of Russia, a forum of the most prominent NGOs leaders, established by the special resolution of the State President. This argued that there is a very untypical, contradictory civic society in Russia, with some elements of the former soviet mentality.[42]

According to the new legislation, which came into effect on 18 April 2006, all current NGOs should re-register with the State. Of course, the process of negotiation between the registering authority and individual NGOs can sometimes be difficult. On the other hand, it is often not a matter of any great importance. For example, if a group of friends wish to form a society for the colonization of the Sun, but do not bother to register it officially, this is hardly a matter of juridical concern by the State. Many experts consider that the new legislation will not seriously affect either the broad missions or the day to day activities of NGOs and voluntary associations. It does, however, require the elected officers to be open and accurate in ensuring financial probity and in the general governance of the organization.

This is as much in the interest of Russians as individual members of voluntary associations, as it is in their interests as citizens of the Russian State. Moreover, setting such standards of internal governance is part of the process of the non-formal education of the membership and their development as functionally competent citizens. Again, the representatives of the NGOs should learn how to present the purposes and results of their activity to the general Russian public, through the media, explaining the social benefits of what may be described as a third sector to Russian society as a whole. This experience may be useful as a point of comparison in a collection of essays that focuses on the development of NGOs in the People's Republic of China.

Notes

1 N.V. Chekhov. *People's education in Russia* (Moscow: NIVA, 1912), p. 18. This quote is from a letter by the highly influential Count Dolgorukov to the Russian Tsar about Sunday schools for the common people.

2 A. Ferguson, *An essay on the history of civil society* (Edinburgh: Edinburgh University Press, 1966).

3 G.W.F. Hegel, *The philosophy of history* (New York: Dover Books, 1956).

4 K. Marx and F. Engels, *The German ideology* (London: Lawrence and Wishart, 1965).

5 A. Gramsci, *Selections from the prison notebooks* (London: Lawrence and Wishart, 1971).

6 W.J. Morgan, 'Homo Sovieticus: Political education and civil society in the Soviet Union', in *SCUTREA Conference Proceedings 1970–1997* (London: Birkbeck College, 1989), pp. 218–223.

7 W.J. Morgan, 'Public opinion, political education and citizenship', in Morgan, W.J. and Livingstone, S.W. (eds) *Law and opinion in 20th century Britain and Ireland* (Basingstoke, London and New York: Palgrave-Macmillan, 2003), pp. 9–31.

8 A. Rogers, *What is the difference? A new critique of adult learning and teaching* (Leicester: NIACE, 2003).

9 Among the most well known – *Ligovsky Narodny Dom* in St Petersburg, *Narodny Dom* of *Khar'kiv* Society for Literacy, Ukraine.

10 D. Wartenweiler, *Civil society and academic debate in Russia 1905–1914* (Oxford: Clarendon Press, 1999).

11 R.B. McKean, *The Russian constitutional monarchy, 1907–1917* (London: The Historical Association, 1977).

12 W.J. Morgan, *Communists on education and culture 1848–1948* (Basingstoke, London and New York: Palgrave Macmillan, 2003).

13 The State Federal Body for Political Enlightenment.

14 S. Fitzpatrick, *The Commissariat of Enlightenment: Soviet organization of education and the arts under Lunacharsky, October 1917–1921* (Cambridge: Cambridge University Press, 1970).

15 W. Kolarz, *Religion in the Soviet Union* (London and New York: Macmillan and St Martin's Press, 1961); and J. Anderson, *Religion, state and politics in the Soviet Union and the successor states* (Cambridge: Cambridge University Press, 1994).

16 S. Fitzpatrick, *Education and social mobility in the Soviet Union, 1921–1934* (Cambridge: Cambridge University Press, 1979).

17 R. Conquest, *The great terror: A re-assessment* (London: Hutchinson, 1990).

18 J. Muckle and W.J. Morgan (eds), *Post-school education and the transition from state socialism* (Nottingham: The Continuing Education Press, 2001), p. xix; and I. Berlin,

The Soviet mind: russian culture under communism, Hardy, H. (ed.) (Washington, DC: Brookings Institution, 2004).

19 E.P. Mickiewicz, *Soviet political schools: The Communist Party adult instruction system* (New Haven: Yale University Press, 1967); and R. Conquest, *The Politics of ideas in the USSR* (London, Sydney and Toronto: Bodley Head, 1967).

20 D.C. Lee, *The people's universities of the USSR* (New York: Greenwood Press, 1988).

21 www.cultinfo.ru/fulltext/1/001/008/107/010.htm

22 W.G. Miller (ed.), *Toward a more civil society? The USSR under Mikhail Sergeevich Gorbachev* (New York: Harper and Row, 1989); and D.W. Spring (ed.), *The impact of Gorbachev: The first phase 1985–1990* (London and New York: Pinter, 1991).

23 Minxin Pei, *From reform to revolution: The demise of communism in China and the Soviet Union* (Cambridge, MA: Harvard University Press, 1994); and C. Marsh, *Unparalleled reforms. China's rise, Russia's fall, and the interdependence of transition* (Lanham, Boulder, New York and Oxford: Lexington Books, 2005).

24 J. Muckle and W.J. Morgan, *Post-school education and the transition from state socialism*; S. Webber and I. Liikanen, *Education and civic culture in post-communist countries* (Basingstoke and New York: Palgrave Macmillan, 2001); B. Eklof, L.E. Holmes, and V. Kaplan, *Educational reform in Russia: Legacies and prospects* (London and New York: Frank Cass, 2005); and W.J. Morgan, 'Marxism and moral education', editorial, *Communism, post-communism and moral education*, Special Issue of the *Journal of Moral Education*, Vol. 34, No. 4 (December, 2005), pp. 391–398.

25 W.J. Morgan and G.A. Kliucharev, 'From comrades to citizens: Adult education and the transition in Russia', in *Studies in International Adult Education: Civil society, citizenship and learning, Vol. 2* (Hamburg and London: Lit Verlag, Muenster, 2001), pp. 223–248; and W.J. Morgan, G.A. Kliucharev, and E.I. Pahomova, 'Adult and continuing education in post-Soviet Russia: What do Russians need and want?' *Education in Russia, the Independent States and Eastern Europe*, Vol. 20, No. 2 (2003), pp. 50–65.

26 A.B. Evans, L.A. Henry, and L.M. Sundstrom, *Russian civil society: A critical reassessment* (Armonk, New York and London: M. E. Sharpe, 2006).

27 C. Marsh and N.K. Gvosdev (eds), *Civil society and the search for justice in Russia* (Lanham, Boulder, New York and Oxford: Lexington Books, 2002).

28 C. Marsh (ed.), *Burden or blessing? Russian Orthodoxy and the construction of civil society and democracy* (Boston, MA: Institute on Culture, Religion and World Affairs, Boston University, 2004).

29 N.K. Gvosdev, *Russia in the National Interest* (NJ: Transactional Publishers, 2004), p. 25. Given the importance of the Russian Orthodox Church as an NGO, the present authors intend to examine its role as a provider of non-formal and informal education in a separate paper.

30 Q. Ma, *Non-governmental organizations in contemporary China* (London: Routledge, 2006).

31 Federal Law 'On Political Parties' No. 168, adopted 20 December 2004.

32 ucsmr.ru (also available in English).

33 G. Foley, *Learning in social action: A contribution to understanding informal education* (Leicester: National Institute of Adult and Continuing Education, 1999).

34 www.logic.ru/~phil-soc/ (English version is available).

35 Interview with Dr Andrei Korolev, Secretary to the Society, March, 2006.

36 W.J. Morgan, 'Local knowledge and border-less education: Are they compatible?' in Cullingford, C. and Gunn, S. (eds), *Globalization, education and culture shock* (Aldershot: Ashgate, 2005), pp. 35–47.

37 Zakon RF N122-FZ 'Osnovi zakonodatel'stva o kulture' (22 April 2004) (The Legis-

lative Act on Culture in the Russian Federation with amendments of 01 January 2005).

38 R.K. Saubanova, *Organizatsionno-pedagogicheskie uslovija optimizatzii sel'skoi kul-turno- obrazovatel'noi sredy* (*Management and pedagogical recommendation to opti-mization of rural cultural-educational environment*) (Kazan, Tatarstan: State University, 2005).

39 G. Kliucharev and L. Dukachiova, *Informatsionno-obrazovatel'nyi potentzial klub-nikh I kul'turno-dosugovikh uchrezhdenii* (*Informational and educational potential of clubs and leisure-time establishments*) (Moscow: The Center for Social Forecast (*Tzentr Sotsial'nogo Prognozirovanja*), 2006).

40 Electronic version is available at www.tiofest.ru.

41 M. Gorshkov and N. Tichonova (eds), *Sotsial'nie neravenstva I sotsial'naya politika v sovremennoi Rossii* (*Social inequalities and social policy in contemporary Russia*) (Moscow: Nauka, 2007).

42 *O Sostojanii Grazhdanskogo Obzhestva v Rossiiskoi Federatzii* (*On the situation on the civic society in Russian Federation*) – only electronic version available at www.oprf.ru/rus/documents/report.

4 The changing aspects of civil society in China

Jean-Philippe Béja

The study of State–Society relations is an important component of political science and is particularly useful to characterize a political regime. Such an approach is especially fruitful in the study of communist regimes.* The redis-covery of the concept of civil society in the 1970s can be considered a landmark in the development of research on Central and Eastern European regimes. It is therefore quite surprising that most sinologists have been reluctant to use the notions which emerged in Eastern Europe in the 1970s to analyse China before 1989. Only a handful of European observers of the pro-democracy movement during the late 1970s and the early 1980s had regarded the concept of civil society as fruitful for the study of Chinese politics. Paradoxically, it became widespread among China specialists and pro-democracy scholars in exile only after the repression of the 1989 pro-democracy movement. In China itself, it became a "hot" topic when *Social Sciences in China*, the mainland journal pub-lished in Hong Kong, devoted its first issue to a discussion of this concept in 1992.

In the last decade, it was widely used by many Western and Chinese observers. But the reality that it covers is very different from the one that the Eastern European concept referred to. Whereas the latter had more to do with strategy, it is now essentially an analytical concept closer to the Anglo Saxon definition developed in the 1990s, in which civil society designates non-governmental organizations (NGOs). In the last few years especially, many political scientists have devoted much of their energy to compile exhaustive lists of NGOs in China.[1]

In this chapter, I will try to argue that this concept of civil society, referring to an informally structured network of NGOs which have a loose relation with the Party-State, is quite different from the combative structure which had developed in Poland in the 1970s, in Czechoslovakia in the 1980s and, to a certain extent, in China during the first decade of the reforms. And I will argue that the development of such associations does not play the same role as the ones which emerged in Eastern Europe and in 1980s China. In other words, the development of such a "civil society" does not mean that the regime is democra-tizing, nor does it mean that the evolution of China will follow a pattern similar to Eastern Europe.

The social pact for reform

The failure of reform from outside: repression of the Democracy Wall Movement

The civil society strategy appeared after the failure of the institutionalization of a political opposition. In Poland in the 1970s, the brutal repression of the workers riots in Gdansk and Sczeczin convinced part of the rebellious intelligentsia that it was impossible to directly confront the Party in the political field. The most concerned elements founded the *Komitet Obrony Robotników* (KOR) (Committee for the Defence of Workers), which started to help society organize itself and presented itself as a self-limiting social movement.

> [Since the social movements in Eastern Europe] had given up hopes for radical reform of [the power] structures, there was no other alternative but to concentrate the activities of the movements on the democratic self-organisations of social solidarity and cooperation *outside* the institutional framework of the state.[2]

The Chinese evolution was different. In the People's Republic, in the wake of Mao's death and Deng Xiaoping's rehabilitation, an atmosphere of relative freedom was felt in the Chinese Communist Party (CCP) circles. In order to legitimize his policy aimed at achieving the "four modernizations" which needed the support of the intelligentsia, Deng Xiaoping launched a policy of rehabilitation of the "stinking ninth" based on a stated will to carry out secularization. Many thinkers who had been criticized during the last two decades of Mao's reign were summoned by Hu Yaobang who then acted as Deng's representative in the intellectual field and asked to devise Marxist foundations for the new policy. Well aware of the legitimacy crisis facing the regime, Hu launched his campaign for "thought liberation" rallying most audacious thinkers behind his new line. Criticisms of the abuses of the Cultural Revolution were allowed in the official press. After the rehabilitation of the Tiananmen Incident of 5 April 1976, and the Third Party plenum where he defeated the neo-Maoists, Deng launched the Conference on theoretical thought during which the totalitarian nature of the Great Helmsman's regime – designated under the code name "feudalism" – was seriously denounced. Thinkers who criticized the various aspects of Mao's rule (without naming the Red sun) asked for the institutionalization of free debate as an antidote to the excesses of "modern superstition". At the same time, the CCP had relaxed its grip on public expression of opinions, and while discussions were taking place in the Great Hall of the People, in the streets of Peking, Xidan and Tiananmen, victims of Mao's campaigns, and especially members of the Red Guard generation, were denouncing the abuses by cadres and producing analyses of the regime, asking for the institutionalization of supervision by public opinion. As Ye Jianying said at the time, "Xidan democracy Wall is a model of people's democracy"[3] and some of the participants in the Theoretical Thought Conference often took part in meetings organized by the editors of unofficial journals. Some, such as Yan Jiaqi or Guo Luoji, wrote articles for *Beijing zhi chun* (Beijing Spring), an unofficial journal distributed at the Wall. Therefore, a joint pressure was exerted by intellectuals inside the system who enjoyed the support of reformers in the leadership and ordinary citizens who asked for the respect of basic rights. But in March 1979, Deng Xiaoping formalized the limitations imposed on the political debate by stating the "Four Cardinal Principles". Then, from 1979 to 1981, the Democracy Wall movement was repressed, and its main actors were sentenced to long jail terms without causing any reaction on the part of the intelligentsia. This closing of the Wall ended the period of direct participation by citizens in the political field and opened the way to the struggle for a civil society.

Social stability: a condition for the development of civil society

In the countryside, the major success of Deng's new policy was the effective dismantling of the people's communes. This policy satisfied the requests of farmers who represented the vast majority of the Chinese population. By allowing them to sell their products on the free market, and eventually by proceeding to a de facto decollectivization, the CCP succeeded in bringing a long period of stability to the countryside. Until 1985, the standards of living of the rural population grew by leaps and bounds as well as the agricultural production, and it is not until the second half of the 1980s that the situation started to be more contrasted.

In the cities, salary rises and the opening of job opportunities by self-employment (the *geti hu*) considerably alleviated the pressure on the urban population. So did the re-establishment of bonuses for the workers and the rise of the salaries of state-owned enterprise (SOE) workers. As no profound restructuring of SOEs was on the agenda, the new leadership enjoyed a large measure of support among employees and workers. This started to change after the Third plenum of the twelfth Central Committee in 1984 tried to impose the end of the iron rice-bowl (*tie fanwan*) by making firms responsible for their profits and losses. The first wave of semi-privatization which took place in the second half of the 1980s provoked discontent among SOE workers because it allowed some cadres to become quite rich while salaries were stagnating. But not until the end of the 1980s did urban dwellers start to listen to the criticism pronounced in the newly emerging public space.

Contradictions at the top

Although Deng had clearly stated the limitations of the scope of political criticism, the CCP summit remained divided between conservatives who stood for a limited reform of the command economy (a return to the strategy of the 1950s viewed as a Golden era) and reformers who were ready to abandon a large portion of the ideology in order to achieve modernization. Reformers themselves were divided between those who thought that bold innovation was possible only in the economic field and those who believed that the political system had to be deeply reformed. As the paramount leader, Deng Xiaoping arbitrated between the various factions and was careful not to alienate the conservatives.

As the satisfaction of rural and urban society's needs provided the necessary stability, it was possible to leave more space for debate and experimentation on the way forward for the political system. The reform faction which steered the course all along the 1980s could therefore encourage the intellectuals whose support was necessary to achieve modernization to engage in a reflection on the ways to improve the efficiency of the regime. However, there was no question that ordinary citizens would take part in the debate: the latter was to remain circumscribed to the elite.

The Chinese brand of civil society: an intra-elite project

As they realized that the CCP was not ready to tolerate the existence of organizations in the field of politics,[4] but that part of the leadership persisted in its policy of secularization and reform,[5] most of the advanced theoreticians who had helped design the new avatar of the official ideology, ostensibly opted for collaboration with the reformers. This is quite different from what had happened in Poland where only after intellectuals had despaired of the possibility of reforming the system from inside did they start to develop a civil society.

But although they had decided to work with the reformist leadership, Chinese intellectuals were not so naïve. They drew the lessons from the last twenty years of Mao's reign and tried to take some distance from the leaders by helping develop an embryo of civil society and of public space outside the CCP. Taking advantage of their positions at heads of many journals to which they had been appointed after their rehabilitation, the former "stinking ninth" encouraged debates on the nature of the regime and on the factors that had made the tragedy of Maoism possible. Literary journals were instrumental in helping a generation of writers come of age. Former educated youth described the political state of the countryside, denouncing the abuses by local cadres, ex-rightists related the sufferings they had been through just because they had dared state their opinion to help the CCP correct its course, victims of extremism wrote about the large-scale repression that led millions to reform through labour. The writers criticized the Marxist orthodox literary theory[6] and along with the newly appeared social science scholars whose disciplines had just been rehabilitated, helped introduce a number of Western theories and weaken the hegemony of Marxism–Leninism in public life. Numerous conferences held in universities provided opportunities for discussions of the means to deepen political reforms. These ideas were somewhat relayed by the media, which adopted a much freer style than before.

But the field of ideology was not the only locus of creation. The former Red guards were very creative in designing new modes of organization such as the professional associations which rivalled the old ones and gave younger scholars positions of responsibility. As publishing houses were increasingly made responsible for their profits and losses, they were keen to publish the works of audacious intellectuals. They therefore allowed the creation of editorial boards whose members were appointed without the approval of their departments of organization, boards which functioned as quasi-autonomous associations.[7] The members of these boards were often friends who shared a common goal and common ideas on their work. They were keen to publish translations of the newest western books in social sciences and original analyses by young Chinese specialists. This shows that in a sense, the growing importance of the market in the Chinese economy provided the bolder writers with new freedoms.

Besides, many activists organized conferences and debates on all sorts of subjects, including the role of culture in development, the necessity to fight for the recognition of freedoms of speech and assembly, the evolution of political regimes in foreign countries, etc.

Although these structures were less "unofficial" than the "home seminars" that were taking place in Prague or Warsaw during the same period, they served a similar function. However, to the difference of what happened in Eastern Europe, most members of these Boards, specialists associations and "salons" were Party members who worked outside the Apparatus to create an autonomous sphere.

Their lesser autonomy can be accounted for by the fact that, in China, there was no independent structure capable of playing the role of the Polish Church which, thanks to its insulation from the Party and to its international links, had been able to provide an institutionalized protection to the actors of the civil society. In China, the would-be developers of civil society could only rely on the protection of the most radical reformist leaders and therefore could not clearly break with the CCP.

The reformers protected them because they needed new ideas to justify their struggle against the conservatives and neo-Maoists and to consolidate the legitimacy of their policies. They encouraged the creation of think tanks which helped devise new policies. The people who worked in these structures, such as the *tigaisuo*,[8] did not differ much from the audacious scholars who were active in the universities. This is what a well-known dissident intellectual explains: "Communist party reformers and intellectuals were very close, for the Party was very tolerant during the 1980s. It was absolutely necessary for them to work together."[9] On the other hand, some Party leaders established informal links with the founders of autonomous organizations such as Wang Juntao and Chen Ziming, the founders of the autonomous Peking Social and Economic Research Institute:

> One needs to have two "wings", i.e. in practise, one needs to have one hand in the system and one in the pro-democracy movement. During that period, we held meetings which, up to a point, influenced theoreticians and brought many ideas and projects inside the system; we also systematically founded editorial boards, essentially to influence public opinion. On that front, we were quite successful.[10]

Collaboration between reformers, establishment intellectuals and intellectuals outside the system (*tizhi wai zhishifenzi*) worked quite well despite the recurrent campaigns against "bourgeois liberalization" which took place from 1981 to 1989.

At the end of the 1980s, the network of semi-autonomous organizations (professional associations, editorial boards, salons, research centres) constituted a form of civil society – although, at the time, almost nobody in China used that term– which bore some resemblance to the one which had appeared in Eastern Europe a little earlier. As in Eastern Europe, this sector had been born out of the impossibility of creating a political opposition. But, contrary to what had happened in that part of the world, the Chinese civil society was made possible by the protection provided by the reformist faction and could not achieve any measure of institutionalization.[11] Besides, it was exclusively an intra-elite process and never did the actors of the emerging civil society establish contacts with workers or peasants. Intellectuals active in this sphere were working to reinforce the radical reformers and to convince them of the necessity to recognize pluralism in society.

The social crisis

In the second half of the 1980s, the social stability induced by the policies adopted at the Third plenum of 1978 started to erode. In the countryside, the authorities lacked the necessary cash to buy grain from producers and paid them with IOUs which were absolutely useless. Small-scale discontent started to appear in villages.

But it was especially in the cities that the situation started to deteriorate. The decision to make SOEs responsible for their profits and losses and the emerging dual channel which allowed the sons of the *nomenklatura* to make huge profits by trafficking in authorizations[12] provoked discontent among workers and employees of SOEs. In the summer of 1988, after the leadership launched the price reform which resulted in high inflation (14 per cent), discontent among workers peaked. The social stability which had allowed the reformist leadership to launch experimentation in the political realm came under threat.

This coincided with disappointment among the radical intelligentsia following the dismissal of Hu Yaobang. Hu had been viewed as a kind of protector of the intellectuals, and his dismissal for "tolerance towards 'bourgeois liberalism'", the codeword for independence of mind, shocked most liberal thinkers. Many actors of the civil society started to despair of the possibility of reforming the system from inside. At the beginning of 1989, writers and scholars who belonged to the establishment[13] launched petitions to ask for the liberation of political prisoners. This reminded one of the attitudes of Soviet intellectuals during the Brezhnev era. The disappointment of the establishment intellectuals provided the conditions for students to take to the street in the spring of 1989. At the beginning, the majority of intellectuals did not support the students as they were afraid of losing the protection of the CCP reformers who had allowed them to build a semi-autonomous sphere. Nevertheless, they finally decided to join the movement. The student demonstrations had a very strong impact on the discontented urban population who joined the students to denounce corruption and authoritarianism and demand democracy and freedom. The actors of the "civil society" who had finally opted for autonomy from the CCP, repeatedly demanded that the authorities accept to conduct a dialogue with them. This was considered as too much of a challenge by part of the reformers, and a split occurred among them. Deng Xiaoping sided with the conservatives and dismissed Party Secretary General Zhao Ziyang who had been willing to engage in a dialogue with the student movement. The Party leadership opted for repression and the activists were defeated.

As opposed to what had happened in Poland after the proclamation of martial law in December 1981 when the actors of civil society had been able to seek protection from the Church, Chinese intellectuals had nowhere to turn to. Their protectors had been purged, and the Party quickly reinstated its hegemony over the political field. It has been careful not to let any kind of political challenge re-emerge ever since. In a way, one can say that the 1989 pro-democracy movement gave the "coup de grace" to the "combative" civil society in China.

The pact for conservation

The Tiananmen massacre sealed the new pact of the elites.[14] By crushing the attempt at democratization which had developed in society with the help of the radical reformers, the Party leadership saved its hegemony. But force was not enough to restore legitimacy. The cause of socialism had lost its appeal among the masses as was shown by the strong discontent which reigned from 1989 to 1992, when the Conservatives had their way. Therefore, the Party had to find a new type of legitimacy. This was achieved by Deng Xiaoping's trip to the South in 1992. The paramount leader put an end to the struggle between neo-Maoists and reformers, by stating that any policy was good as long as it favoured economic development. He explicitly declared that there should be no unending haggling over whether a policy was capitalist or socialist (*xing she xing zi*), showing his commitment to the achievement of secularization. He was able to rally the whole leadership behind his project which combined the development of a market economy and the reinforcement of dictatorship. And in fact, since 1992, there has been no episode of struggle between diverse political projects in the leadership of the apparatus. A consensus has emerged and it is still effective now.

Avoid social unrest at all costs: stability eclipses everything

The new agenda had new implications: whereas in the early 1980s, economic reform had been supported by the great majority of the population, with only a fraction of the bureaucracy opposing it, since the end of the decade, discontent had appeared in the countryside and in the cities. The new agenda for development, which aimed at transforming the command economy and the large SOEs, was bound to provoke more discontent. In the 1990s, it became clear that economic reform would hurt a great number of workers and farmers. In the mind of Party leaders, it was essential to maintain a strong repressive apparatus and to mobilize the support of all the segments of the elites. This was achieved by making sure that they would be able to considerably raise their standards of living.

Given the risk of social unrest, and the consensus that reigned at the summit of the Party, the leadership considered it had become dangerous to continue to proceed with experimentation in the political sphere. Therefore, the new social pact that the CCP presented to the intelligentsia was different from the one it had proposed in the 1980s. It was not a pact for reform anymore; it was a pact for conservation. This time, the political system had to remain unchanged so that it could enact the new development strategy. Intellectuals would see their standard of living dramatically improve by entering the marketplace, creating private firms, by the revaluation of university salaries, etc. Scholars and professors would be allowed to raise their academic level, to take part in symposiums and conferences abroad, to establish links with the international scientific community, to do research in foreign universities. But, the condition was that they not try to revive the organizations which they had created in the 1980s, whose goal was to push for the transformation of the regime, and, obviously, that they not try to link with the disgruntled portions of the population to help them translate their discontent into political demands. In front of the growing risk of social unrest, authoritarianism had to be reinforced. This was expressed in the slogan: "Stability overrules everything else" (*wending yadao yiqie*).

As time went by, a larger space was granted by the CCP to society's initiative. This has led many observers to write that in China, a civil society has been developing in the 1990s. This is a bit far fetched. In any case, this civil society has been growing in a space designed by the CCP, and it still does not enjoy any kind of legal guarantees that would provide for its institutionalization. In this sense, it does not enjoy a larger autonomy than the one which had emerged in the 1980s, and the scope of its action and reflection is much more disjointed from politics than it had been during that decade.

The success of globalized newspeak

Ironically, it was after the Tiananmen massacre that the term "civil society" made its appearance on China's intellectual scene. Since the end of the 1990s, even the authorities-have used it, often referring to it as the "third sector" (*di sange bumen*). However, it is a completely different concept from the one which had appeared in the 1980s, closer to the one that is prevalent in the West, especially in the newspeak of international organizations. To be provocative, one could say that the CCP has learned how to use the politically correct language of globalization.

In effect, since the fall of the Berlin Wall and the end of the Cold War, conventional wisdom has it that politics have been increasingly replaced by administration. For administration to be efficient, it has to rely on good "governance". Free expression of citizens in the public space, which, under the influence of Eastern European dissidents, had been at the centre of public debate during the 1980s, has given way to discussions among experts on how best to design public policies, and to the newspeak of international organizations. In this approach, mankind's problems can be solved if one applies the right expertise. Scientism, which had characterized the end of the nineteenth century, has made its comeback, albeit under a different guise, at the end of the twentieth century.

It is quite ironical to note that the end of totalitarianism in a large part of our planet has given rise to an increasing depoliticization of the public space. Dissident intellectuals the world over have been replaced by experts, whose legitimacy for action in society is based on "scientific" knowledge. Putting forward the increasing complexity of the problems faced by most countries in the modern world, most government leaders tend to reduce the space for public debate and to expropriate citizens from participation in controversies. In democratic countries, political participation is more and more reduced to voting every four or five years, and ordinary citizens feel increasingly estranged from political life. This disenfranchisement is an explaining factor of the decreasing turnouts which have characterized elections in most advanced democracies.

In this sense, the CCP, which has not gone through the troubles of democratization, has demonstrated an impressive capacity to speak the language of "(post) modernity". In the world of "governance", there are no more political programmes, only concrete problems which must be confronted with "public policies". Technocrats need trustworthy information which they know the bureaucracy is unable to provide. In the West, consultation of "users" and experts is occupying an increasingly large space to the detriment of public debate by the people's representatives in parliaments. In China, one can observe the emergence of a growing number of committees, and in this sense, the regime is becoming increasingly similar to other modern states. The multiplication of committees appears to be one of the characteristics of governance in these countries.

In democratic societies, NGOs which constitute "civil society" are becoming powerful actors, whereas the more traditional organizations such as political parties, trade unions, etc. have seen their role decrease. This civil society, however, is not the combative one that we have discussed above, the objective of which was to give life to social actors. The NGOs that compose it today are mostly humanitarian associations, or one issue groups, which seek to lobby the government to enact public policies which will help resolve specific problems. Instead of putting problems in political terms – in terms of choices that can be debated in public by citizens – governments tend to put them forward as technical problems and tend to create structures of consultation to help solve them. Citizens are being replaced by "users".

The CCP has shown a remarkable ability to adapt to this evolution of the modern state and its leaders have enthusiastically rallied behind the new themes of governance, and even civil society, allowing international NGOs to settle on its soil (organizations such as Médecins sans frontières, Oxfam, Ford Foundation, etc.). It has also started to allow the development of Chinese NGOs (we shall see below that these are acting under serious constraints). In return, international governmental and NGOs congratulate themselves of this leap into modernity by a regime which seemed so reluctant to accept recognize such organizations.

A provider of modern identity for Chinese intellectuals

The majority of Chinese intellectuals have also shown plenty of enthusiasm for these new ideas. They see them as a way to emancipate themselves from the traditional model of the Confucian (or the pro-democracy) intellectual whose action is based on morals, to become "modern" professionals, specialists who play a determining role in the modernization of the country. In effect, as they take part in the various committees set up by local and national governments, they can put their knowledge to use and help adapt policies to the needs of society.

As a matter of fact, since 4 June and even more since Deng Xiaoping's trip to the South, the majority of the intelligentsia have been convinced that they had to collaborate with the CCP to make China a prosperous and powerful country. In return, the CCP gives them consideration and Jiang Zemin had even included the intelligentsia in his "Three represents".[15] Whereas during the 1980s, intellectuals had to fight for democracy if they wanted to be regarded as modern, things have changed with the advent of the (post-)modern state. In the new situation, there is no contradiction between the regime and the intelligentsia. The latter do not have to fight for the transformation of the former in order to attain the common goal of modernization. Collaboration is not only possible, it is desirable if one wants to help China regain its prominent position on the international scene.

However, the CCP does not go so far as to set up consultative structures of the Hong Kong type, where ordinary citizens are directly consulted by the administration on the ways of solving the problems that the State must address. The various echelons of the Party-State have chosen to ask experts to carry out studies in order to gather information on the opinions of the social groups targeted by the policies they want to enact. But, of course, the input from scholars is not binding for the leading cadres who use it at their discretion.

However, scholars are satisfied that the government consults them when it comes to designing new policies. They see it as a kind of recognition of their action as a positive factor in the struggle for modernization. On the other hand, this new relation to the authorities allows them to conciliate the role of the "modern" intelligentsia whose legitimacy is based on expertise with the more traditional functions of the literati such as the "counsellor to the Prince" – a model which is part of their identity – and the "spokespeople for society", which is at the heart of their legitimacy.

Seeing no hope of a return to power of radical reformers eager to transform Party rule, the majority of the intelligentsia have therefore abandoned the struggle to create an autonomous civil society, and most of its members have accepted the function that the Party-State has designed for them. Under these circumstances, many intellectuals, especially economists and sociologists, enjoy real consideration from the authorities. They help develop the new kind of "civil society" as encouraged by the Party-State.

The revival of the model of the "Counsellor to the Prince"

Let us take the example of sociologists. Government at various levels often ask them to take part in all sorts of advisory committees that they set up. They can make their voices heard when the local authorities tackle problems like the situation of the *mingong* (migrant workers), or juvenile delinquency. For example, in the Spring of 2002, the National People's Congress (NPC) put the defence of the vulnerable groups (*ruoshi qunti*) at the top of its agenda. This decision has given rise to the creation of large-scale research programmes on the increasing social polarization. Between 2002 and 2005, many research papers have been written by sociologists on the fate of migrant labour (*mingong*) in the cities. Whereas the denunciation of the negative effects of the *hukou* system by some radical sociologists in 1988–1989 had not led to any concrete change to that system,[16] participation by mainstream sociologists in the various committees set up by the local and municipal governments bureaus in charge of migrant labour (*wailai renkou guanli ju*) has, in certain cases, helped improve the situation. The sociologists justify their propositions for change with arguments based on economic efficiency, they explain to the bureaucrats that the relaxing of controls on *hukou*, by doing away with the discrimination between rural and urban populations, will help set up a modern labour market capable of rationally affecting the workforce to available jobs. Their arguments have convinced some leading cadres, and many municipalities have set up a system of "provisional *hukou*" which allows *mingong* who have a work contract and accommodation in the cities to enjoy almost the same rights as urban dwellers. More recently, their lobbying in the various committees has helped convince cadres of the necessity to do something about the education of migrant workers' children. For instance, under the pressure of sociologists from the Sichuan Academy of Social Sciences, schools for children of migrant workers have rapidly developed in Chengdu. Sociologists' opinions are obviously not the only factor which has allowed these improvements, but they have played an undeniable role. These recent successes show the efficiency of this type of intervention.[17]

However, from the point of view of Party-State–Society relations, one must note that the position of intellectuals has changed, compared to the 1980s. Now they intervene as experts inside the system. They reject the *à la* Solidarnosc model of civil society for reasons of efficiency and do nothing to favour the autonomous expression of the social groups they try to defend, nor do they encourage them to set up the associations that would enable them to defend their interests. Of course, they are well aware that the Party-State will not tolerate the creation of autonomous organizations by the citizens themselves. Besides, its traditional elitism leads the intelligentsia to regard action by the working people with diffidence. Being themselves as wary of disorder (*luan*) as the political leaders, they wilfully agree to silence the ordinary people, whose "quality" – a term meaning a mixture of level of education, politeness, urban behaviour – is too "low" to be able to run the government (*renmin de suzhi taidi* is a very common phrase even among the most pro-democracy intellectuals); therefore, they accept to submit to the government's requirements. By prohibiting public debate and political participation of citizens, by instituting mediation through experts, the Party-State is succeeding in transforming political problems into purely administrative questions, or, to use a "modern" phrase, in questions of "governance". The majority of the intelligentsia has enthusiastically accepted this transformation.

The revival of paternalism

In sum, many intellectuals who, in the 1980s, would definitely have worked within the semi-autonomous organizations, are now very active in what the Party-State terms "the third sector" (*disange bumen*). The so-called "NGOs" which compose this sector are supposed to design solutions to social problems that the Party-State cannot solve for lack of resources, or for lack of will, but under its control. The CCP looks as if it were going back to the nineteenth-century paternalism as it itself is developing ideas which are reminiscent of the ones that had emerged among Christian industrial magnates. It is all the more ironical as the theoreticians of socialism such as Marx or Proudhon had denounced this ideology with great vehemence. By eulogizing the concept of charity, the vanguard of the proletariat asks the privileged to help the victims of modernization without affecting the social structure while trying by all means to prevent the emergence of the disgruntled as a political actor capable of con-tributing to political life and maybe transform it. The creation of this web of associations with the benediction of the CCP is also reminiscent of the action of the Qing Dynasty which used to allow the gentry to create organizations whose function was to solve the social problems induced by natural disasters.

In the 1990s, both for fear of repression, and because they accepted the new social contract proposed by Deng Xiaoping, the intelligentsia has renounced to be the ferment of an autonomous civil society which eventually could set up a dialogue with the CCP (the Solidarnosc model); the most concerned scholars have instead immersed themselves in participation in government-operated non-governmental organizations (GONGOs) active in rural education, health, all sectors which have been abandoned by the government since it launched the reforms. These organizations are often very closely linked to the CCP's "mass organizations". For example, the famous Hope Project (*Xiwang gongcheng*) which helps develop schools in backward rural areas, operates under the aus-pices of the Communist Youth League whereas *Dagongmei zhi jia*, the House of the Women Migrant Workers, which helps organize cultural activities and legal education for migrant women in Peking is closely linked to the All China

Women's Federation.[18] But these organizations of the twenty-first century enjoy a much smaller degree of autonomy than their Qing counterparts inasmuch as they act in an environment which is very strictly controlled by the Party-State.

In other terms, one could say that the intelligentsia, which, during the 1980s, had been seeking to reform the political system in order to promote the prosperity and the maturity of society through the institutionalization of its autonomy, now tends to accept the technocratic discourse held by the Party-State. Instead of helping the weakened categories organize in order to be able to defend their interests, it tries to help them out by providing charity. This is a much less perilous road, as it does not put intellectuals in opposition to the Party-State, while still comforting their image as defenders of the weak. The intelligentsia is all the more confident that this is the right path to follow, as presenting social problems in terms of "poverty alleviation" is strongly encouraged by international organizations, whether governmental or not.[19] This apolitical approach considers that public policies can solve the problems of "poverty" which is presented as a result of some kind of fatality rather than the consequence of the nature of the socio-political system.

A corporatist model?

The rationale behind the encouragement provided by the Party-State to the third sector is that, with the development of the market economy, the State should not try to intervene in all aspects of life, especially in the economy.[20] The new official discourse stands for a "big society, small state" formula. But it reserves to the CCP the right to create the NGOs which represent society. We have seen above how NGOs have been created to help the disgruntled. It is interesting to note that no Party leader has ever acted for the creation of a *mingong* association, for example, whereas they have encouraged businesspeople to enter the Chambers of Commerce (*shanghui*). In other terms, as in Mussolini's corporatist model, the State decides which social categories exist and can be represented, and it itself creates the NGOs which will represent them. The setting up of any such association is subject to its authorization.

However, the situation is not so clear-cut, and sometimes, the CCP is obliged to acknowledge the existence of associations it did not help promote. The case of Aizhi (AIDS) Action Project is interesting. It was founded by Wan Yanhai, who wanted to attract the attention of the population on the serious development of AIDS in China at a time when the government refused to recognize it. When Wan posted detailed information on the AIDS situation in Henan province in August 2002, provoking an outrage all over the world, the authorities arrested him.[21] However, when the UNAIDS functionaries, and a great number of AIDS-related NGOs all over the world protested against this measure, the government freed Wan and allowed him to register his association under the company law.[22]

This shows that the CCP is not omnipotent and that pressure can force it to recognize organizations that it fought. Obviously, this could not have happened in the case of a political party or of an autonomous trade union. But this example shows that the economic sphere can provide a space for the emergence of associations which might become the basis for the development of a civil society in the "combative" sense of the term. Already, many scholars and activists have created firms which actually do carry out research on sensitive problems such as education, accommodation, integration of migrants, etc. There is no comprehensive research on these firms, but it would be interesting to have an idea of their scope. If it is substantial, this could point to the possibility of a politicization of the economic sphere and provide better foundations for the eventual development of civil society.

However, recent experience shows that the CCP is quite reluctant to completely forsake its control on the third sector. The authorities are particularly wary not to let political dissidents try to use these associations either to achieve their agenda, or only to establish contacts with ordinary citizens through them. In some cases, activists who have a sensitive background are prevented from staying in the board of some NGOs, even if they were among the people who founded them. This shows that pressure by the authorities can succeed in eliminating the people whom they consider dangerous. It points to the very tough limitations that the CCP can impose on third-sector associations. But it also shows that the authorities can convince most leaders of even outspoken autonomous organizations to enforce their ban on dissidents. These leaders prefer to keep avowed dissidents out so that they will not be subject to pressures by the security organs, and the result is the increased isolation of these political activists. They do it in good faith, in order to be able to develop their action, but, through this kind of self-censorship, they act as auxiliaries and help the CCP enforce its ban on open dissent.

These developments show the ability of the CCP to integrate large numbers of activists who might otherwise have become dissidents, by giving them the feeling that they can act more efficiently if they accept to stay within the limits it has designed, especially if they abstain from linking the social problems they try to solve to the political situation. Moreover, these activists, in their search for efficiency, accept to break away from political dissidents, thus enforcing the CCP policy and consolidating its legitimacy.

China seems to be evolving along the same lines as the developed world, as consultation of users, recourse to experts, the increasing role of a "civil society" in the narrowest sense of single issue NGOs or charity organizations are replacing the social movements of yesteryears and marginalizing the political intervention of social actors. Is China, therefore, really entering the mainstream of modernity? Will it be able to make a direct transition from totalitarianism – the matrix (and the instruments of control) of which continues to exist – to postmodern governance without going through the stage of democracy? The present regime seems to be evolving towards a kind of post-political authoritarianism which enjoys the support of a large proportion of the elites, including the intelligentsia. It is the first time since 1949 that elites in all fields, whether economic, political or intellectual, have supported the project proposed by the Party-State.

The Right Defence Movement: a new avatar of the struggle for an autonomous civil society?

One interrogation remains: will this pact among the elites be strong enough to resist eventual pressure from the "toiling masses"? Or will these be able to organize and attract the support of part of the intelligentsia in an attempt to change the political system so that it takes their interest into account? This question might well plague the evolution of the political regime of the People's Republic of China for the decades to come. Some indices seem to indicate that disenfranchised groups such as farmers start to organize collective protests. Although these protests remain circumscribed at village or township level, they tend to develop in some regions such as Central China.[23]

Just as Mao Zedong's action in order to "educate the successors to the Revolutionary cause" ended up in creating a generation of blasés or opponents, the new tolerance for NGOs, however limited their scope of action, may have undesired consequences. Some of the leaders of these seemingly respectful organizations have no illusions and use the legal aid and other aspects to heighten the political awareness of the social categories they are working with. Sometimes, their action results in the multiplication of conflicts in which the "vulnerable groups" use all sorts of methods to defend their rights.

The multiplication of conflicts linked to land grabs, to expropriations from city centres, to unpaid salaries or to the degrading conditions of the environment[24] has shown that the sacrosanct stability has been increasingly under threat. Using the officially sponsored discourse on the rule of law, many victims have turned towards the courts to defend their rights. Coupled with the official attention granted to the plight of "vulnerable groups", the discourse on rights has given an excuse to some concerned intellectuals to launch a campaign for the respect of citizens' rights.

The event which sparked the emergence of the Rights Defence Movement (*weiquan yundong*) was the Sun Zhigang affair. In March 2003, a designer from a village in Hubei, Sun Zhigang, was arrested in the streets of Guangzhou. As he could not show his provisional *hukou*, he was taken to a Shelter and Repatriation Centre where migrant workers without IDs are concentrated before being sent back home to their villages. Sun did have regular documents, but he was never given the opportunity to send for them and was beaten so harshly that he died in custody. The story of his death was published in the *Nanfang Dushi Bao* (Southern Metropolis) and provoked an outrage. When the Guangdong CCP Committee ordered the papers not to cover that story, it was already too late, as a great number of infuriated comments had appeared on the Internet. Five legal scholars from Beijing launched a petition asking for the abolition of the Shelter and Repatriation Centres. To their utter surprise, in June 2003, Prime Minister Wen Jiabao decided to abolish them. This was viewed as the first victory of public opinion since 1989. By challenging the legality of a well-established institution, legal scholars, helped by journalists who had denounced the scandal, had succeeded in having it suppressed. After that episode, many legal scholars, lawyers and citizens alike were convinced that the law could be used to defend the rights of ordinary Chinese. Then, many victims of abuse – villagers insufficiently compensated after land expropriation, peasants victims of corrupt Party secretaries – started to hire lawyers and to challenge the governments and their agents in court. With the help of journalists, of ordinary netizens, a network of lawyers and legal scholars specializing in civil rights appeared and is now considered as a tool to challenge abusive cadres. This network is informal, but the people it links help the victims find ways to use the law in order to defend their rights. Thanks to the Internet, it has grown nationwide. An interesting aspect of this network is that it cuts across social classes, allowing for collaboration between intellectuals (such as lawyers, journalists, professors) workers and peasants. During the past year, it has come under attack from the authorities who have targeted some civil rights lawyers, suspending their license,[25] jailing some of them under the pretext of threatening State security. The CCP tends to treat the Civil Rights Movement as it treated the pro-democracy movement in the 1990s. However, it is difficult for the authorities to deny the victims the right to go to court as conflicts multiply and tend to escalate, threatening to become violent and therefore putting the sacrosanct stability in jeopardy. Besides, civil rights activists do not challenge the legitimacy of the State but, on the contrary, take it to its word and ask for the enforcement of the law to check the abuses by officials. The Civil Rights Movement is a test of the determination of the government to establish the rule of law, which it presents as its objective. Will the authorities continue to take repressive steps against its leaders? Or will they consider them as intellectuals committed to help improve the lot of the "vulnerable groups"? Can the network of the right protectors become the embryo of a new civil society? It is still early to tell, but the historical developments which have taken place since the launching of the reforms show that it is difficult for the CCP to prevent the autonomization of society. Of course, it still has very strong assets to check this process.

Be it in the 1980s, when the organizations that the intelligentsia had set up were fighting for a radical transformation of the CCP's rule and for democracy, in the 1990s when it has been working for the development of NGOs, or in the twenty-first century when, together with ordinary citizens, they struggle for the establishment of the rule of law, action by intellectuals has always taken place in a space which was designed and structured by the CCP. In the 1980s, it depended on an alliance with the fraction of radical reformers for its possibilities of expression; since 4 June 1989, it has accepted to restrain its discourse to the one that is officially tolerated by the authorities. If no social group is in a position to overcome these limitations, it will be very difficult for a vibrant civil society to be consolidated in China.

Notes

* An earlier version of this chapter was published in *Social Research*, Vol. 73, Spring 2006, pp. 53–76
1 Surely the best compilation is the one which appeared on China Development

brief website. See www.chinadevelopmentbrief.com/page.asp?sec=2&sub=3&pg=0 (accessed 11 October 2006).

2 Maria Renata Markus, "Decent Society or Civil Society?" *Social Research*, Vol. 68, No. 4 (Winter 2001), p. 1015; emphasis original.

3 Hu Jiwei, "Hu Yaobang yu Xidan minzhu qiang (Hu Yaobang and the Xidan Democracy Wall)", *Zhengming*, Vol. 5 (2004), p. 49.

4 The cardinal principles which insisted on the leadership of the CCP were clear to everybody.

5 The failure of the anti-bourgeois liberalization campaign in 1981 convinced the liberal intelligentsia that at least part of the leadership (especially Hu Yaobang) was ready to protect bold initiatives in the ideological field and to pay the price of a clash with the conservatives.

6 Speeches by authors at the Congress of the Association of Writers in 1984 required freedom of creation.

7 The first of these editorial boards, and one of the most famous was *Zou Xiang Weilai* (*Marching toward the Future*), a collection housed by the Sichuan People's Press (Sichuan renmin chubanshe).

8 Tizhi gaige yanjiusuo (Research Centre on the Reform of the System), which played a very important role in the devising of the rural policy all along the 1980s.

9 Bao Zunxin, quoted in J.P. Béja, *A la recherche d'une ombre chinoise*, Paris: Ed.du Seuil, 2004, p. 110.

10 Zhang Weiguo, "An interview of Wang Juntao", *Zhengming*, Vol. 7, No. 200 (1994), p. 40.

11 There was no such thing as the 1980 Agreement of Gdansk whereby the Polish United Workers' Party (PUWP) acknowledged the existence of Solidarnosc. When, during the 1989 pro-democracy movement, the students' autonomous organizations asked for a public dialogue, the authorities refused bluntly.

12 After 1987, many cadres' children started to sell at market price raw materials and machinery that they bought at State price, making huge profits in the process. The success of these companies (*pibao gongsi*, attaché case companies) outraged the ordinary workers, because their managers needed no other skills than to be able to use a network of relationship (*guanxi wang*).

13 "Open Letter to the Standing Committee of the National People's Congress and to the Party Central Committee", in Zhang Jinyu (ed.), *Ziyou zhi Xue, Minzhu zhi Hua* (*The Blood of Freedom, the Flowers of Democracy*), Taipei: Guoli zhengzhi daxue, guoji guanxi yanjiu zhongxin, p. 53.

14 One can compare the function of this massacre with the repression of the "June Days" (journées de juin) after the 1848 revolution in France. This massacre provided the conditions for the social pact which supported the Second Empire, during which France became an industrial power.

15 The second one of these is "the most advanced culture" and who else represents culture?

16 Cf. Gong Xikui, "Zhongguo xianxing huji zhidu toushi (Perspectives of the system of residence registration in China)", *Shehui kexue*, Vol. 312, No. 2 (1989), pp. 31–35, translated in Jean-Philippe Béja, "La crise sociale en Chine (China's Social Crisis)", in *Problèmes politiques et sociaux* (*Social and Political Problems*), Paris: La documentation française, 1989.

17 On this subject, see Chloé Froissart, "Escaping from under the Party's thumb", *Social Research*, Vol. 73, No. 1 (Spring 2006), pp. 197–218. The author details the changes in legislation on migrant workers and the new discourse of the Party after the sixteenth congress.

18 See Chloé Froissart's article.

19 Cf. for example, Ray Cheung, "Change of focus urged in efforts to tackle poverty", *South China Morning Post*, 25 May 2004.

20 "If intermediary organisations are not developed, it is impossible to enact the reform of institutions …. The development of a socialist market economy necessarily entices an autonomous society beside the State", Wu Jinliang, *Zhengfu gaige yu di san ge bumen fazhan* (*The Reform of Government and the Development of the Third Sector*), Beijing: Zhongguo shehui kexue chubanshe, 2001, p. 20.

21 Cf. Nicolas Becquelin, "Pioneer in aids fight is in trouble", *South China Morning Post*, 14 September 2002. Just before, the authorities had resorted to all sorts of means to silence Dr Gao Yijie, who had tried to attract its attention on the seriousness of the situation.

22 Cf. "China permits activist to register AIDS institute", *AFP*, Beijing, 19 October 2002.

23 For peasants protests in Anhui, cf. Chen Guidi, Chu Tao, *Zhongguo nongmin diaocha* (*A Survey of Chinese Farmers*), Beijing: Renmin wenxue chubanshe, 2004, and Yu Jianrong, "Nongmin youzuzhi kangzheng jiqi zhengzhi fengxian: Hunan sheng H xian diaocha (Farmers'organized resistance and political risk. A survey of Hunan H district)", *Zhanlüe yu Guanli*, Vol. 58, No. 3 (2003), pp. 1–17.

24 The authorities have announced that there had been 87,000 collective protests in 2005, an increase of 13.4 per cent compared to 2004. See Irene Wang, "Incidents of social unrest hit 87,000", *South China Morning Post*, 20 January 2006.

25 Gao Zhisheng, one of the most famous right defence lawyers, saw his firm closed by the authorities in early 2006. See Gao Zhisheng, "Chosing the battles", *China Rights Forum*, No. 3 (2006), pp. 43–45.

5 NGOs in China

Development dynamics and challenges

Yiyi Lu

Since the late 1980s, the concept of civil society has gained great international prominence.[1] It routinely features in public debates, academic writings, media reports and policy analyses on almost any issue of current concern. Civil society organizations, notably non-governmental organizations (NGOs), have also enjoyed a spectacular growth over this period, receiving increased support from multilateral institutions, governments, the corporate sector and the general public.

China watchers have always shown great interest in the development of civil society in the country, largely because of its widely perceived potential for bringing about democratic political change. But they have also attached importance to civil society, especially NGOs, on account of the other vital functions they are supposed to be able to perform, such as providing social services, promoting community development, protecting vulnerable and marginalized social groups and generating debate on public policies. Much hope has been pinned on their role in helping to meet the enormous development challenges which China faces.

Is such hope well placed? Can Chinese NGOs live up to expectations? This chapter offers an assessment based on detailed field research over several years.

Defining NGOs in China

The official Chinese term for NGOs is 'popular organization'. This comprises two sub-categories, 'social organization' and 'private non-enterprise unit' (PNEU). Both types of organization are non-profit-making, but social organizations are membership-based whereas PNEUs are not.

Chinese researchers and practitioners often divide Chinese NGOs into 'officially organized NGOs' and 'popular NGOs'. The former are initiated by the government and receive government subsidies. Their staff are often on the government's payroll, and their leadership positions are often held by government officials. By contrast, popular NGOs are initiated by private citizens and receive no government subsidies. Their staff are not government employees, and they do not have officials occupying their top management positions.[2] Officially organized NGOs are also frequently called 'top-down NGOs', while popular NGOs are referred to as 'bottom-up NGOs'.

Although the official Chinese term is 'popular organization', 'NGO' and two other terms – 'non-profit organization' and 'third sector organization' – are also frequently used in China. Technically, these terms have different nuances, but they are often used interchangeably.

The growth of NGOs since the reforms

The emergence of an NGO sector in China has been a direct consequence of the changes to both the Chinese state and the society since the beginning of the reforms in 1978. Reforms have not only led to a relaxation of state control over the economy and society, but have also seen the state actively creating and sponsoring NGOs in order to transfer to them certain functions which it used to perform itself under the command system. In the economic sphere, the government has sought to reduce its direct management role by establishing intermediary organizations, such as trade associations and chambers of commerce, to perform sectoral coordination and regulation functions. In the social welfare sphere, the government wants to foster an NGO sector onto which it can offload some of the burden of service provision.[3] In the social development sphere, the government hopes that NGOs can mobilize societal resources to supplement its own spending.[4]

Meanwhile, societal actors have been quick to exploit the greater social space and the non-state-controlled resources now available to them to pursue their independent interests and agendas. NGOs provide an important channel for such pursuits. With the impetus to the formation of NGOs coming from both the state and the society, the number of NGOs has increased rapidly in the reform era. Ministry of Civil Affairs (MCA) statistics show that before 1978 there had been only about 6,000 social organizations in China. By the end of 2006, their number had reached 186,000. The number of PNEUs, which did not exist before the reforms, reached 159,000.[5] Moreover, the social organizations that existed before the reforms were fully controlled by the state and mainly served the state's objectives, whereas many NGOs that have emerged since the reforms enjoy considerable autonomy and work to promote societal interests. A good example of such NGOs is those that are 'organized around marginalized interests',[6] such as self-help groups formed by people living with HIV/AIDS, or organizations championing labour rights.

Despite the rapid growth of NGOs, many factors have prevented them from effectively performing public-benefit functions. These factors range from government policies on NGOs to the characteristics of political participation in China. Some key factors are discussed below.

Government policies

Wary of the potential threat to its authority and rule posed by organizations such as the *Falun Gong*,[7] the government has adopted a policy of forestalling the formation of NGOs which might challenge it politically, weaken its control over society or constrict its autonomy in formulating economic and social policies. For example, a set of internal guidelines followed by civil affairs departments in considering applications to establish NGOs stipulates that no NGO set up by 'specific social groups', such as migrant labourers, laid-off workers or ex-servicemen, should be allowed to exist.[8] Apparently, the government fears that these often disgruntled social groups would cause it big trouble once they are able to organize themselves. In a collection of MCA documents, several reports by provincial governments highlighted their achievements in thwarting attempts by members of these social groups to form their own organizations. For example, a report from Shanghai mentioned that some rural migrants employed at a Shanghai factory had formed a union which sent a letter of petition to higher authorities demanding reduced working hours and increased pay and threatened further action if their demands were ignored. The report said that the local government successfully persuaded the union to disband.[9]

Not only does the government proscribe NGOs that are liable to make difficult demands on it or challenge its policies, it also wants to prevent any NGO from growing too big and powerful by developing an extended organizational network. This is demonstrated by several clauses in the current government regulations for NGO management and registration. For example, one clause prohibits NGOs from establishing regional branches. This means that national NGOs cannot set up any branch outside Beijing, while provincial and county-level NGOs must confine their organizations to the provincial capital city or the county seat. NGOs carrying out the same activities can exist simultaneously at all the different administrative levels, but they must remain separate organizations.

Many NGOs complain that this clause has seriously curtailed their growth potential. After successfully setting up and running a popular NGO that provides innovative social services, several founders interviewed for this study have tried to establish similar organizations in other cities, in order to make the services available to more people and to spread their ideas. However, because of the 'no regional branch' rule, any extension of the original organization in other locations must be established as an independent NGO. In other words, the services they set up in different places cannot be run as a unified operation under a single leadership, making the scaling-up of the services more difficult.[10]

The government's regulation of the NGO sector has also been guided by a professed desire to improve efficiency and eliminate unproductive competition between NGOs. While these appear to be sensible objectives, the means whereby the government tries to achieve them – one of the most heavily criticized clauses in the current NGO regulations – has often amounted to further cramping of NGOs' space. This clause states that the government will not allow any new NGO to be established if in the same administrative area there is already an NGO doing similar work. This stipulation has meant not only that many popular NGOs have been denied approval for establishment, but also that some existing ones have been forced either to disband or to be incorporated into officially organized NGOs. For example, since the Disabled Persons' Federation

(DPF), a semi-official organization, already has local chapters in every city, popular NGOs formed by disabled people have not been allowed to register, even though many disabled people and their relatives are dissatisfied with the DPF and feel that it has done a poor job in representing their interests. In one city, a popular membership NGO for disabled people had existed alongside a similar NGO that was affiliated with the DPF for over 10 years, but after the central government ordered an overhaul of the NGO sector in 1998, the local civil affairs department refused to renew the popular NGO's registration and forced it to merge with the organization affiliated with the DPF. As a result, the popular NGO's ability to promote the interests of its members was constrained.[11]

Government capacity for NGO administration

The government's tight regulation of NGOs is just one side of the story. Its desire to keep effective control over NGOs has not been matched by its capacity to enforce its policies. Researchers have observed that in this particular arena the familiar problem of the central government in Beijing experiencing increasing difficulty in securing compliance with its policies from local governments has once again manifested itself. As Saich wrote, '[L]ocal governments will approve social organizations or other non-state bodies that contribute to the local economy and well-being. This is irrespective of formal regulatory requirements.'[12] In fact, to look at the problem in terms of the centre versus the localities simplifies the situation. The central government is not dealing with recalcitrant local governments as single entities on this issue. Rather, the challenge it faces is how to discipline myriad individual government agencies from the national all the way down to the lowest administrative level, which often put their narrow departmental interests before the overall strategic interest of the state. As an MCA official said in an interview, many government units simply use the cover of NGOs to create agency slush funds and to make money through charging illegal fees or extorting donations from enterprises. Apparently, these agencies have every incentive to circumvent central government policies in order to protect their NGOs.[13]

On the one hand, individual government units often fail to discipline the NGOs under their sponsorship, and on the other hand, Civil Affairs, the agency charged with policing NGO activities, is seriously constrained in its ability to perform this duty. The MCA's Popular Organization Management Bureau (POMB) only has a few dozen staff, who in addition to developing and coordinating NGO-related policies, drafting strategic plans for the sector, investigating and prosecuting illegal NGO activities, and providing guidance and advice to local civil affair departments, are also responsible for registering and conducting annual reviews of all national and cross-regional NGOs as well as foreign NGOs that operate in China. As one Chinese researcher commented, the POMB staff did not even have time to read the annual reports of all the NGOs under their supervision, let alone effectively monitor and review their activities.[14] The situation at provincial and lower levels is similar or even worse.

Many provincial civil affairs bureaux have only about six to eight staff working on NGO administration, who must oversee thousands of NGOs. Below the provincial level, many civil affairs bureaux have such limited human resources that they cannot dedicate a single full-time staff member to NGO-related work. Therefore, as many civil affairs officials openly admitted, and indeed complained, they are woefully ill-equipped for the NGO management duty which the state has laid on them.[15]

Given its limited capacity, the government appears to have given priority to monitoring and controlling NGOs which it distrusts on political and ideological grounds, while worrying less about NGOs that are guilty only of economic misdeeds. The combined effect of the state's NGO policy and its limited policy enforcement capacity is that certain types of NGO, particularly those that are likely to perform the political functions often ascribed to civil society organizations, such as challenging state policies, championing the rights of disadvantaged social groups and promoting pluralism and diversity, have limited space to pursue their activities. Meanwhile, many NGOs that engage in economic corruption and malfeasance – in other words conduct that constitutes the antithesis of civil society virtues – have been able to continue their operations unhindered.

NGO dependence on the government

Both officially organized and popular NGOs depend on the government for vital support and resources. For example, thanks partly to the government's attempt to restrict their size, most NGOs lack the organizational capacity to implement even medium-scale projects. They therefore need to collaborate with the government and rely on its administrative network to implement their projects. NGOs are vulnerable to obstructive and predatory behaviour by individual government agencies or officials, which can jeopardize their work. In such situations, they often seek support from other government agencies and officials and rely on their protection to solve their problems. Because of the government's lack of transparency, NGOs rely on good connections to the government to obtain information on its policies and practices which directly affect their work. In short, even if NGOs do not receive any funding from the government, they are still dependent on it for their ability to operate.

This dependence on the government has limited NGOs' usefulness as champions of interests and values that are different from those of the government. Consider the example of a popular NGO active in the field of women's rights. It has collaborated with local radio and television stations to make programmes that educate women about their legal rights. The programmes proved to be extremely effective in raising the awareness of these issues not just among women but also in the local population at large. Despite the tremendous impact of the media, however, the NGO failed to fully harness its power in the service of its cause, because it was afraid of offending the government. The television programmes it produced featured typical cases in which women's rights had been trampled. The NGO was very circumspect in choosing the topics for these programmes. It covered stories such as extra-marital affairs resulting in husbands abandoning their wives and children, but avoided others which would show the local authorities in a bad light. For example, a policeman and his colleagues beat up a woman after she had a fight with his girlfriend. The woman sought justice but the local police force ignored her complaints. Although it tried to help the woman through its government connections, the NGO decided not to expose the case in the media, as it would antagonize the police department whose goodwill the NGO needed.[16]

NGOs' dependence on the government not only constrains their actions but also affects their attitude towards the vulnerable and disadvantaged people who are supposed to be their raison d'être. Many NGOs consider their relationship with government agencies and officials as the most important of all their relationships. In contrast, their clients, who tend to be the most powerless among NGOs' contacts and who depend on them for services, are often treated as the least important people. NGOs themselves are not unaware of the contradictions involved in such a ranking of their relationships, but they argue that this is unavoidable and think that they have got their priorities right. As one NGO manager said:

> If you are very close to the government and your work is praised by the government, it is beneficial. But it can also have a downside. Ordinary people will think that you are the same as the government. Those people who distrust the government will not support you any more. They will think that you are wallowing in the mire with the government. But if you don't curry favour with the government you cannot get things done. In the end, the support of the government is far more important than the support of the common people. Besides, people have different views. There are also those who will support you because you enjoy an excellent relationship with the government.[17]

Dependence on the government has also been the reason for many officially organized NGOs' poor record in fulfilling useful functions on its behalf. Officially organized NGOs are often created to assist with the administrative tasks of government agencies and to facilitate the implementation of government policies. Some government-initiated foundations, for example, are set up to raise money from non-governmental sources to fund government-identified programmes. However, the performance of these NGOs has been very uneven. A considerable number of officially initiated foundations have failed to raise any funds. In the government's own assessment, among national-level officially organized NGOs, only one-third had been 'useful', one-third had been 'of limited use', and one-third had been 'completely useless or even worse', i.e. they actually created problems for the government rather than playing any useful role.[18]

Why have so many officially organized NGOs been ineffective tools for the government? As part of its reform programme, the national leadership has encouraged government agencies to transfer some of their functions to NGOs, but many agencies at the local level are reluctant to do so, as it would reduce their power and resources. Therefore, although they have set up new NGOs in response to the call from higher levels, they have not handed over any real responsibility to them.[19] This is one of the main factors accounting for the limited impact of these NGOs.

In addition, many officially organized NGOs are staffed by serving or retired government employees whose incomes and job security are not tied to the fortune of the NGOs. Some of these NGO staff have displayed considerable entrepreneurial flair and raised money themselves to undertake projects, but there are also others who will only carry out activities if they receive project funding from the government. When there is no money, they do nothing. After a field trip to a western province, a Beijing-based NGO researcher found that many staff of officially organized NGOs he interviewed there were unperturbed by the fact that they were sitting idly in their offices all day long. The general secretary of one such NGO said that they were 'on strike', because the local government was in financial crisis and had no money to give his organization.[20] NGOs like this have continued to exist because they do not need to earn their living. By creating the dependency of such organizations, the government has only itself to blame for their ineffectiveness.

Motives of NGO practitioners

As mentioned above, many officially organized NGOs at local levels are simply tools for local government agencies to create agency slush funds. NGOs allow these agencies to set up bank accounts where they can put their off-the-book income. Obviously, such NGOs cannot be expected to make a genuine contribution to the public interest. Some popular NGOs have also been set up by people whose real motive is profit. Loopholes in the government's NGO management system have made it possible for profit-oriented organizations to register as NGOs, especially at the local level. Many fee-charging social service organizations, such as private nursing homes and childcare institutions, fall into this category.

Even if their motive is not profit, many NGO practitioners still have self-serving purposes. According to one outspoken women's NGO activist, a university lecturer, there were four reasons why she took part in NGO activities: they provided her with data for her teaching and research; they allowed her to make useful new friends, thereby expanding her social network; they brought some extra income and they gave her opportunities to go on foreign trips. This woman considered her case to be typical. She had worked for several well-known women's NGOs in China and knew many inside stories. She was very cynical about the motives of most leaders of women's NGOs, believing that they had similar goals to hers but that in addition they were after fame.[21]

As this woman pointed out, it was not that these NGO leaders did not believe in what they were doing. They did care about the causes they had chosen for themselves and had worked energetically to promote them. However, they were not exactly value-driven. Their NGO activism did not necessarily spring from deeply held beliefs or ideals. It was motivated as much by personal gain as by anything else. This interest in personal gain was reflected in the way these leaders managed their organizations. There was often a total lack of transparency and democratic decision-making. The leaders wanted to control everything and were reluctant to share opportunities and acclamation with their staff. Consequently, they all had difficulty retaining talented people. Furthermore, this woman argued, because the leaders' actions were not founded on a passion for such ideals as equality, democracy and the empowerment of women, they could hardly inspire others with these ideals. In fact, they often showed little regard for these principles in their treatment of the NGOs' beneficiaries. As to the NGOs' ordinary staff, they had not experienced much equality, democracy or empowerment themselves because of their leaders' autocratic style, so how far were they able to go in embodying these values in their own interactions with the NGOs' clients?

This woman's opinion was shared by many other NGO workers. They often complained that their leaders treated the NGOs as their private property. As one proof of this, many cited the fact that their leaders were extremely reluctant to set up boards of directors to supervise their actions. Some staff felt that they were working for the fame of their leaders rather than a public cause. Many said that their leaders did not allow them to represent the organizations in external meetings for fear that they would start to make a name for themselves, and many were disgruntled at the monopolization of opportunities by their leaders. One person said that she was only able to go on a study tour to a foreign country because the donor agency that funded the tour specifically invited her, as it was directly related to the work she was doing. This greatly annoyed her manager, who tried unsuccessfully to find excuses to prevent her from going on the trip. Not surprisingly, many staff also complained that their leaders would tolerate no disagreement, let alone criticism.[22]

Despite the complaints of their staff, to conclude that many NGO leaders started out with selfish gains in mind, such as fame, professional opportunities or material rewards, is probably doing them an injustice, for at the beginning many of them simply did not know exactly what they would achieve with the projects they were embarking on. On the other hand, many founders of popular NGOs did admit that self-fulfilment was their main motivation. Many of them were not satisfied with the jobs they were doing and were looking for ways to put their talent to better use.

While there is nothing wrong in seeking self-realization through NGO work, the fact that the original motivation of some NGO leaders is self-realization rather than passion for the specific issues addressed by their NGOs does tend to present problems for the organizations later on. It is true that wanting a fulfilling career and a sense of personal achievement is not the same as having specific selfish aims, such as fame or professional advancement. However, in practice one tends to associate the latter with the former. It seems that, once their work has brought them rewards such as fame and professional opportunities, some NGO leaders do attach great importance to them and are unable to convince those around them that they care about the NGOs' missions more than these personal gains. At the same time, their success is dependent on their being portrayed as high-minded individuals who put self-interest aside to pursue public causes. This discrepancy between the public image and the actual behaviour of NGO leaders as observed by their colleagues appears to be an important reason for the cynicism among NGO staff about the motives of their leaders and the purposes of their organizations.

The cynicism prevalent among NGO staff has contributed to an internal culture in many NGOs which is characterized by a lack of trust and openness between leaders and other members, a lack of institutional loyalty, much back-biting and incessant power struggles. While many NGO staff complain about the self-serving behaviour of their leaders, many of them also inadvertently reveal that they themselves do not always put the interest of their organizations above their own. For example, many have no scruples about badmouthing their leaders to donors and clients, which often serves to undermine the latter's confidence not just in the leaders but in the organization as a whole. It is not uncommon for staff members to make contact with donors and other key supporters behind their leaders' backs to promote their own schemes. Quite a few of them admit that they plan to start their own NGOs or projects and to this end are secretly exploiting the resources of the organizations for which they currently work.

Just as NGO staff are often full of complaints about their leaders, so NGO leaders also have plenty to say about the cynical tactics of their staff. One leader said that two senior staff in her organization never disagreed with any of her decisions at staff meetings. However, if they did not like these decisions, they would go afterwards to the NGO's patron in the government to make mischief, so that he would pressure her to change her decisions.[23] Another leader said that her deputy had tried to oust her through backstage manoeuvres rather than an open challenge. The deputy supplied clients with details of various behind-the-scenes activities in the NGO, which served to foment their dissatisfaction with her leadership. Eventually, some of the clients joined forces to demand that she hand over the helm to the deputy.[24] Many NGO leaders feel that their staff often have personal agendas and do not share information with them.

In short, while it would be unrealistic to expect all NGO workers to be good Samaritans who are without selfish concerns, motivational issues appear to have contributed to a very unhealthy internal culture that has plagued many Chinese NGOs. This culture has not only undermined their public-service performance but also threatens their organizational sustainability, as is attested by the internecine wars that have crippled many NGOs.

Political culture

Various qualitative and quantitative studies of China's political culture have identified a number of features that are not conducive to collective action and civil society activism. These include elitism, fatalism and lack of cooperative spirit and group solidarity.[25] These features cannot be attributed to a single cause. Rather, history, ideology, customs and tradition, and past and present political institutions have all played a part in producing these features.

Both qualitative and quantitative studies of political culture have intrinsic limitations; therefore, simply using the conclusions of such studies to explain the weakness of Chinese NGOs would not constitute rigorous analysis. Furthermore, the existence of cultural traits that are not conducive to civil society activism does not mean that such activism cannot develop in China. Nevertheless, in analysing the problems frequently encountered by Chinese NGOs, insights from studies of Chinese political culture and political behaviour can be useful, although they should be applied with caution. The cultural attributes and behavioural patterns identified by these studies do seem to have some bearing on NGO performance. Many Chinese NGOs in different sectors and different geographic locations seem to face a number of similar obstacles, and the relevance of cultural factors therefore needs to be considered.

Among many popular membership-based NGOs, there appears to be widespread pessimism (or realism) about what they can achieve through their actions. This pessimism is apparently responsible for many people's lack of interest in engaging in advocacy activities to challenge the status quo, especially current government policies and practices. Many people stress that NGOs should not set unrealistic goals for themselves and should be sympathetic to the government's position. For example, the leader of an association of parents of disabled children remarked:

> When so many able-bodied people have been laid off, how can we realistically expect the government to give subsidies to families with disabled people, or find jobs for disabled people? My brother lives in New Zealand. I have heard from him that in New Zealand the government takes care of everything for disabled children. There are special provisions for them so they receive more benefits than normal children. If we want China to do the same, I am not even sure if it can be achieved 50 years from now, so I don't blame the government. There is no point in pressuring it to do what it is incapable of doing.[26]

The leader of another NGO which seeks to reduce the use of pesticide said:

> The pesticide problem cannot be solved quickly. Reducing pesticide usage will require major changes on a number of fronts. For instance, reform of the current agricultural chemical distribution system is necessary, since at present many people make a living by selling pesticides. Viable alternatives to pesticide must be found and offered to farmers, whose livelihood will otherwise be affected. Consumers' awareness needs to be substantially raised so that they will reject polluted agricultural products. A system of quality and safety control must be installed to keep polluted products out of

the market. The government will not be able to make all these changes overnight even if it wants to. Even if the government drafts new regulations banning the use of pesticide, implementing them will be difficult. Therefore there is no use asking the government to develop new policies. Eliminating the use of pesticide will inevitably take a long time.[27]

Even if they are not completely pessimistic about their ability to make a difference, most people want quick solutions to their problems and are unwilling to devote time and energy to any activity that does not promise immediate returns or concrete benefits to themselves. Most revealing is the remark of a participant at a national conference of parents of mentally disabled children. The remark was made in response to another participant's suggestion that they contact representatives to the People's Congress to ask them to introduce new legislation on social services for disabled children:

> It is too slow a remedy to be of any help. Even if we can make the People's Congress adopt new legislation to provide social services for disabled children, it may take five years for it to happen, but we cannot wait that long. By then our children will have grown up. So let us focus on practical issues instead.[28]

At the same conference, several parents from different cities all mentioned that the preoccupation with their individual short-term needs had prevented many parents from taking part in collective actions to pursue long-term goals. In one city, some parents of autistic children set up an association which effectively lobbied government special education schools to accept their children, who used to be denied access. However, once the problem of their own children's schooling had been solved, some initial members of the association, including its two founders, pulled out of the organization instead of continuing the fight for new parents joining the association recently who still faced this problem.[29]

In another city, a parents' association was set up with the encouragement of a local NGO leader who consciously tried to promote civil society activities. Its objective was to organize parents to influence government policies on welfare provision for disabled people, but it was unable to mobilize active participation from many parents. As the president of the association said:

> The Chinese people are very practical. They only make investments when they are assured of returns. If there is going to be a 50% gain, people will give you 50% support, otherwise they give you nothing. Because they did not see any material benefits, parents were not keen on the association. The two vice presidents and I made ourselves very busy but achieved nothing.[30]

Fear of incurring the displeasure of authorities is common among members and potential members of popular NGOs and presents a further impediment to the development and effective functioning of these bodies. At the above-mentioned conference of parents of mentally disabled children, some parents, when encouraged to organize themselves, were afraid that the authorities would accuse them of participating in illegal activities. For example, at a group discussion, after hearing parents complaining that they received little support from either the government or society, a teacher suggested that families living close to each other could form small groups and meet regularly to exchange information and engage in mutual aid. Even such an innocuous scheme scared some parents, who feared that they would be found guilty of setting up illegal organizations.

In a public speech in 2002, Meng Weina, an NGO activist for nearly 20 years, argued that the development of civil society in China might have been hindered more by the people than by the government. Over the years, she and colleagues in her organization had used various means to push the government to provide more welfare for disabled people. Although the government was often annoyed by their sharp criticism, it had by and large responded favourably to these legitimate demands. On the other hand, her open criticism of the government and bold challenge to existing policies and practices had frightened many members of her own organization as well as other NGOs, who had tried to distance themselves from her and accused her of being overly political. As a result, Meng Weina felt that she had faced more pressure from 'the people' than from the government.[31]

Meng Weina's charges were at least partially borne out by comments from those who had worked with her. In dealing with the government, Meng Weina had not shrunk from confrontational strategies. For example, she once led some parents of disabled children on a demonstration outside the municipal People's Congress to demand that the government provide financial assistance to disabled children in non-governmental schools. Some people who had taken part in the demonstration later argued that Meng Weina was wrong to involve them in such activities. One parent said:

> In retrospect I think she had no consideration for our safety. China has its specific situation. What if the government arrested us? She should have thought about protecting us. If she organized the demonstration now I would not have taken part in it.

A former colleague of Meng Weina's said, 'She is too emotional and tactless. We should take strong measures only after courteous ones fail. We should try to get what we want from the government through friendly negotiations rather than confrontational strategies.'[32]

Such views were disputed by a disabled woman who set up a club for disabled youth with the help of Meng Weina. As this woman remarked, 'Many people criticize her for using radical measures, but if she had not taken radical measures the government would not have paid attention to her.' Her experience of trying to make the government approve the club had convinced this woman that they would not have succeeded if they had not followed Meng Weina's advice and put some pressure on the government:

If we did not fight for our rights we would never have succeeded, because they told us we did not need to organize our own club. They said they would organize things for us through the disabled persons' federation. If we had listened to them, we wouldn't have the club today. After Meng Weina staged the demonstration the government immediately sent over 10 officials to her school to discuss their demand and they agreed to give the school 100,000 yuan every year. If Meng Weina had not taken that action, how could they receive the money?[33]

Despite similar expressions of support for Meng Weina's 'radical actions', most people were afraid of taking part in such actions. Some even maintained, in the face of evidence to the contrary, that Meng Weina's actions had had no positive effect on government policies and practices. Others agreed with Meng Weina's argument that her efforts had forced the government to improve its care for disabled people, but nevertheless thought that her strategies were likely to cause 'misunderstanding with the government' and were therefore not suited to 'the political environment of China'.

To Meng Weina, her NGO colleagues' and clients' fear of offending the government was a major constraint on her ability to engage in civil society activism. To respect their wishes, she was forced to channel her energy into service delivery rather than advocacy work. Faced with similar problems, some other activists who shared Meng Weina's dauntless spirit had decided to abandon group-based actions altogether in favour of individual action. Some anti-AIDS campaigners, for example, felt that as individuals they were less fearful of criticizing the government and exposing its mistakes, and therefore they could carry out more effective advocacy than organizations. The conclusion they drew from this was that they did not need any organization to support them.[34] While this may be the case, it demonstrates once again how many disincentives for collective action exist at present.

Scholars have pointed out that whereas the institutional arrangements in many societies make it difficult for ordinary citizens to influence policies at the implementation stage, thereby forcing them to pursue their interests by targeting the agenda-setting or policy formulation stages of the policy process, the institutional design in China is such that the reverse is true. In China, policies are usually not formulated in a precise form, and lower-echelon bureaucrats often enjoy considerable discretionary power in interpreting and implementing policies according to local situations. Such an institutional design induces people to focus on influencing the decisions of individual officials rather than the policy-making process itself in order to obtain the desired benefits from the government. This in turn encourages them to take individualized actions such as developing patron–client ties with officials or using *guanxi* (personal connections), which is often more cost-effective than investing in group-based political activities.[35]

Many examples bear out the above analysis of the characteristics of political participation in China. A story related by a member of a parents' association serves to illustrate this point. This parent and a fellow member of the association paid a visit to the municipal government's Charity Fund which had provided financial aid to various people in need. However, it had not provided funding for families with disabled children, as it did not have such a funding category. These two parents argued that many families with disabled children also experienced financial difficulties, so the Charity Fund should create a new category for such families. The Charity Fund official who received them said that this was not possible. However, he offered to help the two parents with their individual needs.[36] One can see from this example how tempting it is for ordinary people in China to approach officials with their individual problems rather than trying to obtain benefits for a whole group of people.

NGOs are often undermined by internal strife, which tends to break out whenever the opinions or interests of their members are not in total alignment. Not a single NGO interviewed for this study has been free from such strife. Two NGOs in the HIV/AIDS field saw their members disagreeing with each other as to which priority issues their organizations should be addressing. In each case, rather than trying to resolve their differences, members simply pursued their own interests with little regard for the unity of their organization and the coherence of its goal. One NGO organized a national conference of people living with HIV/AIDS (PLWHA) in order to bring such people in different parts of the country together for joint action. However, PLWHA who had no higher education felt snubbed and rejected by those who did. Efforts by an internationally funded HIV/AIDS prevention programme to encourage people at high risk of contracting HIV, such as homosexual men and commercial sex workers (CSWs), to form their own organizations also encountered much difficulty, as homosexual men tended to form many small circles based on similar educational background and socio-economic status and did not wish to be associated with those outside their circles, while CSWs often saw other CSWs as competitors rather than allies.[37]

In recent years, as they start to carry out more advocacy as opposed to service delivery activities, Chinese NGOs are increasingly aware of the need for joint action. On environmental issues, for instance, NGOs may need to challenge government policies which prioritize economic growth over environmental protection or oppose large infrastructure projects backed by powerful ministries and giant state-owned enterprises, or they may seek to change the life-style of millions of people, advocating a new consumption mode which is more energy efficient. Individual NGOs working on their own are unlikely to win such huge battles, so they need to pool their resources and join hands with other like-minded people and organizations. However, NGO cooperation has been plagued by incessant competition for leadership positions and the spotlight, with most good initiatives unable to sustain themselves over an extended period of time. In one case, several NGOs campaigning on an issue together agreed to rotate the chairmanship. However, after the first year, the serving chair was unwilling to hand over to the next organization and the joint campaign fell apart.[38] In another case, a donor-funded project aimed at encouraging NGO cooperation invited several NGOs to jointly implement a project. Although they all signed a contract agreeing to share resources and support each other, the NGOs in fact treated their relationship as a zero-sum game and were reluctant to share even basic information with each other, let alone other resources.[39] In the last few years, several attempts to organize environmental NGO alliances have been made, but they all fizzled out. In a recent workshop to discuss NGO cooperation on environmental issues, participants all agreed that a database of environmental NGOs would facilitate cooperation, but instead of agreeing to jointly construct a database, the NGOs which could contribute resources to such a project all wished to start their own databases instead of joining other organizations' effort.[40]

Conclusion

This chapter has discussed some major problems that have affected the ability of Chinese NGOs to perform the benevolent functions which are generally expected of them. This suggests that the effectiveness of NGOs either as service providers or as advocates for the interests of their constituencies cannot be automatically assumed but must be empirically proved.

Most of the problems faced by Chinese NGOs have no quick or easy solutions. Many of them stem from the political and institutional arrangements that currently exist in China, such as the way state–society relations are structured. Organizational capacity-building for Chinese NGOs has been high on the agenda of many donor agencies. Partly as a result of donor interest, many organizations and individuals have been busy organizing training programmes for these NGOs. However, as this chapter has sought to demonstrate, the problems afflicting Chinese NGOs cannot simply be removed by, say, teaching them some modern management techniques, or the importance of working together with other NGOs. The situation is far more complicated. To help Chinese NGOs better fulfil their potential, interested parties need to look beyond the NGOs themselves and to direct more effort at improving the general environment for the development of these organizations.

Efforts to overcome the challenges faced by Chinese NGOs also need to be aided by better research. Studies of Chinese NGOs have tended to go to two extremes. Either they apply 'macro' political theories such as civil society and corporatism, which are of limited use in explaining the actual behaviour of NGOs,[41] or they invoke management theories which have evolved from studies of non-profit organizations in western countries and therefore cannot take into account the specific political, legal and institutional situation in China.[42] Studies of Chinese NGOs need to move beyond macro political theories, but they must not neglect political analysis altogether, as many existing NGO studies which focus on management issues have done. To fully understand the motivations of Chinese NGOs, the way they operate, their vital relationships and the impact they make, we need more data from detailed qualitative research, but above all we need to relate NGO studies to such issues as state capacity, political culture and the evolving state–society relations in China.

Notes

1 Most of the field research for this chapter was funded by the Ford Foundation. Additional research was carried out when the author did consultancy work and implemented projects in China for various international organizations. Field research involved a large number of interviews with leaders, staffers, members and clients of NGOs, as well as government officials and Chinese NGO researchers. Over 40 NGOs were studied. They were located in different parts of China and worked in different sectors. Information on the interviewees is withheld in order to protect their identities, except in a few cases when interviewees did not mind having their names mentioned. An earlier version of this chapter appeared as a Chatham House Asia Programme Briefing Paper.
2 The distinction between officially organized and popular NGOs is not always clearcut. For example, some popular NGOs have staff who are able to work for them while retaining their status as government employees.
3 For example, see Linda Wong, *Marginalization and Social Welfare in China* (London and New York: Routledge, 1998).
4 For example, see Jude Howell, 'NGO-State Relations in Post-Mao China', in David Hulme and Michael Edwards (eds), *NGOs, States and Donors: Too Close for Comfort?* (London: Macmillan Press Ltd in association with Save the Children, 1997), pp. 202–215.
5 http://www.mca.gov.cn/artical/content/WGJ_TJGB/2007129141632.html, accessed 11 March 2007. It should be noted that the MCA statistics only include registered NGOs. Current government regulations require NGOs to register with the government in order to exist lawfully, but many unregistered organizations are still able to operate owing to the government's limited capacity for controlling unregistered organizations. There are also NGOs that register as businesses, since the registration requirements for businesses are easier to meet. Therefore, the real number of NGOs is higher than the MCA statistics show.
6 Jude Howell, 'New Directions in Civil Society: Organizing around Marginalized Interests', in Jude Howell (ed.), *Governance in China* (Lanham, MD: Rowman & Littlefield, 2004), pp. 143–171.
7 *Falun Gong* is a semi-religious sect related to *qigong* (traditional breathing and meditation exercises) that took the government by surprise when 10,000 of its followers surrounded the headquarters of the state apparatus in central Beijing for 13 hours on 25 April 1999 to protest against media criticism of its practice. The government subsequently launched a nationwide crackdown on *Falun Gong* and eventually banned it as 'an evil cult'. The *Falun Gong* incident reminded the government that it had not maintained effective control over the activities of NGOs; therefore, it took steps to tighten NGO registration and supervision following the incident.
8 These guidelines were mentioned in several speeches by high-level Civil Affairs officials.
9 Popular Organization Management Bureau, Ministry of Civil Affairs, *Minjian Zuzhi Guanli Zuixin Fagui Zhengce Huibian* (*Collection of the Latest Regulations and Policies on the Management of Popular Organizations*), 2000.
10 Interviews between 2000 and 2002.
11 Interview, May 2000.
12 Tony Saich, 'Negotiating the State: The Development of Social Organizations in China', *China Quarterly*, No. 161 (March 2000), p. 140.
13 Interview, October 2001.
14 Interview, May 2000.
15 Interviews, 2000, 2001 and 2007.
16 Research on this NGO was carried out in 2000.
17 Interview, April 2000.

18 Talk by a POMB official at Tsinghua University in January 2000.
19 For example, see Kenneth W. Foster, 'Embedded within State Agencies: Business Associations in Yantai', *China Journal*, Vol. 47 (January 2002), pp. 41–65.
20 Interview, August 2000.
21 Interview, November 2001.
22 Interviews between 2000 and 2006.
23 Interview, August 2000.
24 Interview, February 2006.
25 For example, see Alan P.L. Liu, *Mass Politics in the People's Republic: State and Society in Contemporary China* (Boulder, CO: Westview Press, 1996); M. Kent Jennings, 'Political Participation in the Chinese Countryside', *American Political Science Review*, Vol. 91, No. 2 (1997), pp. 361–372; Yang Zhong, Jie Chen and John M. Scheb II, 'Political Views from Below: A Survey of Beijing Residents', *Political Science and Politics*, Vol. 30, No. 3 (1997), pp. 474–482; and Suzanne Ogden, *Inklings of Democracy in China* (Cambridge, MA: Harvard University Asia Center, 2002).
26 Interview, May 2000.
27 Interview, May 2005.
28 March 2000.
29 Interview, March 2000.
30 Interview, March 2000.
31 Speech at Tsinghua University in May 2002.
32 Interviews, May 2000.
33 Interview, May 2000.
34 Interviews, October 2002.
35 Tianjian Shi, *Political Participation in Beijing* (Cambridge, MA/London: Harvard University Press, 1997).
36 Interview, July 2000.
37 Interviews, October 2002.
38 Informal discussion, January 2007.
39 Discussions with people involved in the project in 2006.
40 Beijing, January 2007.
41 For example, see Vivienne Shue, 'State Power and Social Organization in China', in Joel S. Migdal, Atul Kohli and Vivienne Shue (eds), *State Power and Social Forces: Domination and Transformation in the Third World* (Cambridge: Cambridge University Press, 1994), pp. 65–88; Jonathan Unger and Anita Chan, 'Corporatism in China: A Developmental State in East Asian Context', in Barrett L. McCormick and Jonathan Unger (eds), *China after Socialism: In the Footsteps of Eastern Europe or East Asia* (Armonk, New York: M.E. Sharpe, 1996), pp. 95–129; Timothy Book and B. Michael Frolic (eds), *Civil Society in China* (Armonk, New York: M.E. Sharpe, 1997); and Howell, 'NGO-State Relations in Post-Mao China', pp. 202–215.
42 For example, see Wang Ming, Liu Peifeng *et al.*, *Minjian Zuzhi Tonglun* (*A General Survey of Nongovernmental Organizations*) (Beijing: Shishi Publishing House, 2004). The chapters in the book have such titles as 'NGOs' evaluation system', 'NGOs' human resources management', 'NGOs' financial management', etc., and they focus on management theories instead of political or sociological analysis.

6 The state, firms and corporate social responsibility in China

Zheng Yongnian

China's crisis in corporate social responsibility

The concept of corporate social responsibility (CSR) has been widely recognized, but there has not been a widely accepted definition in the academic circles. Generally speaking, CSR refers to that while firms are responsible to maximize their profit and their shareholders' interest, they should also commit themselves to the responsibilities to their employees, costumers, environment, and communities where they operate their business. It includes business ethics, operation safety, occupation health, protection of workers' legal rights and interests, environmental protection, engagement in charities, donation to public welfare, and aid to social weak groups.

From whatever perspective, CSR in China is in serious crisis. Take the cost of people's life as an example. According to official statistics, over 263,500 people died in industrial accidents in two years (2004–2005). In the coal mining sector alone, nearly 6,000 minders died in 2005.[1] Nevertheless, it seems that the central government has had difficulty in enforcing effective policies to bring the situation under control.

Let us begin with mining accidents. During his 2005 New Year visit to Chenjiashan Coal Mine, Tongchuan, in China's Northwest Shaanxi Province, Premier Wen Jiabao shed tears with the family of a dead miner as he listened to their memories of the deceased. A few days before Wen's visit, the worst coal mine accident in the past 44 years took place and claimed 166 lives. Wen's posture was expected to generate some political significance. China's official newspaper commented, by sharing his tears with others, Wen tried to convey his sympathies for those who had suffered from accidents; his tears were not only for the victims of the Tongchuan coal mine disaster, but also for other lives lost in the country's frequent coal mine accidents; while the public was touched by Premier's tears, it was also expected that the state could better regulate the coal production system in order to curb such incidents.[2]

Wen must have been frustrated by rising numbers of mining accidents. Since he became China's Premier in 2003, he had repeatedly emphasized the importance of coal production safety. His administration had set up the State Safety Production Supervision and Management Administration and attempts had been made to implement various regulations to improve the safety level of coal production. But apparently, the situation has not improved. Official Statistics show that in 2004, there were 3,639 coal mine accidents in the country, causing the death of 6,027 people.[3]

Despite its ever greater efforts, it is almost impossible for the Chinese central government to regulate the country's huge coal production network. Until today, there are more than 600 large state mines, 2,600 provincial mines, and 22,000 township or private mines in China. As a giant producer of coal, China has been plagued with frequent coal mine accidents. The death rate for every million tons of coal produced in China is 100 times that of the United States and 30 times that of South Africa. One recent mine accident took place on 20 November 2005 in Heilongjiang province and claimed 164 lives. Another one took place on 7 December 2005 in Tangshan, north China's Hebei province, claimed 90 lives.

The frequent mine accidents are only the tip of the iceberg. China faces mounting problems with discharging CSR. While the central government has attempted to perform its role in achieving CSR, both local governments and firms have not. The central government's attempts to improve safety are frequently compromised by local authorities and firms ignoring unsafe production. In 2004 alone, more than 130,000 people died in industrial accidents.[4]

While industrial incidents could be regarded as extreme cases in CSR, irresponsible firm behaviours, such as labour rights violation, environmental degradation, and the absence of the spirit of charity, are widespread in China. Take labour rights as an example. Workers' rights are routinely violated. Workers are often required to work far more than 40 hours a week, have few days off, paid below the minimum wage, and not paid required overtime compensation. Physical abuse of workers and dangerous working condition are also common.

Irresponsible firm behaviours have become one of the major sources of rising labour disputes in recent years. How to create a good environment for CSR has become an important agenda for China's top leadership. Although the term of CSR was not specifically used, CSR was among the themes of the eleventh Five-Year Plan, suggested by the Fifth Plenum of the Chinese Communist Party (CCP) in October 2005 and approved by the National People's Congress in March 2006.[5]

It was the first major policy package by the Hu Jintao-Wen Jiabao leadership. The plan aims to achieve sustainable development by addressing mounting problems China faces, consequences of previous single-minded pursuit of rapid economic growth. Apparently, China's rapid development has borne heavy environmental, social, and even life costs. Such a development mode is not only unsustainable, but also likely to result in social instability.

According to this plan, the CCP will seek to build a society where resources are better conserved and where the environment is better protected. The ultimate political goal is to build a "harmonious society" (*hexie shehui*). The plan stressed that China should maintain a stable and rapid economic growth, with the target to double, by 2010, the per capita gross domestic product (GDP) achieved in the year 2000. Meanwhile, more attention should be directed to social justice and solving the problems related to ordinary people's interests.

This new policy thinking is in the line with the various discussions on CSR both inside and outside China. The Chinese leadership has mapped out the different roles that the state and firms should play, respectively, in achieving such a grand goal.

But compliance is far from assured. This chapter attempts to place China's CSR in the context of the relationships among the state, firms, and society and analyse why China's CSR lacks a good regulatory frame. It argues that the Chinese state does not have strong capacity in regulating the market players effectively. Lacking good foundation in the rule of law, the leadership faces the daunting task to ensure success of this new policy. To make prospects even bleaker, civil society in China has yet developed an effective mechanism to voice grievances and exercise influence on firm behaviours.

The state, firms, and CSR

To understand China's problem in performing CSR, it is important to first look at the relationship between the state and private firms. Take mine incidents as an example again. China's central government has repeatedly emphasized the work safety and made regulations, but firms, together with local governments, more often than not ignore these regulations. The lack of work safety, poor management, and the corruption of officials have led to the frequent occurrence of industrial incidents. China vice director of the work safety committee of the State Council Zhang Baoming once commented that "almost every accident is associated with corruption."[6]

Every time after a serious accident takes place, the central government will issue new instructions to related officials at all levels to engage in dealing with the accidents, blame is then laid and officials either resigned or punished. But accidents persist.

Why is China's central government not capable to achieve what it has wanted to achieve? Take mine incidents as example again. It is not difficult to find out what has gone wrong with CSR in China. In almost all cases, four key factors were involved, namely, firms, the government, workers, and society. To investigate irresponsible corporate behaviour is to explore how these four factors interplay in shaping CSR in China.

Where does CSR come from? Although definitions of CSR vary, there is much common ground. It is often reviewed as to how companies manage their core business to add social, environmental, and economic values in order to produce a positive sustainable impact for both the society and the business.[7]

Among others, main types of responsible corporate behaviour include:

a   CSR is committed to and promoted by the board.
b   Local laws and tax rules are followed.
c   Stakeholders' opinions are taken into account.

d   High labour standards and measures to protect the environment are adopted.
e   Firms' economic, social, and environmental performance and impact are monitored and reported to the public.
f   High standards of employee training and steps aimed at raising awareness of the company's responsibility are adopted.[8]

For firms to adopt CSR, there must be a right environment, which usually include the consumer, the investment climate, society, and the workplace.

In a well-developed market economy, the pressure for businesses to adopt CSR can come from consumers and society. Since consumers can freely choose corporate products, they create a social environment for firm competition and thus bring about pressures for firms to adopt CSR. Firms can benefit from the market by providing better corporate products and services. As the company reaps the rewards, this puts pressure on their competitors to do likewise.

However, this can hardly be materialized. The lack of accurate information, or open competition, or distortions from subsidized sectors, can lead to a breakdown in the market-led process. Market mechanisms are even more problematic in developing or transitional economies, where there are no right environments for competitive business, and regulations governing business practices are difficult to enforce.

The role of governments thus becomes important. The government has to make sure that conditions are right not only for investments, but also for making investments more responsible.

More specifically, governments can (a) regulate against persistent poor performance; (b) facilitate processes, information, and cooperation to bring about changes to help the poor; (c) form partnership with businesses and society; and (d) endorse best practice and transparency.

Changing state–firm relations and their impacts on CSR

China is a transitional economy as well as a transitional society. To understand the country's CSR environment, the first task is to see how the market-oriented reform has affected the relationship between the state and firms and the behaviour of the latter.

Firms in modern western sense did not exist in the pre-reform China. In the West, while firms could be owned by the state, they have to operate on market principles. In China, all firms were not only owned, but also managed by the state. Accordingly, no market existed and all resources were allocated by state plans. Consequently, there was no functional differentiation and no boundaries between the state, firms, and the society. Firms had to perform social functions and were responsible for cradle-to-grave affairs for workers.

Meanwhile, there was no room for civil society. The party-state identified itself as a party for workers (also peasants). There was an implicit social contract between the party-state and the workers. While the former provided the latter with various services, the latter accepted and recognized the legitimacy of party rule. In such a system, there was little question concerning what is now called CSR. When such a tacit agreement between the party-state and workers was acceptable to both parties, neither of them should have an incentive to break it. The maintenance of labour peace required relatively little use of overt coercion.

Such a situation also determined that there was no need and room to develop CSR. Indeed, firms performed the functions what either the state or the society should perform. Nevertheless, the market-oriented reform since the late 1980s has rapidly changed the relations between the state, firms, workers, and society.

In the state sector, the market reform means that the state gradually withdraw from economic affairs. But radical privatization did not take place in initial stages. The central government decentralized economic power to local governments at different levels. Local governments became de facto owners of state enterprises and played a role of what the scholarly community called "state corporatism."

Moreover, in pursuing high economic growth, local economic performance became the most important indicator for the central government to evaluate local officials. This evaluation system provided local officials with great political incentives to be interventionists. Close ties between local governments and firms made it extremely difficult for the government to regulate firms' behaviour.

Since the mid-1990s, partial privatization has taken place under the policy of *zhuada fangxiao* (focusing on large firms and letting small firms go) by the Zhu Rongji administration. While firms of medium and small size are privatized, efforts have been made in establishing a regulatory regime over big state firms [state-owned enterprise (SOE)]. These reform measures have had mixed impacts on CSR. Privatization did not lead to improvement in CSR since local governments are unwilling to regulate these firms as they too can benefit from local economic development.

In big state firms, the development of the regulatory regime pushes the firms to improve their corporate governance and thus become more socially responsible. Still, the performance of CSR varies. State firms that are managed by central authorities tend to have fewer labour rights violation, while these managed by local governments tend to violate labour rights more frequently. For instance, many mine accidents have taken place in decentralized state firms.

The market-oriented reform and open-door policy have also led to rapid development of the non-state sector, including privately owned firms, foreign-funded firms, and township–village firms. In the non-state sector, CSR performance varies in different types of firms. As is the case of privatized state firms, both domestic private firms and township–village firms perform badly, because of either local protectionism or the lack of enforcement of regulations. Labour rights violations are widespread in these firms. As in decentralized state firms, mine accidents have also taken place in non-state firms.

Large firms with direct investment from, and management by, western companies tend to have fewer violations since these firms are more likely to stress the importance of labour law compliance. Firms owned by Hong Kong Chinese, Taiwan, and South Korean firms tend to have more blatant labour violations largely because these firms are able to develop substantial *guanxi* (connections) with Chinese local governments, connections that have emboldened them to violate workers' rights and compromise Chinese regulations.

Both corporatization and privatization have pushed Chinese firms to make profit maximization their only goal without considering the externalities of their behaviour. Increasingly, intensive competition among firms and among local governments has worsened the situation. Inter-firm competition has not lead Chinese firms to be socially more responsible. Although in the long run, CSR can enhance firms' competitiveness and make their development sustainable, it still remains a concept alien to most firms in China.

It is also worth noting that Chinese firms have not developed a spirit of charity, an important aspect of CSR. According to China Charity – China's largest charity organization – 70 per cent of the donation it has received came from outside China, and less than 15 per cent came from domestic firms. To date, there are over ten million registered domestic firms in China, and less than 100,000 firms, or 1 per cent of the total, have donated in some way.[9]

Workers' power weakened, other social forces yet to play a great role

Another major actor which can play an important role in CSR is social forces. As discussed above, the complicated relations between the state and firms make it difficult for the state to regulate firms' behaviour. But if social forces, be they workers or consumers, can exercise their power over firms, the latter could become more socially responsible. Viewing from this perspective, China also lacks a right environment for CSR.

The reform policy has changed not only state–firm relations, but also state–society relations. Take workers' role as example. The political and economic status of workers has declined significantly. The party-state has made efforts to reform SOEs to rationalize their economic activities. While private entrepreneurs become politically significant, workers are no longer seen as the only force that the party relies on for legitimacy and economic development.

While SOE reforms have increased the power the management, the power of the trade union continues to be greatly constrained. In the pre-reform period, the trade union was subordinate to party leadership. It is now subject to management. For years, the trade union has tried to advance the economic interests of workers, but it lacks effective institutional means. For example, the workers' council, which was re-instituted in 1981, is supposed to have the right to participate in almost all enterprise decisions. But in practice, it does not have the final say on important issues. The selection of council members is controlled by the top leaders within a firm, and chosen council members often lack knowledge of the firm's operations and are thus unable to make useful suggestions.

The tension between management and workers often results in workers' resistance. Nowadays, the interaction between workers and the party as well as the government are often confrontational. The party is placed in an awkward position in dealing with workers' resistance. It cannot entirely ignore workers, nor can it cease reform measures which often undermine workers' interests. To continuously promote economic development, the party-state has adopted a cooptation strategy to deal with private business people. But so far the party has not found out a way to co-op workers' interests.

The role of other social forces in facilitating CSR has been mixed. While the government is gradually withdrawing from direct economic management and service provision, it has tried to pass the buck to social forces. Over the years, laws and government regulations have begun to appeal to these social forces and let them play a role in delivering CSR.

In the last two decades, the government has established a number of official charitable organizations, some of which have been able to mobilize substantial private funding. A wide-cited example is the China Youth Development Foundation's flagship Project Hope, which since 1989 has raised enormous amount of money to build rural schools and provide scholarships for students from poor areas. While much of the funding has come from corporations and overseas Chinese, fully 64 per cent of ordinary urban Chinese citizens have also contributed.

This is especially true for the case of poverty reduction. The government has mobilized social organizations, NGOs, and private enterprises to participate in a wide spectrum of aid-the-poor activities, such as the Cause of Glory, Aid-the-Poor through Culture, Happiness Project, Spring Buds Program, Young Volunteers' Project of Supporting Education in Poor Areas in Relays, and Poor Peasant Households' Self-Support Project.

International organizations such as the World Bank, the United Nations Development Program (UNDP) have also been mobilized in poverty reduction. These organizations have cooperated extensively with China in aid-the-poor work. Other foreign governments and organizations that have successfully carried out aid-the-poor projects in China include the European Union, the governments of the Great Britain, the Netherlands and Japan, the German GTZ, the Asian Development Bank, the Ford Foundation, the CARE of Japan, the Japan Bank for International Cooperation, the World Vision International, and the Hong Kong Oxfam.

Nevertheless, the role of civil organizations and NGOs in facilitating CSR should not be overestimated. Most domestic NGOs in China remain governmental or semi-governmental, namely, governmental "non-governmental organizations." These NGOs will have to perform their role in the line of the government, namely their role as a helping hand, and can hardly play an independent role. Without autonomy, NGOs are not empowered to have a meaningful impact on corporate behaviour, let alone governmental behaviour.

Due to lack of autonomy, the political influences of China's NGOs vary widely across different areas and as well as between different NGOs. In some areas such as poverty reduction, charity, and environmental issues, NGOs are encouraged to play a greater role. But in other areas such as religious issues, ethnicity, and human rights, the influence of NGOs is virtually absent. Also, some NGOs are more powerful than others. Most commercial organizations are extremely powerful in influencing the government's policy-making process. It is not difficult to find business people sitting in the People's Congress and the Chinese People's Political Consultative Conference at different levels of government. But workers and farmers are not allowed to organize themselves and thus do not have any effective mechanisms to articulate and aggregate their interests.

When powerful social groups can organize themselves, they become ever more powerful. There is no way for weak social groups such as workers and farmers to push for CSR. This is so partly because China is in an early stage of economic development and development is given higher priority than political participation. Workers and farmers might be able to play a more important role with further economic progress. But at this stage, it is difficult to say that growth and development of NGOs can facilitate CSR.

China: not a regulatory state yet

Needless to say, among many factors associated with poor performance in China's CSR, the most fundamental one is that China has yet become a modern regulatory state. Before such a modern regulatory frame comes into being, CSR is highly improbable in China.

To say that China is yet a regulatory state should not imply that the country does not have any regulations over firms. With the development of market economy, the Chinese state has been transforming from one that highly reliant on political control to a regulatory one. The rule of law has been the political motto ever since the reform and open-door policies. Thousands of laws and regulations have been passed, aiming at establishing a modern regulatory state.

But building a modern regulatory state has not been an easy task for the Chinese leadership. In order to regulate corporate behaviour, there must be a clear boundary between the state and firms. Although the state has been gradually downsizing and withdrawing from direct economic management, it is still highly interventionist. While privatization in rich coastal areas has been quite smooth, SOEs continue to dominate the poor and western provinces. The banking system remains politically directed, making it hard for private entrepreneurs to access credit.

Moreover, entrepreneurs are constrained by the lack of adequate legal framework and even more so, by the absence of an effective judiciary. Within firms, the CCP elite continue to enjoy broad, discretionary powers, inviting corruption, and other forms of irresponsible behaviour.

More important is that China lacks the infrastructure of modern regulatory states. In developed countries, laws, regulations, and contracts often mean the *end* of business. Once made, they are binding and governments and firms have to follow. But this is hardly the case in China. China never realizes a system of rule of law. For China's governments and firms, laws, regulations, and contracts often mean the *beginning* of business. Extensive bargaining between the governments at different levels and between the government and firms is a mandatory process for the enforcement of laws, regulations, and contracts. Legal fragmentation is a fundamental part of China's political system.

Legal fragmentation makes it extremely difficult, if not completely impossible, to enforce laws, regulations, and contracts. Take Chinese labour law as an example. The labour law is, by and large, not at odds with either the International Labour Organization (ILO) core labour standards or the basic content of most corporate codes of conduct. As a matter of fact, China has ratified more of the ILO conventions related to these standards than the United States.

The Chinese labour law is comprehensive, covering labour contracts, working hours, wages, worker safety, child labour and labour disputes, among other subjects. Government regulations provide additional details and rights. For example, the law currently mandates a maximum workweek of 40 hours. Minimum wages are established locally, and wages cannot be deducted or delayed without reason. If employees must work more than 40 hours, overtime pay at fixed rates is mandatory. Workers are guaranteed at least one day off each week. Working conditions are required to be safe.

In reality, all these rights of Chinese workers are routinely violated. When violations take place, there are no effective mechanisms to correct them. For example, China, a country with more than 1.3 billion people, has only about 110,000 trained lawyers. Of these, only a few are sufficiently trained to handle labour disputes.

The lack of law enforcement also gives firms an incentive *not* to perform CSR. For example, corporate codes imposed on factory owners could raise costs, so owners have a financial incentive to ignore code requirements. Although the government occasionally sends teams for inspections, factory owners are becoming increasingly adept at circumventing inspections, through practices such as double book-keeping and coaching of workers. As a result, inspectors are often deceived.

Local governments are supposed to help the central government in promoting CSR. In reality, they often hide information on firms within their jurisdictions from the inspection teams due to their close connections with local firms. For example, the Tangshan mine incident, which took place on 7 December 2005, was due to ignoring the order of closure from higher authorities.[10] The mine was ordered to close down on 18 July 2005, but the owner of the mine apparently ignored the order. Huge profits provide greater incentives to the owners of mines to take risks on human losses.

The fact that China is a transitional economy also often makes it difficult for the state to make needed regulations. Take migrant workers as example. Before the 1990s, China was virtually a fixed society, and the government employed the household registration system to guarantee social stability. But rapid industrialization and urbanization have undermined the household registration system, and people are free to move. Today, China has over 100 million migrant workers, or the so-called floating population.

The existing system is apparently not prepared for new social conditions such as floating population. Consequently, these conditions cannot be managed by the system. Until major events such as the SARS and the bird flu epidemics did the government realize how important to take these new factors into consideration. Nevertheless, compared to workers, the rights of migrant workers are more frequently violated. Moreover, China has a virtually inexhaustible supply of migrant workers, most of whom are ignorant of their rights under Chinese laws and are willing to work under any conditions without protest.

Helping hand from multinational companies

CSR is a new concept both from most Chinese firms and for government officials as well. Arguably, it was a concept imported from the developed West. Despite huge obstacles in the way of implementing CSR, however, there are reasons for optimism over time. One way to understand China's poor performance in CSR is that the country is in transition. Many problems are transitional, and it takes time for both government bodies and firms to find solutions. Other problems are situational. For example, the frequent coal mining disasters in recent years have been exacerbated by China's energy crisis. With further economic development, working conditions can be expected to improve and workers' rights to be more respected. Many factors are facilitating the development of CSR in China.

One important source for better CSR is economic globalization. China has since the early 1990s become the world's most favoured destination in comparison with all other developing countries. By early 2005, China had attracted a total of US$580 billion in foreign direct investment (FDI). Not surprisingly, over 80 per cent of the world's 500 largest companies and top 100 information technology firms have set up businesses in China.

Such heavy investment of western businesses in China is a forceful push for China's CSR. Many foreign firms went to China to take advantages of China's unregulated markets and often tended to ignore their CSR, even commit some immoral affairs.[11] But many others have strived to bring capital, technology, and management know-know to the country. They have tried to introduce their best CSR practice to China.

To give a few examples.[12] IBM has pumped tens of millions of US dollars into learning centres at Chinese kindergartens, schools, and universities, supplemented by teacher and scholar training programmes. Ascott Group, an international firm that manages luxury-serviced apartments, has opted to help pupils in Guangxi, in collaboration with World Vision, by donating funds to provide immunizations and nutritional lunches for more than 400 children. The company also contributed funding to renovate the school kids' dormitories, which until then require students to share bunks, at times as many as three students in each bunk.

Other foreign firms tend to pay more attention to integrating CSR practices into business objectives and, above all, redefining the role of a company in society and its environment. For example, HSBC has implemented comprehensive anti-money laundering standards across its entire business line. The firm uses careful identification procedures for opening accounts, close monitoring of transactions, and a worldwide network of control officers for tracking and reporting. The firm also conducts money laundering awareness programmes for every new member of staff and refresher courses where relevant.

Since 1989, Microsoft China has provided nearly US$542,000 to support computer skill training projects for laid-off and migrant workers in Liaoning, Sichuan, Guangdong, and Shanghai.

All these practices in one way or another influence CSR performance among China's domestic firms. These practices have informed the Chinese government that adopting CSR will strengthen Chinese corporations' international competitiveness. The Chinese government is increasingly taking a proactive position on the issue of CSR. Furthermore, Chinese firms can learn from these practices that adopting CSR can make corporate development sustainable.

The state as a feasible solution

But a more important factor is the transformation of the Chinese state. To promote CSR, the state has to regulate firms' behaviour. While market principles are becoming increasingly important in regulating the behaviour of Chinese firms, the development of CSR cannot rely on voluntary steps by firms to meet social needs. To regulate firms' behaviour, the Chinese state will have to facilitate the growth of the social forces which have promoted firms to develop CSR elsewhere – including a strong and independent media. Fortunately, there are good signs indicating a better relationship between the state and society in China.

It is true that China's legal infrastructure continues to be inadequate. While there are great difficulties for top-down legal enforcement, bottom-up social participation is not allowed. The government prohibits any independent trade unions, leaving workers without representatives to discuss violations with the management. Workers who have tried to form independent unions or lead labour protests have been imprisoned. Nevertheless, even the stodgy, government-dominated All-China Federation of Trade Union (ACFTU) has recognized a need to take a more activist approach to workers' rights.

The central government has realized that something must be done to improve its legal infrastructure. The government's attitude towards workers' rights is under change. China is now facing a rising tide of labour disputes, which could destabilize Chinese society and thus undermine the political legitimacy of the CCP. Therefore, there is a need for employers to better understand and honour their obligations under China's labour laws. In an apparent reflection of this new attitude, at the 2003 annual ACFTU congress, the federation made a direct appeal to multinational retail corporation Wal-Mart Stores, Inc. to allow its workers to establish trade unions.

More importantly, China's top leadership has realized that the single-minded pursuit of GDP growth ever since the reform and open-door policy is associated with economic inefficiency, environmental degradation on a colossal scale, lack of industrial innovation, income disparities, and social conflicts. All these factors have made China's development unsustainable.

Therefore, the eleventh Five-Year Plan (2006–2010) calls for efforts to address social ills, land dislocation issues, inadequate rural social security and health care, and to industrialize the rural sector.[13] Given the fact that political mobilization remains important in China, overall policy shift at the central level will create a better political environment for local governments to change their behaviour in pursuing local GDP growth and thus create a better environment for firms to perform their CSR.

Notes

1 Xinhua News Agency, "Li Yizhong zai quanguo anquan shengchan gongzuo huiyi shang de jianghua" (Speech by Li Yizhong on National Conference on Work Safety), Li is the Director of the State Administration for Work Safety, www.xinhuanet.com, accessed on 26 January 2006.
2 *People's Daily* (English version), "Learning from the Premier's Tears," see http://english.people.com.cn/200501/07/eng20050107_169966.html, accessed on 7 January 2006.
3 *People's Daily*, "10 Key Words Depicting China in '10th Five-Year Plan' Period," 28 September 2005.
4 "China Mine Blast Death TOLL jumps," *BBC News*, 28 November 2005.
5 Yongnian Zheng, "The New Policy Initiatives in China's 11th 5-Year Plan," *Briefing Series*-Issue 1, China Policy Institute: University of Nottingham, November 2005; and Yongnian Zheng, Zhengxu Wang and Sow Keat Tok, "China's National People's Congress 2006: Policy Shifts Amidst Growing Dissatisfaction with Existing Development Patterns," *Briefing Series*-Issue 7, China Policy Institute: University of Nottingham, March 2006.
6 *China Daily*, "Learning from the Premier's Tears," 7 January 2005.
7 Other terms used include "socially responsible business" and "corporate citizenship" to mean the same thing.
8 This discussion is based on Department for International Development, *DEID and Corporate Social Responsibility*, London: DFID, no publication date.
9 http://politics.people.com.cn/GB/30178/3923802.html, accessed on 7 December 2005.
10 *Mingpao*, Hong Kong, 12 December 2005.
11 The Academy of International Trade and Economic Cooperation, the Ministry of Commerce, "Some Multinational Firms Evade Social Responsibilities in China," http://news.xinhuanet.com, accessed on 25 March 2006.
12 This description is based on CorpWatch, China: Corporate Social Responsibility, *China View*, 13 May 2005. www.corpwatch.org, accessed on 14 November 2005.
13 For an analysis of the eleventh Five-Year Plan, see Zheng, "The New Policy Initiatives in China's 11th 5-Year Plan."

7 The media, Internet and governance in China

Gary D. Rawnsley

> If there are any persons who contest a received opinion, or will do so if law or opinion will let them, let us thank them for it, open our minds to listen to them, and rejoice that there is someone to do for us what we otherwise ought, if we have any regard for either the certainty or the vitality of our convictions, to do with much greater labour for ourselves.
>
> (John Stuart Mill, *On Liberty*)[1]

> Free and untainted information is a basic human right. Not everyone has it; almost everyone wants it. It cannot by itself create a just world, but a just world can never exist without it.
>
> (Elizabeth Wright)[2]

For students of how communications interact with political processes, actors and institutions, China offers a fascinating case-study. The People's Republic is today concerned with questions of governance, political and economic efficacy, authority and legitimacy that strike at the very core of its continued leadership. Given that these issues are affected by communications processes, it is not surprising that the government devotes considerable attention to how the media should and do operate.

The glass is either half-empty or half-full depending on one's evaluation of the present situation. International websites, chat rooms, discussion groups and newspapers published outside China provide a colossal amount of (often anecdotal) evidence that there is reason to be pessimistic: almost daily we learn of Chinese journalists being sacked, imprisoned or beaten up; of newspapers forced to close because they have been too critical or have challenged an ideological position; of the Great Firewall that blocks access to the World Wide Web for information-starved Chinese.[3] *Southern Weekend* in 2001 was criticised for publishing reports that were detrimental to good governance and so its editor-in-chief was removed. In March 2003, the *21st Century World Herald* was closed, and in March 2004, staff at the *Southern Metropolitan Post* were subjected to official investigation. The list continues ad nauseum.

However, the glass is also half-full, and optimists point to recent reports that have suggested the outbreak of a "guerrilla war" between journalists and the Publicity Department of the Communist Party, implying that the media are now prepared to challenge central control over their work. After all, they recognise a discrepancy between a state-controlled media increasingly dependent on ratings and advertising to survive. The "guerrilla war" came to a head over the closure of *Bingdian* (*Freezing Point*), a popular supplement of the *China Youth Daily*. Thirteen veterans of politics and propaganda in China, including Mao Zedong's former secretary, responded by publishing a letter in which they called for the easing of censorship and new laws to protect press freedoms:

> History [they wrote] demonstrates that only a totalitarian system needs news censorship, out of the delusion that it can keep the public locked in igno- rance. Depriving the public of freedom of expression so nobody dares speak out will sow the seeds of disaster for political and social transition.

Optimists are inclined to perceive such outbursts as a crucial step in China's evolution of political communications. Communist Party veterans hold a revered position within political society, and their interventions contribute to a spirited open debate that is difficult for today's leaders to ignore. In other words, the media – their problems, need for reform and their explicit involve- ment in the political process – are added to the political agenda. In the imme- diate terms, such eruptions of criticism may provoke the government to tighten its control over the communications process and expose journalists and media to ever tighter rules and regulations. The Chinese leadership is unlikely to create or tolerate the existence of a critical public sphere that will challenge party power and which may fulfil the expectations of democratic theorists.[4] However, there are potential long-term benefits if the critical media are pre- pared to wait. The reason is that the Chinese leadership may finally realise that free speech and freedom of publication are indispensable for governance and are especially crucial for the continuing success of China's programmes of development and modernisation.

Governance and the media

The centre of democratic procedure is inhabited by political communication. Polit- ical communication provides a vertical channel of dialogue and information between governments and governed, elected and the electors. Political communi- cation helps to structure the participation and competition that characterise demo- cracies. For supporters of direct democracy, a renewed system of political communication is the way to energise citizens in an increasingly apolitical environment.[5] They advocate greater opportunities for deliberation and discussion of political issues, popular mobilisation and increasing the possibility to pressure governments (through devolution, referendums and grassroots civil-society activ- ity). This, they say, is the recipe for the creation of a new civic-minded population:

> First, deliberation requires that one be well informed about proposed legis- lation. This includes being knowledgeable about competing – and minority

– ideas, needs and perspectives. Second, it requires that this information be thoughtful and rationally considered rather than reacted to emotionally.... Third, deliberation requires that one be able to exchange views on proposed legislation with other decision makers, if one chooses. Fourth, deliberation requires open-mindedness. One's preferences must be revisable in light of discussion, debate and new information.[6]

Dialogue is important for accountability as it requires opinions to be defended. In an ideal society, dialogue therefore encourages people to think through their views and have a clearer understanding of why they hold those opinions. It is essential to the formation of public opinion that may conform to or challenge the prevailing political order.

This means that a fully informed critical public opinion is essential for good governance. For democratic political systems that derive their authority from electoral procedures, the consent of the governed, and their performance between elections, a watchful public that is supported by media systems unafraid and able to scrutinise the decisions taken by politicians may moderate governments' behaviour. Transparency, accountability, critical engagement and challenging ideas all help to make governments work better and therefore better service providers. In short communication is crucial to the health of civic society and therefore to governance. There must be freedom of speech, of expression and to dissent because cynicism nourishes democratic debates and processes.

So the media offer a voice to a range of actors located both inside and outside the political process, thus constructing a clearly defined public sphere in which public opinion can be assembled, articulated and debated. However, if we are to fully understand the power of modern communications processes, this simple idea requires elaboration. The power of the media is such a core concern in modern politics because we are compelled to acknowledge the media as political actors in their own right. No longer mere reporters or observers of political events, the media have assumed a central position within political society. Duncan McCargo has described how the media can be agents of stability (supporting the status quo), agents of restraint (checking and balancing political society) or agents of change. Through close examination of the media in selected Asian societies, McCargo demonstrates that these roles are not mutually exclusive. Rather, the media perform all these roles at different political moments.[7] The merit of this agency-based approach is not only that it recognises the power that the media possess, but also suggests that they are in constant strategic negotiation with other political actors, all enjoying access to their own resources.

The media do not like to admit they are political actors, as this would compromise the functions they believe they fulfil in a democratic society.[8] It also implies that there is little to separate the media – ostensibly working on behalf of the powerless and voiceless – from the politicians they try to expose. Only once they and we accept the (in many ways disturbing) notion that the media in democratic societies are political actors, do we understand that the media do not simply transmit information or offer entertainment, but rather have the propensity to be ideologically influential through the imagery they present. The media provide the cues and the frameworks which determine political discourse and which influence our perception and reaction to social and political reality. "In the conduct of politics," noted Colin Seymour-Ure in 2001, "media are primary and political institutions secondary. The media can live without politics; indeed, surveys show that politics is one of the least appealing subjects to readers and audiences. But politics cannot live without the media."[9]

So the media not only contribute to and provide a vital service *to* governance, they are political actors that are centrally involved *in* the process of governance. They help to disseminate the policies and positions determined by political elites and governments, and they frame the political debate and mobilise civil society around the requirements of the legislative process. In short, they can and often do make and break governments.

The media and governance in China

Although they remain fundamental to the political process, the media in China fulfil very different functions and responsibilities. Their autonomy is limited, and they have little opportunity to openly challenge state power; rather the Chinese media are required to play specific roles *on behalf* of the state. This facilitates authoritarian-based governance, but societies following a programme of modernisation and development require a more democratic model of media involvement in the political process.

It is difficult to imagine how authoritarian governments could survive without devoting serious resources to influencing and controlling systems of communication. Lacking the political legitimacy enjoyed by democratic governments, authoritarian regimes depend on communications to reinforce their political and coercive power. Systems of communication rarely extend beyond transmitting, framing and interpreting for the audience the decisions and actions of the government. They facilitate political recruitment, socialisation and mobilisation; hence, communications have distinct social and political responsibilities of social control and nation-building that are consistent with the development priorities and ideological assumptions of the regime. For example, in 1999 C. Rozzario, Director of the Public Affairs Division (Singapore Ministry of Home Affairs) justified his government's strict management of communications by claiming that, "In a multi-racial and multi-religious Singapore, we cannot put at risk the racial harmony and sense of public order, peace and safety built up over the years."[10] Hence, the state called for the adoption of a nationalist ideology to forge a common bond among its people. This ideology, communicated through media and education, is built around five pillars that reflect the collectivism at the heart of Singapore's commitment to "Asian values," namely nation, family, community, consensus and harmony. This ideology is justified as a "safeguard against undesirable values permeating from developed countries."[11] Singapore is one of many authoritarian regimes, including China, that worry about the chaos that pluralism and freedom of information may introduce to their country, upsetting not only its development strategies, but also its cultural foundations (national communications are therefore tasked with resisting "cultural imperialism"). Many regimes have therefore decided that nationalisation of the media allows the most efficient form of state management. Since 1960, the Cuban state has owned and controlled all media to serve its political agenda.[12] Suharto's government in Indonesia designed its national television network in 1962 around a specific developmental programme that required its people to identify closely with the regime. The Indonesian government required the media to help foster a sense of national unity, with television sets located in village halls across the country showing state-controlled programming.[13] This meant that the government-decided broadcasting could encourage national identity and unity through the communal experience of watching centrally planned programming.

Alternatively, state control of the media may help to depoliticise and demobilise a population, sapping their energy, generating passivity and depriving people not only of a voice, but also of stimuli that might activate them. In authoritarian Spain, for example, "the primary result of media control was to secure the *passive acquiescence* of the Spanish population rather than to resocialize the citizenry into active participatory roles" (emphasis added).[14] Hence, television stations produce and broadcast cheap entertainment programmes devoid of any meaningful content, or the government sanctions the controlled importation of (ostensibly) harmless foreign programmes. The 1970s British drama, *The Onedin Line*, was one of the most popular programmes ever shown in Romania during the 1980s. Ceaucescu's decision to remove it from the airwaves in favour of North Korean-inspired propaganda was one factor that contributed to the activation of citizens against the regime. Gunther, Montero and Wert are particularly scathing about this attempt by the Spanish Fascist regime to create an inert audience: "Regime maintenance," they write, "was facilitated by communications policies that effectively bored most Spaniards into passivity and acquiescence and deprived them of stimuli that might have triggered political mobilization."[15] But as Sükösd notes, this strategy can backfire, as it did in Romania: in Hungary, the "official importation of Western popular culture resulted in a spiralling of demand for the forbidden fruit."[16] The forbidden fruit is always the most attractive variety, as the reaction in Chinese chat rooms to the suppression of news about Zhao Ziyang's death demonstrates (see p. 126).

Authoritarian governments exercise a variety of mechanisms to pressure, influence and, in the most extreme cases control communications, at the same time as demonstrating intolerance of alternative political opinions, autonomous and spontaneous popular mobilisation, information and channels of communication, but we can identify the following characteristics:

- Important appointments within the media are decided on political rather than professional grounds.
- The news agenda and news coverage are politically controlled to reflect the political agenda.

- Laws and legal systems are created to influence the media (targeting source, media actors and/or audiences).
- However, the media, journalists and editors are often subject to cycles of extra-legal abuse and intimidation.
- The idea that the media operate within an autonomous public sphere is absent.
- Civil society lacks autonomy; its mobilisation is tolerated only in service of the state-decided agenda.
- Primary groups too are expected to serve political functions; church, youth groups, schools, art, even family-life are pressed into service to communicate the state's political agenda.

Although it has embarked on a comprehensive programme of economic and social reform, the Chinese communist regime preserves its authority in civil society and over the media anxious that liberalisation serve, not challenge, the regime's agenda (including economic modernisation and the preservation of the party's power[17]). The leadership has created new layers of bureaucracy to enforce their management of the media. In its March 2006 issue, the *Far Eastern Economic Review* revealed the existence of a "shadowy group of Communist Party officials entrusted with tremendous power and almost no accountability" called the News Commentary Group (NCG, created in 1994) to "clean house at major newspapers."[18] This group, claim the authors, was responsible for the closure of newspapers, including *Bingdian*, and the purging of editors documented at the beginning of this chapter:

> The NCG … is a reinvention of censorship that allows the Party to ensure "guidance of public opinion" in the midst of an unruly market. Party leaders can use the NCG as their hatchet men and at the same time confuse, for the sake of China's international image, the issue of exactly where they stand on censorship.[19]

The Chinese media are required to disseminate the message as decided by the Communist Party,[20] a responsibility that the *People's Daily* reaffirmed in 2000:

> We should pay special attention to the use of modern tools of the mass media, such as the press, the radio, the television and the Internet, bring into play their role as the main channel of ideological education, and make continuous efforts to create lively forms that can reach people's ears, brain and heart.[21]

Earlier in October 1996, Jiang Zemin, then President of China, General Secretary of the Communist Party and Chairman of the Military Commission toured the Chinese media to offer his guidance on their work and organisation. The *People's Daily* (3 October 1996) recorded his requirements under the title "On the Correct Direction of Public Opinion":

1   The press must be guided by the Party's basic theory, basic line, and basic guideline, and keep politics, ideology and action in conformity with the Party Central Committee.
2   The press must firmly keep to the standpoint of the Party, adhere to principle, and take clear-cut stand on what to promote and what to oppose on cardinal issues of right and wrong.
3   The press must adhere to the party's guideline with stress on propaganda by positive examples, sing the praises of people's great achievements, and conduct the correct supervision of public opinion that should help the party and state to improve work and the style of leadership, solve problems, enhance unity, and safeguard stability.
4   The press must ... hold patriotism, collectivism and socialism on high, and use best things to arm, direct and mould the people.

Here, President Jiang affirmed beyond doubt that the Chinese media are and must remain *part* of the political system; they must conform to party lines, directives and requirements, and they have a responsibility to work *with* the system, not against it.

Hu Jintao's accession to power as the Chinese Communist Party (CCP) General Secretary in 2002 was accompanied by an overwhelming sense of optimism. In particular, he seemed committed to introducing more transparency in government, resulting in *Xinhua* publishing details of Political Bureau Standing Committee meetings. This connects with Hu's agenda to focus more than his predecessors on the growing wealth gap and the problems of uneven development (as suggested by reports of the Tenth National People's Congress in March 2006). Recognising that corruption is also a hindrance to governance print and media journalists have been encouraged to investigate allegations of corruption and mismanagement of local affairs by local officials, though criticism of national leaders remains prohibited. China's handling of the SARS crisis in 2003 was a turning point for the government–media interface as the problems of a tightly controlled media were exposed to international scrutiny.

At the same time, we must accept that Hu Jintao is anything but a liberal and has maintained the characteristic hard-line of communist practice where political reforms are concerned. Rather, Hu's goal is the strengthening of the Communist party to make it more efficient. As we mentioned earlier, media censorship has not abated; rather it has increased with the government tightening its grip over newspapers and television stations in often innovative ways. Websites are now more frequently blocked than previously or are made to compromise their objectivity before being allowed to enter the lucrative Chinese market (such as Google). Filtering software allows a greater degree of control over the web pages that surfers can access, while a so-called Internet police force trawls the web for subversive content. Meanwhile, in November 2005, the *South China Morning Post*, published in Hong Kong, learned that the Publicity department of the Chinese government had ordered newspapers to seek approval from authorities before publishing reports on new outbreaks of the disease or any deaths.[22]

Perhaps most disturbing are published allegations that Hu instructed propaganda officials in September 2004 that they should learn from Cuba and North Korea, two political systems not renowned for their records of good governance.

Moreover, a succession of ambiguous regulations (including Articles 51, 53 and 54 of the Constitution, the 1989 Protection of National Secrets Law and the 1992 Regulation on the Protection of Secrets for News and Publication) actively discourage journalists from reporting and publishing information that might actually contribute to better governance. While the vagueness of this legislation is already a serious barrier to full reporting, the cost of navigating the bureaucracy – and thereby potentially exposing oneself to the charge of criminal activity – can be too high, making journalists over cautious and too eager to engage in self-censorship (exacerbated by the Sword of Damacles wielded by the News Commentary Group).[23] Typically confusing were Premier Wen Jiabao's remarks at the conclusion of the Tenth National People's Congress on 14 March 2006:

A people's government should accept the democratic supervision of the people .... Only if a government is subject to the supervision of the people will it not dare to be indolent. [But] Every citizen must also consciously abide by the law and order, and must protect the interests of the country, society and the collective.... The websites should be able to convey the right message and information. The websites should refrain from misleading the public or exerting an adverse impact on social and public order...

Every citizen in this country has the freedom of speech and freedom of publishing. At the same time, every citizen in this country needs to abide by the laws and safeguard the national and social interests ... we ... need to educate and properly guide the general public so that they can more and more realise that their legitimate concerns need to be expressed through legal channels and in lawful formats.[24]

The statement lacks clarity and precision, deliberately leaving arbitrary what is permissible and how prohibited activity is defined. This is a classic technique adopted by authoritarian governments at all times and in all places, regardless of ideology. It helps strong government but not good governance.

Governments wishing to control the flow of information in the service of their authoritarian agendas face considerable risks. In particular, they are exposed to the pressures exerted by modern communications technologies which make increasingly difficult the opportunity to hermetically seal their borders and prevent their citizens from receiving and conveying uncomfortable news and information. The short-wave radio, for example, was a source of alternative information throughout the Eastern Bloc during the Cold War.[25] As I discovered in my earlier research on international communication in that period, audience have a stubborn curiosity about information that governments do not allow them to receive and will actively seek out alternative sources of information, often at considerable risk to their own safety. This is as true in 2006 as it was in 1956.

For instance, anecdotal evidence available to researchers today suggests that the Chinese government's blatant media censorship only whets the popular appetite for forbidden information. When Zhao Ziyang, to many a hero of the 1989 Tiananmen Square demonstrations, died after fifteen years of house arrest in January 2005, the Chinese government controlled coverage of his passing and his funeral. Information was scarce: "I live in Guangzhou, and that night I wasn't able to access two Hong Kong TV stations, so I realised immediately that something major had happened ..."; "... today ... my grandmother said, 'Zhao Ziyang died, why isn't the news or the papers reporting it?' I was curious, so I went searching on the Internet, but I found I couldn't open many Web sites, which made me think something was strange ..."; "This morning, I couldn't connect to any overseas web sites, and I realised that something had happened..."; and "Putting aside Zhao's merits and faults for the time being, we have already completely lost the right to speak, and to hear about him! What kind of world is this?"[26] These concerns surfaced in chat rooms and on other discussion sites on the Internet, suggesting that the information revolution may continue the trends set by short-wave radio and help curious users circumvent the officially managed media.

China, the Internet and public space

A striking feature of political life in China is the growing evidence that the Communist party's governance is increasingly challenged by a progressively vocal civil society. However, this civil society's critical voice is not present in the newspapers or on Chinese television, for few independent public spaces exit within the mainstream media environment to lend them the autonomy required by a questioning critical media. Rather, the Chinese are discovering new public spheres to engage with each other and with the political system, and the Internet is increasing in popularity and use as a space in which the public may express their restlessness and dissatisfaction.

Since its invention the Internet has been associated with democratic political communication. One of the most vocal optimist for the power of the Internet, Howard Rheingold, noted in 1993: "The Internet ... if properly understood an defended and understood by enough citizens, does have democratising potential in the same way that alphabets and printing presses had democratising potential."[27] The widespread use and potential of the Internet (along with other new information communication technologies, such as mobile telephones and SMS messaging) has suggested nothing less than a revolution in political communication: its speed, promise of greater levels of interactivity and connectivity, the absence of hierarchies and the possibilities offered by an unfettered and unmediated source of communication have together contributed to the Internet's appeal to democratic theory. Idealists claim that the Internet has the capacity to transform political life by creating networks of globally or locally active citizens and by developing public spheres where they can participate in decision-making and help set the political agenda.[28] They believe that the Internet offers the opportunity to rejuvenate direct democracy through the creation of "virtual forums" or new public spaces. This is because the Internet bestows upon civil society a selection of fundamentally new communication strategies that have the capacity to transform their more traditional approaches to political behaviour. Groups can and do use Internet technologies to mobilise support on a national, regional and even global scale and can do so with less financial resources and attention to the demands of other electronic media. At the same time, social movements can despatch and publish their information, material, letters of protest, communiqués and press releases quickly and, because of the precise targeting allowed, efficiently to media organisations, governments, corporations and possible sympathisers. Vast political "rhizomes"[29] are created as groups share information, create links (virtual and real) with each other and post information about each other's activities on their own websites. It is therefore unsurprising that some have predicted the Internet promises the dawn of a new political age. Grossman,[30] for example, theorised that after the great epochs of classical Greek and representative democracy, technological changes place us on the verge of a third new period of electronic or "strong" democracy as described by Barber:

> Strong democracy is defined by politics in the participatory mode: literally it is self-government by citizens rather than representative government in the name of citizens. Active citizens govern themselves directly here, not necessarily at every level and in every instance, but frequently enough ....
> Self-government is carried on through institutions designed to facilitate ongoing civic participation in agenda-setting, deliberation, legislation, and policy implementation ...
> ... strong democracy relies on participation in an evolving problem-solving community ... [where] ... public ends ... are literally forged through the act of public participation, created through public deliberation and common action[31]

Embedded in this quotation is an assumption that a strong democracy based on participation, deliberation and "problem solving" can contribute to good governance. It is not difficult to see why advocates of the wider application of the Internet in political life have anchored their beliefs in the normative standards offered by such thinkers as Barber. Particularly empowering is the opportunity for all users to be simultaneously author, publisher and audience of news, information and opinion in a global market place of ideas. This is realised most dramatically in the rapid emergence of the "blogger" culture, the posting by anyone with access to the Internet of online diaries that allow readers a glimpse into the lives of their authors. Bloggers can undermine official news sources and propaganda and offer alternative perspectives on events from those provided by other media following their own news agendas and reporting stories according to particular framing devices. Most attractive about blogging is that it represents a genuine bottom-up process of unmediated and unfiltered communication. Bloggers can also challenge prevailing social orders.

And there is evidence (in addition to that offered by blogging) that the Internet has evaded and undermined traditional forms of political control and challenge established patterns and hierarchies in the organisation, flow and content of political communication. Well documented, for example, is the way the Zapatista movement used the Internet to bring international public pressure down on the Mexican government.[32]

Rheingold's assessment about the potential for empowerment through the Internet is largely correct. In fact, we might go further and note that Internet use and availability have proliferated at a faster pace than previous communications inventions: in less than a decade the Internet reached fifty million users worldwide; it took the telephone seventy-four years, radio thirty-eight years and television thirteen years to reach comparable levels of distribution.[33] However, there are serious flaws in the belief that the Internet is universally empowering and democratising. First, the visionaries make two major assumptions:

1   that people want to participate in the political process and
2   the current channels of political participation are defective.

Both are common beliefs, and while I support the first if we stretch the definition of the political process beyond voting to include new social movements and civil-society activity (the global protests against the 2003 war in Iraq is a good example), the second is more problematic. Traditional methods of participation are failing in some parts of the world and flourishing in others making generalisations impossible. The difficulty arises when, in accepting the first two assumptions, the idealists consent to a third: that the Internet is the solution to these problems in political communication. How accurate is this?

Let us begin with the idea that everyone can be publisher and recipient. If this is the case, we are confronted not only with an explosion in the amount of information we must confront, sift and process,[34] but with a fundamental question that defines the democratic approach to political communication: whose truth are we receiving? How can we check and guarantee the accuracy of the information? Does this mean that the responsibility for determining the truth falls to the consumers rather than producers? If we are already concerned with how the traditional media have the capacity to distort the truth and present a one-dimensional, biased or superficial picture of political issues, processes and institutions, won't we become more anxious with information that is unmediated, unedited and unverifiable? The Internet provides more information, but it does not guarantee the quality of information. Perhaps this really is a case of better the devil you know ...?

Second, available evidence seems to suggest that the Internet confirms long-held suspicions that communications reinforce rather than change political behaviour, habits, attitudes and opinions. Those who use the Internet for political purposes are already active and plugged into the political universe through regular use of such channels of communication as media, parties and groups. This reinforcement becomes a factor of access to the Internet itself, the technology, and fluency and security in using it. Hence, critics lament the fact that cyberspace is dominated by the same social elites and actors we find in other areas of political life, and this provokes a suspicion that the Internet allows groups to preach to the converted. After all, first one must be interested in a particular issue, group or party to take the time to find their website (we all have experience in using a search engine and know that finding the correct search term is only the beginning of what can be a frustrating process which may involve sifting through several thousand entries to find a relevant site), and it is unlikely given the strength of the reinforcement thesis of public opinion that these users will actively seek out the counter opinions offered by alternative groups and individuals.

We have to concede that the greatest obstacle to the democratic potential of the Internet remains non-technological, namely governments who consider this communications system a threat to their political power and thus seek to constrain its use. Of course, the glass may be half-full; this threat assessment may be a positive indication of the Internet's potential strength. Governments only attempt to ban and suppress technologies, information and people they judge dangerous and subversive. Nevertheless, the reality of attempted political containment contradicts the utopian aspirations of Netizens who once believed that it is impossible to censor or regulate Internet content, and that individual states had no authority or legitimacy in cyberspace. Across vast portions of the world, Internet content or access to the Internet is at best regulated and at worst denied by states pursuing interventionist or isolationist policies towards the information revolution. This situation also highlights how the vision of a globalised world characterised by the declining relevance and sovereignty of nation-states, especially in cyberspace, is misplaced. Rather, individual states are determined and able to control the Internet within their own borders, reinforcing and preserving their dominion.

Many authoritarian governments, including the People's Republic of China (PRC), face a serious predicament. Pursuing developmental agendas requiring interaction with an increasingly open and interdependent world, these governments must embrace new communications technologies for their economic promise while minimising their democratic potential. Kalathil and Boas have baptised this a proactive strategy, with governments "guiding Internet development and usage to promote their own interests and priorities."[35] Regimes try to contain Internet use among the intellectual and scientific elites, that is, those required to access and publish information on behalf of national development. Singapore's founder and first Prime Minister, Lee Kuan Yew, reinforced this agenda when he admitted that only the "top 3 to 5 percent of a society" is able to handle the chaos and plurality of information offered by the Internet.[36] The rest of society must access the Internet via "proxy servers" that deny users the right to see officially blacklisted sites, a management strategy shared by other authoritarian governments.

Iran, too, has faced similar difficult choices. In 2001, the government closed most of Iran's Internet cafés, known as "Coffeenets." The reason was a curious mixture of business concerns and political posturing: the popularity of VoiceChat, the instant messaging service that allows Internet users actually to speak to each other meant that state-owned telephone companies started to lose revenue. Iran's theocracy had initially embraced the Internet revolution, seeing the application of new technologies as a way of spreading the word of the Prophet, but then worried about the proliferation of the "immoral" effects of western culture that Internet users could easily download from unregulated sites. In May 2003, the Iranian government began to block pornographic and other sites it judged subversive or obscene. Around seventy young users were arrested in March 2003 for meeting through an illegal online dating service, clearly suggesting that the authorities had monitored the chat rooms used.[37]

Chinese sources (especially those produced by the government and its news agency, Xinhua, such as the *People's Daily* and the English language *China Daily*) provide mounting evidence to suggest that the government is convinced that the Internet can make a positive contribution to the country's development. Hence, it is to China's credit that it has been at the forefront of the information revolution, promoting widespread access to the Internet and investing US$500 billion in the information technology industry by the end of 2005 in order to provide access to their benefits across the entire country. Yet, the Chinese government is also infamous for the regulations it imposes on this information revolution, trying to "limit the medium's potential challenges through a combination of content filtering, monitoring, deterrence and the promotion of self-censorship."[38] Internet cafes are required to use software that restricts access to particular websites and to keep records of their users and the sites they have visited. These measures outwardly undermine the principle that the Internet is a technology free from interference.

When one considers the way some scholars and observers have discussed the potential impact of the Internet, it is not difficult to see why China is worried. Among the first to pronounce on the democratising possibilities of the Internet was US Secretary of State James Baker in 1991:

> No nation has yet discovered a way to import the world's goods and services while stopping foreign ideas at the border. It is in our interest that the next generation in China be engaged by the Information Age .... For this we determine the US feels that the Internet and information technology is a way in which democratic ideas will flourish and assist in managing the change that will come some day.[39]

Baker was followed by Gordon C. Chang who, in his 2001 book predicting *The Coming Collapse of China*, noted that "the regime may patrol cyberspace," but "it cannot help but be changed by the process."[40] Jianhai Bi concurred, suggesting that China's need to enter the information age would collide with the Communist party's determination to preserve its power, concluding that political change was inevitable.[41] With so many suggesting that the Internet will force the eventual collapse of the CCP, it is little wonder that the regime feels under siege.

It therefore imposes control on Internet use, believing that hostile nation-states might harness the Internet in a propaganda offensive and therefore China must be "battle-ready" to meet that threat.[42] In 2000, the Chinese State Council approved the "Measures for the Administration of Internet Information Services," and it makes interesting reading. This lists the web content that the Chinese government has declared illegal, including information considered contrary to constitutional provisions; information that endangers national security; information that threatens national honour; information that spreads rumours or undermines social stability; other information prohibited by the law and/or administrative regulations. In other words, the regulations lack specificity – a common technique whereby authoritarian states are able to exercise political expediency. As in other media systems, this ambiguous legal framework, reinforced by familiarity with the severe penalties for violation, encourages a culture of self-censorship. Anecdotal evidence suggests that the regulations have instilled a sense of caution among Chinese Internet users in the services they access; Internet providers are equally cautious about the information they publish on their websites.

Yet, there are grounds for optimism. A growing body of factual-based evidence suggests that Chinese Internet users are both circumventing restrictions and forcing the government to follow discourses that are determined and shaped by popular opinion expressed online. The downing of a US spy-plane on Hainan island in April 2001 generated what we might consider some of the most critical discussions allowed in China. These completely changed the government's official response to this dramatic event and created a new momentum of nationalism that the government at first had tried to avoid.[43] Moreover, the death of Zhao Ziyang in January 2005 demonstrated the Internet's potential to ferret out forbidden information and express grievances with government-controlled censorship: the Internet "has only endowed citizens with a heightened awareness of the amount of information that is being blocked."[44]

The basis of communist party control over information is centralisation and vertical communication; the Internet, however, is designed to facilitate the *decentralised* spread of information and make possible *horizontal* communications. The lesson we can draw from this is that the Internet may be a communications system that is completely incompatible with communist political and social organisation. The connectivity associated with the Internet has the capacity to break down spatial and temporal relevance while undermining existing hierarchies. Predictably, these tensions worry governments, such as the CCP, that are determined to maintain a grip, however tenuous, on large populations.[45]

We can also learn another sobering lesson from the Chinese experience. The argument for the emancipating power of the Internet is attractive and exciting but not particularly convincing nor grounded in empirical evidence. While it is possible to find a correlation between access to the Internet and political freedom, it is less easy to find proof of *causation*. It is one thing to say the Internet reduces the ability of states to check and control flows of information, but it is quite another to claim that the Internet weakens or reduces the political power of states. While great swathes of the democratic and non-democratic world remain outside the Internet revolution (either by political choice or by economic necessity) democratic forces cannot depend on the Internet to engineer political change. For democratisation to occur, there needs to be a whole series of other changes taking place within society, such as freedom of the press, of assembly, electoral competition and accountability. In other words, the Internet is not necessarily liberating, empowering or democratising, but it can help to strengthen governance and the institutions charged with the task of government and civil administration.

The momentum for political change lies with other factors, particularly with the choices made by political elites or within civil society. The Internet may contribute to the mobilisation of these forces and the distribution of ideas – little more. Certainly, Howard Rheingold, too often falsely criticised as the father of the utopian approach to the Internet, provides a fitting summary of why the Internet is limited as an instrument of civic renewal: "We temporarily have access to a tool that could bring conviviality and understanding to our lives and might help revitalise the public sphere. The same tool, improperly controlled and wielded, could become an instrument of tyranny."[46]

Conclusion

We are faced in China by a complex network of contradictions: an open economy, a closed political system; an economic miracle based on market forces that depend on the free flow of information, ideas and debate, but an environment where the flow of information is tightly controlled; a government committed to the potential of the Internet as a tool of governance, but also anxious to restrain the use of the Internet and contain its power. Ultimately, the problem for Chinese-style governance is that the CCP now bases its legitimacy on performance and delivery, not on dogma,[47] but as the existence of the News Commentary Group demonstrates is still willing to use dogmatic methods of exercising power. Chinese face a growing social divide that aggravates social tension and thus the discrepancy between the message and reality becomes ever more apparent, thus creating a credibility gap. The forces that the Chinese government has unleashed in developing the economy have also planted the seeds of social unrest. Some might argue that they have always been present, just contained. However, in an age of global media with information immediately available to everyone with access to a computer – and despite the Chinese government's best attempts it *is* possible to circumvent the Great Firewall – it is becoming less and less easy to manage information and the new public spaces that are materialising in cyberspace. Michel Hockx is correct when he says that Internet censorship "does not necessarily confront Chinese writers and readers with an unfamiliar situation. Censorship is the norm, rather than the exception."[48] But this should not and does not preclude value judgement of censorship or the possibility of change. Censorship may be "a fact of life" and as observers we may be guilty of "foregrounding censorship" which means "highlighting what does not appear on the Chinese Internet" and drawing attention away "from what does appear."[49] But the mechanisms of censorship reveal much about the architecture of government, elite opinion and the perception of the power of communications. In accepting censorship as the norm, we are in danger of overlooking one important detail: what is good for governance in China – the free flow of information and ideas – is ultimately bad for the Chinese government. With the proliferation of media, publishers and audiences, and a print industry ever more determined to challenge the government (as demonstrated by the example of *Bingdian*), a centrally created and disseminated message is unable to compensate a society ever more willing to protest and express their grievances in public spaces.

Notes

1 Quoted in Mary Warnock, ed., *Utilitarianism* (London: Fantana Press, 1969), 172–3.
2 "Postscript: broadcasting to China," in *Reporting the News from China*, ed., Robin Porter (London: RIIA, 1992), 18–29.
3 Some of these stories are disturbingly similar to those told about purges in the media and propaganda institutions of the Communist party during the Cultural Revolution. See Alan P. Lui, *Communications and National Integration in Communist China* (Berkeley: University of California Press, 1975).
4 Jurgen Habermas, *The Structural Transformation of the Public Sphere* (Cambridge: Polity, 1992).
5 Benjamin Barber, *Strong Democracy* (Berkeley: University of California Press, 1984); Benjamin Barber, "Three Scenarios for the Future of Technology and Strong Democracy," *Political Science Quarterly*, 113, no. 4 (1988): 573–90.
6 L.A. Baker, "Direct Democracy and Discrimination: A Public Choice Perspective," *Chicago-Kent Law Review*, 67 (1991).
7 Duncan McCargo, *Media and Politics in Pacific Asia* (London: RoutledgeCurzon, 2003).
8 Timothy E. Cook, *Governing with the News: The News Media as a Political Institution* (Chicago: Chicago University Press, 1998).
9 In Anthony King, ed., *Britain at the Polls, 2001* (London: Chatham House, 2001), 119.
10 Quoted in *Straits Times*, 28 January 1999.
11 Singapore's Ministry of Information, Communications, and the Arts, *Our Shared Values*, 2002, at www.sg/flavour/value.asp.
12 John Spicer Nichols and Alicia M. Torres, "Cuba," in *Telecommunications in Latin America*, ed., Eli M. Noam (New York: OUP, 1998), 17–35.
13 B. Shoesmith, "Asia in their Shadows: Satellites and Asia," *Southeast Asian Journal of Social Science*, 22 (1994): 125–41.
14 Richard Gunther, José Ramón Montero and José Ignacio Wert, "The Media and Politics in Spain: From Dictatorship to Democracy," in *Democracy and the Media: A Comparative Perspective*, eds, Richard Gunther and Anthony Mughan (Cambridge: Cambridge University Press, 2000), 38.
15 Ibid.
16 Miklós Sükösd, "Democratic Transformation and the Mass Media in Hungary: From Stalinism to Democratic Consolidation," in Gunther and Mughan (eds), *Democracy and the Media*, 39.
17 See Hugo de Burgh, *The Chinese Journalist: Mediating Information in the World's Most Populous Country* (London: RoutledgeCurzon, 2003); Peter Hays Gries, *China's New Nationalism: Pride, Politics and Diplomacy* (Berkeley: University of California Press, 2004).

18 David Bandurski and Lin Hui, "China's Shadow Censor Commissars," *Far Eastern Economic Review*, 169, 2 (March 2006): 28–33.
19 Ibid., 30.
20 Ching-chang Hsiao and Timothy Cheek, "Open and Closed Media: External and Internal Newspapers in the Propaganda System," in *Decision Making in Deng's China*, eds, A. Doak Barnett, Carol Lee Hamrin and Suisheng Zhao (New York: ME Sharpe, 1995), 76–90.
21 Quoted in Robert J. Perrins, ed., *China Facts and Figures Annual Handbook* (Gulf Breeze, FL: Academic International Press, 2001), 313–14.
22 "Beijing Tightens Control on Media Reports," *South China Morning Post*, 2 November 2005.
23 Oswald Spengler in his 1918 *Decline of the West* noted even a free press "could condemn any 'truth' to death simply by not undertaking its communication to the world – a terrible censorship of silence which is all the more potent in that the masses of newspaper readers are absolutely unaware that it exists."
24 "Chinese Premier addresses media on major issues," *People's Daily*, 15 March 2006.
25 Gary D. Rawnsley, *Radio Diplomacy and Propaganda: The BBC and Voice of America in International Politics, 1956–64* (Basingstoke: Macmillan and New York: St. Martin's Press, 1996).
26 Emily Parker, "Cracks in the Chinese Wall," *The Asian Wall Street Journal*, 26 January 2005.
27 Howard Rheingold, *Virtual Communities: Homesteading on the Electronic Frontier* (London: Addison-Wesley, 1993), 279.
28 Ibid.; Nicholas Negroponte, *Being Digital* (London: Hodder & Stoughton, 1995); Lawrence K. Grossman, *The Electronic Republic: Reshaping Democracy in America* (New York: Viking, 1995); Ed Schwartz, *Netactivism: How Citizens Use the Internet* (Sebastapol, CA: Songline Studios, 1996); Ian Budge, *The New Challenge of Direct Democracy* (Cambridge: Polity Press, 1996); Kees Brants, Martine Huizenga and Reineke Van Meerten, "The New Canals of Amsterdam," *Media, Culture and Society*, 18 (1996): 223–47; Roza Tsagarousianou, Damian Tambini and Cathy Bryan, eds, *Cyberdemocracy: Technology, Cities and Civic Newtorks* (London: Routledge, 1998); Michael Dertouzos, *What Will Be: How the New Marketplace Will Change our Lives* (San Francisco, CA: HarperCollins, 1997).
29 I am grateful to Dr Andrew Robinson of the University of Nottingham for bringing to my attention the use of rhizomatic theory in explaining political organisation and behaviour. See his 2005 paper, "The Rhizomes of Manipur," available at www.nottingham.ac.uk/iaps/manipur%20illustrated.pdf.
30 Grossman, *The Electronic Republic*.
31 Barber, *Strong Democracy*.
32 An excellent discussion of the Zapatista movement and its use of the Internet is Harry Cleaver's detailed study, "The Zapatista and the Electronic Fabric of Struggle," available at www.eco.utexas.edu/faculty/Cleaver/zaps.html.
33 Andrea Goldstein and David O'Connor, *E-Commerce for Development: Prospects and Policy Issues* (Paris: OECD Development Centre, 2000).
34 W. Russell Neuman, *The Paradox of Mass Politics* (Cambridge, MA: Harvard University Press, 1986).
35 Shanthi Kalathil and Taylor C. Boas, "The Internet and State Control in Authoritarian Regimes: China, Cuba, and the Counterrevolution," 2001, available at www.firstmonday.dk/issues/issue6_8/kalathil.
36 Victor Mallet, *The Trouble with Tigers: The Rise and Fall of South-East Asia* (London: HarperCollins, 1999), 85.
37 A full discussion of the Internet in Iran, together with analysis of the theological debates that rage within Islam about and on the Internet is found in Marcus Franda,

Launching into Cyberspace: Internet Development and Politics in Five World Regions (Boulder, CO: Lynne Rienner, 2002), 76–80.

38 Kalathil and Boas, "The Internet and State Control in Authoritarian Regimes."

39 James Baker, "America in Asia: Emerging Architecture for a Pacific Community," *Foreign Affairs*, 70, no. 5 (1991/1992): 16–17.

40 Gordon C. Chang, *The Coming Collapse of China* (New York: Random House, 2001), 90.

41 Jianhai Bi, "The Internet Revolution in China," *International Journal*, 56, no. 2 (2000): 421–41.

42 See Gary D. Rawnsley, "Old Wine in New Bottles: Taiwan-China Information Warfare and Propaganda," *International Affairs*, 81, no. 5 (2005): 1061–78.

43 Gries, *China's New Nationalism*.

44 Parker, "Cracks in the Chinese wall."

45 G. Traubman, "A Not-so World Wide Web: The Internet, China and the Challenges to Nondemocratic Rule," *Political Communication*, 15 (1998): 255–72.

46 Rheingold, *Virtual Communities*, 14.

47 Sujian Guo, *Post-Mao China: From Totalitarianism to Authoritarianism?* (Westport, CT: Praeger, 2000).

48 Michel Hockx, "Virtual Chinese Literature: A Comparative Case Study of Online Poetry Communities," in *Culture in Contemporary China*, eds, Michel Hockx and Julia Strauss (Cambridge: Cambridge University Press, 2005), 151.

49 Ibid., 149.

8 Dissecting Chinese county governmental authorities

Yang Zhong

Introduction

There are over 2,000 counties and 427 county-status cities in China covering all rural areas and approximately 900 million peasants.[1] County authorities as a basic level of governmental organ and authority have survived without interruption in China for over 2,000 years. The county government has served for centuries as the most important intermediary linking the central and provincial government and the people. The central government has relied heavily on county governments for implementing its policies and maintaining local stability. Historically, the county government throughout Chinese history has performed similar functions and has been charged with the comprehensive responsibility of administering local affairs concerning justice, public order, tax collection, economic development, agriculture, education, defense and promotion of culture and traditions. County officials in China have often been referred to as "father and mother officials" (*fu mu guan*) who are expected to take care of their subjects in all aspects of their lives.

Given its importance, the level of county government has not been adequately and systematically studied in the field of China studies. Local politics in the People's Republic of China (PRC) is mostly studied in association with central–local relations, the focus of which tends to be the central government. In fact, in China studies the term "local government" often refers to the provincial government. "Localism" and "regionalism" are often used interchangeably. This chapter attempts to understand county government and politics by focusing on county governmental institutions and institutional relationships between the county on the one hand and higher governmental authorities and township/town government on the other. Since county authorities were placed under the authority of municipal government in China, the county government has steadily lost its power and authority over personnel and economic decisions. Due to the fact that most money-making and fee-collecting agencies have been "verticalized" or made *tiao tiao* agencies subject to the jurisdiction of higher authorities, the fiscal problems encountered by county governments have seriously increased and they have thus had to find alternative resources of funds. This chapter also discusses the recently proposed experimental practice of putting county authorities directly under the jurisdiction of the provincial government. Problems facing this new institutional arrangement include extreme reluctance on the part of municipal governments to relinquish their power, the inability of provincial governments to exercise authority over county governments and county governments are not trusted to use their newly gained power properly.

County government authorities

County as an important level of administration was maintained after the Chinese Communist victory after 1949, even though the name was formally changed to "county people's government." Initially, the county government was run democratically and with wide representation. A people's representative assembly (*renmin daibiao huiyi*) composed of peasants, democratic party members, mass organization representatives, military officers and county magistrate/deputy magistrates was established to elect key county officials, supervise the county government and ratify the county's budget.[2] The current county Party and governmental structure was established after the adoption of a new state constitution in 1954. Since then, the county government gradually lost its democratic features. For example, beginning in 1953 county people's representative assembly members were elected indirectly by lower-level people's representative bodies, while the representative assembly lost much of its legislative and decision-making power to the county government.

During the Cultural Revolution, the county government structure prescribed in the 1954 constitution was suspended and replaced by an all-powerful and centralized "county revolutionary committee" consisting of military representatives and rebel leaders from various mass organizations such as the Red Guards, factory workers and peasants. Most of the regular functional governmental agencies and related organizations such as the county judicial system were suspended or radically restructured. The 1975 constitution stipulated that "the county revolutionary committee" was both a legislative body and the executive governing branch at the county level. Four years later, the county revolutionary committee was abolished, and the former county people's government structure was restored. The constitutional status of the county people's government was codified in a new constitution adopted in 1982.

County governmental authorities in China are composed of five sets of organizational bodies (the so-called *wu tao banzi*), i.e. the county people's government, the county Party committee, county Party disciplinary inspection committee, county people's congress and county people's political consultative conference. Of these, the county Party committee is no doubt the most influential decision-making body even though the county people's congress is constitutionally the power center, and the county people's government is constitutionally the executive body. Consequently, the county Party secretary rather than the county magistrate is the most influential decision-maker at the county level even though his/her role is not specifically defined in the constitution.

County people's government

County people's government is the most convoluted and over-staffed organization among all the five sets of governmental and Party bodies at the county level. According to official regulations, the number of county governmental units should be between 24 and 26 for large counties (population over one million), 22–24 for medium-size counties (between half million and a million) and around 20 for small counties (under half a million).[3] But in practice all county governments in China exceed their stipulated size. Most county government agencies number between 40 and 50, and some reach around 80.[4] Table 8.1 lists all the governmental agencies, offices and bureaus in "P county" (with a population of 440,000) in an eastern province.[5] The complex county bureaucracy is often divided into seven areas in terms of function, i.e. general, political/legal, agricultural/irrigation industrial/transportation, basic construction/development, finance/trade and education/public health.

Table 8.1 County governmental agencies, offices and bureaus in P County, Jiangxi province·

General
    Administrative reform commission (*tigai wei*)
    Audit bureau (*shenji ju*)
    Bureau of civil administration (*minzhen ju*)
    Bureau of labor and personnel (*laodong renshi ju*)
    Bureau of local tax (*dishui ju*)
    Bureau of religions (*zongjia ju*)
    Clean government office (*liangzhengban*)
    County government administrative office (*xianzhengfu bangongshi*)
    Planning commission (*ji wei*)
    Section of rule of law (*fazhi ke*)
    Statistics bureau (*tongji ju*)
    Supervision bureau (*jiancha ju*)
Industry and transportation
    Bureau of electric power (*dianli ju*)
    Bureau of postal service (*youzheng ju*)
    Communications bureau (*dianxin ju*)
    Commission of economics and trade (*jingmao ju*)
    Industry bureau (*gongye ju*)
    Transportation bureau (*jiaotong ju*)
Commerce and finance
    Association of supplies and sales (*gongxiao she*)
    Bureau of foreign trade (*waimao ju*)
    Bureau of industrial-commercial management (*gongshang guanli ju*)
    Bureau of tobacco sales (*yancao zhuanmai ju*)
    Commerce bureau (*shangye ju*)
    Finance bureau (*caizheng ju*)
    Grain bureau (*liangshi ju*)
    Investment bureau (*zhaoshang ju*)
    Medicine bureau (*yiyao ju*)
    Price bureau (*wujia ju*)

Table 8.1 Continued

Salt bureau (*yanwu ju*)
Tourist bureau (*luyou ju*)
Agriculture
   Agriculture bureau (*nongye ju*)
   Bureau of fishery (*shuichan ju*)
   Bureau of land administration (*tudi guanli ju*)
   Bureau of township enterprises (*xiangqi ju*)
   Bureau of weather forecast (*qixiang ju*)
   Commission of agricultural economy (*nongjing wei*)
   Forestry bureau (*linye ju*)
   Irrigation bureau (*shuili ju*)
   Station of agricultural machinery (*nongji zhan*)
Law enforcement
   Brigade of traffic police (*jiaojing dui*)
   Brigade of armed police (*wujing dui*)
   Bureau of public security (*gongan ju*)
   Justice bureau (*sifa ju*)
Science, education and health
   Bureau of public health (*weisheng ju*)
   Culture bureau (*wenhua ju*)
   Commission of family planning (*jisheng wei*)
   Education commission (*jiao wei*)
   Science commission (*ke wei*)
   Sports commission (*ti wei*)
Mass organizations
   Association of elders' sports (*laoti xie*)
   Artists' association (*xi lian*)
   Chamber of commerce (*gongshang lian*)
   Elders' commission (*laoling wei*)
   Labor union (*gonghui*)
   Scientists' association (*ke xie*)
   Writers' association (*wen lian*)
Miscellaneous
   Bureau of urban construction (*jianshe ju*)
   Bureau of housing management (*fangguan shuo*)

Note
Banks of various kinds and bureau of state tax (*guoshui ju*) are not included in this table.

In addition to these formal governmental units, the county government also runs a large number of *shiye* (service-oriented) units such as schools, hospitals, hotels and movie theaters and *qiye* (enterprise) units such as shops, factories and companies. Each higher governmental unit is mirrored by at least one corresponding unit at the county level, albeit smaller in size. In fact, there were only 63 governmental units under the State Council in 2000. In terms of governmental structure and functions, the county people's government resembles that of the central government so much that it looks indeed like a miniature state at the local level.

The proliferation of county government bureaucracy has been a gradual process culminating in the 1980s. To take Wannian county (population:

480,000), Hainan province as an example (see Table 8.2). Between 1954 and 1990, county government units increased fourfold. The first wave of county bureaucratic expansion occurred in the late 1950s with collectivization in the rural areas, followed by a further wave in the early 1960s. However, county bureaucracy (in the form of county revolutionary committees) shrank during the Cultural Revolution period as a result of Mao's deliberate and irrational efforts to destroy formal governmental bureaucracy. The post-Mao reform era saw an increase in county bureaucracy due to various factors, the first being efforts to restore the former county government that existed prior to the Cultural Revolution. The second was Deng Xiaoping's emphasis on bureaucratic rationality that stresses bureaucratic structural differentiation and specialization, such as the efforts to separate the Party organization and its functions from those of the government. The third was the expansion of economic activities at the county level and the government's efforts to regulate them. An additional reason is the common tendency for a bureaucracy once in existence to sustain itself even when its rationale can no longer be defended. For instance, the office of spiritual civilization in Pengze county, Jiangxi was created during the Spiritual Civilization movement in the mid-1980s, and it continues to survive even after the movement has long since expired.

An inevitable result of bureaucratic expansion is the increase in staffing and a ballooning of governmental budgets. County Party and government employees had already reached two million by 1989.[6] Among the half million extra Party and government employees (*chaobian renyuan*) by the early 1990s, about 60 percent were found at the county government level.[7] It was estimated in the early 1990s that 80 percent of county expenditure nationwide was spent on salary and benefits for county Party and government employees while only about 17 percent went to local economic development.[8] On average, between 3,000 and 4,000 people are on government payroll or "eating imperial grain" (*chihuangliang*) in a Chinese county.[9] As a result, more than half of Chinese counties were in debt in the mid-1990s.[10]

The county people's government is headed by a magistrate and a number of deputy magistrates (more than ten in some counties).[11] County government daily affairs are run by a general office or *xianzhengfu bangongshi*, which plays secre-

Table 8.2 Evolution of Wanning county government

Year	Number of county governmental units
1954	12
1959	23
1966	34
1972	21
1990	64

Source: Xie Qinkui *et al.*, eds, *Xianzhengfu guanli: wanning xian diaocha* (*County Government Management: The Case of Wanning*) (Beijing, China: China Broadcasting and Television Press, 1994), pp. 96–101.

tariat and coordinating functions. The head of the county government general office occupies an important position since he is one of the closest to the crucial decision-makers of the county government. Yet, all major decisions made by the county people's government must be first approved by the county Party secretary and county Party committee. The county people's government is charged with making specific plans for policy implementation.

There are three policy-making mechanisms or levels of meeting within the county people's government.[12] The first is the magistrates' business meeting (*xianzhang bangong huiyi* or *xianzhang changwu huiyi*) convened by the county magistrate and formally attended by deputy magistrates and the head and deputy head of the county general office; sometimes relevant county bureau chiefs are also invited to attend as non-voting members. These meetings, which are held regularly and formally, discuss, propose and make decisions on county matters. This is the main formal decision-making body of the county people's government.

The second type of meeting is the general county people's government meeting (*xiangzhengfu quanti huiyi*). These are held irregularly and attended by county magistrate, deputy magistrates, leading officials from county government bureaus and offices and township mayors and deputy mayors. The aims of these meetings include: passing on important documents and policies from higher governmental authorities, announcing concrete implementation measures at the county level and promulgating major county economic development plans and strategic measures to implement the plans. The third type of meeting comprises informal meetings among county magistrates and deputy magistrates (*xianzhang pengtouhui*). The main aims of these meetings are to have preliminary discussions on county issues and to try to achieve a consensus on proposed county government policies.

According to the PRC constitution, the county people's government executes policies on behalf of the county people's congress and higher governmental authorities. In reality, however, a county government is solely responsible to and is supervised by its superior authority, i.e. the prefectural government. The county people's government is officially charged with performing the following key functions: planning local economic development, managing and guiding local public enterprises, collecting taxes, controlling land appropriation, running the local educational system, providing public security and promoting social welfare.

Among these functions, developing the local economy has no doubt been the central task for the county people's government since the late 1970s. On a macro-level, the county government is responsible for overseeing the overall economic development of the county. One of its key roles is drawing up a comprehensive economic development plan for the county based upon central government policies and guidelines. Since the decentralization policies carried out by the central government since the early 1980s, the county people's government has been given autonomy to set short-term, mid-term and long-term economic development goals and blueprints with specific targets, such as the economic growth rate, production quotas of industrial as well as agricultural products, tax revenue and personal income.

One important change in the economic role of the county people's government after two decades of economic reforms and decentralization is its relations with county-owned or previously county-owned public enterprises. Chinese county governments have adopted three types of policies vis-à-vis county-owned enterprises: privatization (in part or whole), leasing and continued control. Privatization and leasing of county-owned enterprises have occurred primarily in more developed areas and coastal provinces where the county government mainly collects taxes and leasing fees from these enterprises. In many inland and less developed provinces and areas, however, county governments have yet totally separated themselves from these economic enterprises and still have the power to appoint managers and directors even though the county government is less involved in the micro-management of these enterprises.

County party organizations

The county Communist Party committee is the power center of county governance in the PRC. The committee, the size of which varies from one county to the next depending on population size, is officially elected by the county Party congress held every five years. The county Party apparatus usually consists of the following key organizations: county Communist Party standing committee, general office, Party disciplinary inspection committee, organization department, propaganda department, united front department, office of policy studies and county Party school office. Most county Party committees also have a few more auxiliary offices. Table 8.3 shows the organizational structure of Party apparatus in P county.

At the heart of the county Party apparatus is the standing committee of the county Communist Party committee. The size of this committee varies from county to county. Central Organization Department regulations stipulate that

Table 8.3 Party apparatus in P County, Jiangxi Province

Standing Committee of County Party Committee
General office (*dangwei bangongshi*)

Office of policy studies (*zhengyan shi*)	Organization department (*zhuzhi bu*)
Bureau of confidential documents (*jiyao ju*)	Office of Taiwan affairs (*taiban*)
Office of supervision (*ducha shi*)	Office of politics and Law (*zhengfa shi*)
Bureau of veteran cadres (*laoganbu ju*)	Bureau of cadre files (*dangan ju*)
Office of anti-feudalism (*fanfengjian shi*)	Propaganda department (*xuanchuan bu*)
United front department (*tongzhan bu*)	Office of party schools (*dangxiao*)
Office of civilizations (*wenming ban*)	Office of receiving complaints (*xinfang ban*)
Office of party history (*dangshi ban*)	
Women's association (*fulian*)	Communist youth league (*gongqingtuan*)

larger counties should have about eleven members and seven to nine for smaller counties and the committee is headed by one Party secretary and two to three deputy secretaries.[13] But in most places the committee consists of nine to fifteen members including the Party secretary and three to four deputy secretaries. Each of the deputy secretaries is in charge of a specific area such as industry, agriculture, mass organizations, etc. The first deputy Party secretary is always the county magistrate. Beginning in 2006, a new institutional policy has being implemented to reduce the number of deputy party secretaries to two: the first party secretary (who is the county magistrate) and an executive deputy party secretary.[14] This will no doubt significantly reduce the number of senior party officials at the county level.

Members of the county Party standing committee always include the head of the organization department, the head of the propaganda department and the secretary of the county Party disciplinary inspection committee. Under the Party constitution, the county Party standing committee is the Party's executive body in running the daily affairs of the county Party apparatus. The county Party standing committee functions like the Political Bureau at the national level. In some counties, the committee holds regular meetings (e.g. once a week or once a month) while in others it holds meetings whenever necessary. All major county government decisions are discussed and made by this committee first and are formally adopted by the county government and relevant agencies. More importantly, the committee is also in charge of personnel matters concerning non-leading county and township officials.

Below the standing committee of the county Party committee are a number of functional and administrative offices headed by one office chief and usually two deputy chiefs. One of the most important offices is the general office (*xianwei bangongshi*), officially a secretariat organ and the de facto headquarters of the county Party apparatus. The head of the office is an unusually powerful person since he has direct access to the county Party secretary and the other key county officials, and he is also one of the most informed people about county Party/government affairs including personnel changes. The office is often staffed with two deputy heads and about a dozen office workers. Another power office of the county Party committee is the organization department that handles cadre appointment and promotion. The official responsibilities of the Party organization department include preparing the cadre reserve list (*houbei ganbu mingdan*) and making recommendations for key cadre appointment and promotion at the township level (Party secretaries, mayors, deputy Party secretaries and deputy mayors) and county government bureau level (bureau chief and deputy chiefs). Even though the power of appointment and promotion ultimately resides in the hands of the county Party secretary, key officials in the organization department are usually involved in the appointment and promotion process and therefore have inside information about who is likely to be promoted to what position prior to the formal announcement. Due to their importance, both the general office and the organization department of the county Party committee are heavy targets for networking and backdoor dealings.

Prior to 1989, attempts were made to separate, to a certain degree, the county Party apparatus from the people's government and its agencies. In Deng Xiaoping's words, "It is time for us to distinguish between the responsibilities of the Party and those of government from top to bottom, and promote a better exercise of government functions and powers."[15] The expectation was that through this separation, Party officials could concentrate more on Party affairs and interfere less in day-to-day governmental business in order to raise the organizational efficiency of both the Party and the government. The rationale behind this reform measure is compatible with a Weberian model of bureaucracy that emphasizes functional specialization and differentiation. This reform was suspended after the 1989 Tiananmen Square crackdown, an event whose occurrence was partially blamed on the weakened city Party structure in Beijing. Since 1989 the county Party committee was once again made the predominant power in managing county governmental affairs. In fact, in many places the county Party secretary serves concurrently as the county magistrate. This is said to be a positive move in strengthening the county government. Furthermore, the county Party committee and the county people's government are often housed in the same building. Indeed, the key county Party officials and county people's government officials work as one team. Together they form what Jean Oi calls "the local corporate state" or "a board of directors" with the Party secretary serving as the CEO.[16]

The county Party committee and its secretary are heavily involved in economic matters. All major economic decisions, such as mapping out a county economic plan, starting major economic projects, attracting foreign investment and budgeting county expenses, are decided by the county Party standing committee led by the county Party secretary. County Party secretaries often participate in business negotiations and business trips promoting local products even though legally only the county magistrate can represent the county government in signing legal documents such as contracts. Two reasons are behind the involvement of county Party committee and Party secretary in economic matters. One is that economic development has been defined and treated as a central *political* task for the whole Party since the late 1970s. Therefore, the county Party committee and its secretary are expected and required to be involved in local economic affairs. In fact, developing the local economy is a crucial performance evaluation criterion for county Party officials. A second reason is that the Party committee and its secretary in particular are specifically charged with checking and monitoring whether the economic decisions taken by the county people's government and its agencies are in accordance with the principles and policies of the higher state authorities.

The institutional setting of Party dominance presents a paradoxical situation for central–local relations in the PRC. There used to be three main mechanisms by which the center controlled local government: Party discipline, ideology and the central economic planning system.[17] The latter two have been significantly weakened as a result of reforms in the past two decades. The only viable control mechanism that the center now counts on is Party organization and discipline.

This is the main reason that the center has always stressed the importance of Party leadership at various levels of government and organizations and why the local Party organization and Party secretary have been given so much power. However, this power can be easily abused by local Party chiefs, who can effectively build "independent kingdoms" that give them the latitude to disobey higher authorities or to drag their feet in carrying out the center's policies, particularly in the absence of an effective monitoring system. The system is such that few people dare challenge the Party's authority; in fact, there are substantial incentives for them to follow their local Party boss's orders. Numerous reports on corruption reveal that officials tend to protect each other and that subordinates do not dare to speak out against illegal activities of superior officials for fear of retaliation. In this institutional setting, the Party control system becomes a double-edged sword: it can strengthen the center's control of the localities, but at the same time it can also undermine the center's ability to bring localities into line.

An example in point was a serious mining accident that occurred in Nandan county, Guangxi province on July 17, 2001 and caused 81 fatalities. According to a State Council regulation, local officials are supposed to report immediately to the higher authorities such serious accidents. However, fearing bad publicity and jeopardizing his political career, the county Party secretary conspired with the county magistrate and deputy county Party secretaries and decided to cover it up and successfully kept the accident a secret from higher authorities for almost a month. Due to the high fatality rate, the incident was eventually uncovered by the media and higher governmental authorities. A year later the county Party secretary was sentenced to death and other key county government officials involved in the cover-up were given lengthy prison terms.[18]

The county people's congress

As mentioned above, the county people's congress, which is a county/department (*xian chu ji*) unit in the official organizational structure, is constitutionally the highest decision-making (legislative) body in Chinese counties. According to laws governing the functioning of local people's congress, the county people's congress has 15 official functions including administratively supervising the county government, discussing and deciding county government policies concerning local political, economic, educational and cultural developments, approving county government budget, electing county magistrates, deputy magistrates, chief county court and county procuratorate officers, and appointing county government bureau chiefs.[19] Officially, the county people's government is under the dual leadership of the higher state government authorities and the county people's congress. The county people's government is expected to carry out policies, laws and regulations passed by the county people's congress.

Local people's congresses, like the National People's Congress, were first established in 1954 with the promulgation of the first constitution of the PRC. In the 1950s and the 1960s, representatives of the county people's congress were indirectly elected by township people's congresses. The work and structure of the county people's congress were seriously disrupted during the Cultural Revolution. The structure and role of this organization were redefined and further strengthened, at least on the paper, during the reform period. Since 1979, representatives to county people's congresses have been directly elected. There are strict and detailed rules and regulations on how county people's congress representatives are elected.[20] The size of the county people's congress varies depending on the local population, with a minimum of 120 representatives and a maximum of 450. Representatives serve a five-year term and can be re-elected.

The county people's congress convenes once a year for three to four days (usually in January or February). The main items on the agenda of the annual meeting of the county people's congress include listening to, discussing and approving (by majority vote) work reports of the county people's government, the county people's court, and the county people's procuratorate office, approving the county government budget, passing legislation and electing or appointing key county government officials. A number of committees consisting of five to seven representatives are also established within the county people's congress to work on special issues such as meeting procedures of the county people's congress and county finance.

The key organ within the county people's congress is the standing committee, with membership ranging between 11 and 29 and headed by a chairman and a number of deputy chairmen. Since the county people's congress only convenes once a year for three to four days, the standing committee is the decision-making body when the county people's congress is not in session. Two major responsibilities of the standing committee are appointing key county officials and supervising the county people's government when the county people's congress is not sitting. The daily affairs of the standing committee are run usually by a general office (*bangongshi*) and four sections (*ke*) including a secretariat, liaison section, political section and legal section. The four sections are under the leadership of the general office. In some counties, sections are replaced by special offices that are on a par with the general office of the standing committee. The overall number of officials and staff of working for the standing committee of the county people's congress ranges from 15 to 25, though over-staffing is also a common problem in county people's congress.[21]

The county people's congress in the PRC has a long way to go in becoming a meaningful legislative, supervising and representative democratic institution in spite of some recent progress at county, provincial and national level.[22] By and large, county people's congresses are still rubber-stamp organizations controlled and manipulated by the county Party committee and the county people's government.

County deputies are often referred to as "three-hands" representatives since all they can do in their official capacity is raise their hands (to approve county government policies and personnel appointments), clap and shake hands (with county Party/government officials). Decisions concerning county governmental affairs are primarily made by the county Party committee and the county people's government and are then sent to the county people's congress for formal approval.

In most counties, the chairmanship and vice-chairmanships of the county people's congress are treated as semi-retirement positions for former county leading cadres (e.g. county Party secretary, deputy secretaries, county magistrate and deputy magistrate) who have yet to reach the age of 60 for complete retirement. Often the chairman of the county people's congress is not even a member of the standing committee of the county Party committee – the real power source of county authority in China. In many other counties, the county Party secretary serves concurrently as the chairman of the county people's congress. The joint appointment is said to be a measure to strengthen the role of the county people's congress given the powerful "first-hand" position of the Party secretary. Even though this arrangement may help in empowering the county people's congress vis-à-vis the county people's government, it also further consolidates the control of the county people's congress by the Party secretary. Also, the Party secretary is often too busy to pay much attention to the affairs of the county people's congress.

Election and appointment of key county people's government officials are supposed to be a major function of the county people's congress. But this role is poorly served by the county people's congress. Personnel matters of key county people's government officials are the prerogatives of the county Party committee and its organizational department. The Party-approved/nominated candidates are usually approved by the county people's congress or its standing committee without any challenge. In recent years, there have been reported cases in which Party-nominated candidates for county government bureau chiefs have been rejected by the county people's congress. In some cases, county Party committee officials have applied pressure or outright coercion to "persuade" deputies who are Party members to change their mind and vote for the initially rejected Party-nominated officials in the second round. In other cases, the county people's government has simply appointed the rejected candidate as acting bureau chief, which procedurally does not need the county people's congress's approval, and leaves the bureau chief positions vacant.[23]

For a while in the 1980s, there were always two candidates for the position of county magistrate. The Party set up a straw candidate to make the election appear more competitive and democratic. However, sometimes when the real candidate was from outside the county while the straw candidate was local, the straw candidate won. Therefore, ever since the late 1980s the Party has limited its nominations for these posts to one candidate per post. However, the number of candidates nominated for the positions of deputy county magistrates sometimes outnumber the positions available (*cha e xuanju*), thereby making the competition slightly more meaningful.

Deputies to the county people's congress have also yet to become genuine and active representatives. The first problem is the way deputies are elected. Even though the election laws and procedures are fairly democratic and clear-cut in theory, practice is another matter. Deputies are primarily nominated by the

Party and the majority of deputies are Party members. In fact, a substantial number of deputies (over 40 percent in some places) are government officials.[24] There are virtually no campaign activities on the part of nominated deputies, even though their names are publicized prior to the elections. Being nominated as a deputy is still considered an honor and is often accorded to individuals such as model workers, local leaders and even private entrepreneurs. Deputies to the county people's congress are also supposed to reflect the composition of the local population in terms of gender, occupation and ethnicity in order to make the congress look more representative. Quota systems are often employed to achieve this goal. Even with this deliberate effort, women are still seriously under-represented in county people's congresses in China.[25]

One area in which the county people's congress has made noticeable progress is that many congress deputies have become more outspoken about local problems, especially during the annual convention of the congress. It is not uncommon to hear deputies complaining about what the county government has failed to do and what should be done. Unfortunately deputies to county people's congresses can do little more than complain. They have not been given enough power and authority to effectively affect and change county government policies.

Due to the limited power of county people's congress, few people take them or elections to them seriously. The annual general meeting of the county people's congress is often perceived and handled as a burden by the county Party committee and the county people's government. Eligible voters usually show little enthusiasm in participating in the election of deputies to the people's congress. According to the election laws, each election can only be valid when more than half of eligible voters participate in the election and each deputy receives at least half of the eligible votes cast. However, due to the low level of interest, government election offices often have to set up mobile voting stations (*liudong toupiao zhan*) to solicit votes after the first round fails to produce the crucial number. According to a study of political participation in rural Jiangsu province, only about a third of eligible peasant voters took part in county people's congress in the late 1990s, far short of the official 50 percent threshold.[26]

Relationship between county government and higher governmental authorities

Administratively, the immediate superior authority that the county government is subject to is either the provincially administered city (*shengjishi* or *dijishi*) or the prefecture administrative office (*difang xingzheng gongsu*). Even though these are on the same administrative level, they are different in one respect: while the provincially administered city is a formal level of government with a comprehensive and complete governmental structure and people's congress, the prefecture administrative office is supposed to be only a representative governmental office or organ on behalf of the provincial government. Prefecture administrative offices are set up for areas where there are no major urban centers. By 2000, prefecture administrative offices existed in 22 provinces and about half of all counties were placed under the aegis of the prefecture administrative office.[27]

The prefecture administrative office was created in the 1930s under Nationalist rule. Prior to that, China only had three levels of government: central, provincial and county. The prefecture-level administration was created mainly to allow the provincial and central governments to monitor the county government more effectively, especially with regard to maintaining local stability and preventing Communist subversion.[28] Since the prefecture administrative office was not a formal and comprehensive level of government, it only had a small number of governmental organs with limited staff: 4–5 sectional offices with, on average, 25 governmental staff members.[29]

The Communist government maintained and expanded the prefecture administrative level after 1949. Counties are theoretically under the direct administration of the provincial government. But since the 1950s, the prefecture administrative office, even though a representative body on behalf of the provincial government (*sheng paichu jiguan*), has become de facto a formal level of government with comprehensive governmental agencies paralleling those at provincial and county levels even though according to the current PRC Constitution and Laws of Local Organizations (*difang zuzhifa*) the prefecture administrative office is still, in theory, a representative body supervising and coordinating county governmental activities on behalf of the provincial government and not a formal level of government.[30] (Only the since-rescinded 1975 constitution recognized officially the prefecture administrative office as a formal level of government.)

About half of Chinese counties are under the direct administration of the provincial city government (*shengjishi* or *shengxiashi* or *dijishi*), which, unlike the prefecture administrative office, is a formal level of government according to the constitution. City as an administrative unit and one level of government emerged in the early days of the Republican period. A law passed by the Nationalist government in 1930 divided Chinese cities into two categories: special status cities under the administration of the Executive Yuan (or Executive Council) and regular cities under the aegis of the provincial government. This system was basically maintained by the Communist government after 1949. Chinese cities today are divided into three categories: centrally administered or provincial-status cities (i.e. Beijing, Shanghai, Tianjin and Chongqing), provincial cities (cities under the administration of provincial governments) and county-status cities (whose administrative ranking is the equivalent of counties). By the late 1980s, 168 provincial cities governed 712 rural counties, more than one-third of all counties in China.[31] Putting counties under the direct jurisdiction and governance of provincial cities was not widely practiced until the late 1970s. It was part of the government's effort to integrate rural areas into urban centers under its urbanization policy. The goal was to promote the economic development of the Chinese countryside. What has happened since the 1980s is the large-scale merger of prefectures and county-status cities to create more provincial cities to govern the counties.

Counties under either the administration of prefecture government or municipal government have gradually lost their power and autonomy in the last two decades due to the growth in power of the prefectural authorities, economic development and expansion of urban areas in provincial cities and the "hollowing out" of the county government. Even though the prefectural administrative office is intended to be an intermediate governmental organ that primarily plays the relaying and supervising functions, in most places it has de facto become a whole level of government with full governmental functions and structure. A central government circular issued in 1983 clearly stipulated that Party and governmental offices and staff at prefecture level should not exceed 25 and 1,000, respectively. Yet, by the early 1990s, the average number of Party and governmental offices was around 50 and the average number of officials and staff exceeded 2,000.[32] Most county government departments and offices have a corresponding office at the prefecture level. Much of the power (in areas such as economic planning, finance, personnel and resource allocation) previously held by the provincial government over the county government has been shifted to the prefectural administrative office, albeit to different degrees in different provinces and regions. An obvious result of this new development has been the creation of a new layer of bureaucracy.

Another contributing factor to the declining autonomy of the county government is the expansion of the urban areas of provincial cities and the economic incorporation of counties into the economic life of provincial cities. China experienced its largest expansion of urban areas in the 1980s and 1990s. In fact, many of the rural counties near urban centers have been turned into urban districts (*qu*) and become part of the urban areas. For counties that are close to urban centers, their economy has been integrated with the economy of the towns to various degrees. Many state-owned enterprises in urban areas have outsourced their production to township and town enterprises (TVEs) which serve as economic links between rural counties and cities.

A third factor causing the decline of county government power is the fact that many county government offices and bureaus in the areas of banking, utilities, communications, transportation, salt production and sales, tax collection, postal services, public security and courts have been removed from the control of the county government and placed under the administration of higher governmental levels (or "verticalized"). Most of these offices and bureaus were previously cash cows for the county government. The verticalization of money-making offices and bureaus has seriously undermined the financial footing of county governments in China.

A new institutional arrangement that has been trialed in several provinces is the placing of the county government more directly under the jurisdiction of the provincial government. This experiment was first introduced in Zhejiang in 2002 and has yielded positive results. In fact, the central government in its first policy circular of 2006 stated that this new structure should gradually be introduced nationwide. This was reaffirmed in the eleventh Five-Year Plan unveiled at the National People's Congress annual session in March 2006.[33] This institutional change is part of the government's new emphasis on developing China's vast and backward rural areas. The goal is to give more economic authority and incentive to the county government and to eliminate one more bureaucratic layer (i.e. the municipal government) in the policy implementation process. It is no secret that under the current arrangement municipal government officials tend to focus their attention on and put their resources (part of which are extracted from rural counties) into the development of the urban areas.

In fact, there are a number of reform proposals on the table. The minimum proposal envisages putting the county government under the fiscal jurisdiction of the provincial government, thus giving more economic power to the county level. The most ambitious and drastic reform plan proposes the elimination of the municipal government and putting county governments squarely and directly under the provincial governmental authorities.[34] Supporters of the latter proposal primarily want to bring back the traditional Chinese governmental structure that existed between the Yuan and Qing dynasties when there were only three levels of government, i.e. central, provincial and county.

Placing the county government under the direct administration of the provincial authority is not without challenging problems, which is why this measure has only been implemented on an experimental basis in a limited number of areas. It has met strong opposition and resistance from municipal governmental officials since it would result in their losing much of their power.[35] More importantly, municipal governments will lose fiscal revenue generated from rural counties. For example, in the fall of 2005, Jiangsu provincial government planned to choose five counties as experimental cases placed under the direct fiscal control of the provincial government. However, this plan has yet to be put into practice due to strong resistance from the municipal governments involved.[36] A second problem is that the provincial government is seriously inadequate in personnel in managing the counties. If this reform proposal is implemented province-wide, the administrative burden of provincial bureaus will be tremendously increased. In addition, the provincial government does not have enough trained and qualified personnel to handle rural issues. Third, it is highly questionable whether the provincial government can exercise efficient and sufficient supervision over the county government. It is well known that the county government is one of the most corrupt levels of government in China. Giving more power and authority to county government officials risks providing them with more opportunities for corruption. Due to these problems, it is not clear how quickly this reform will be adopted nationwide.

Relationship between the county government and the township/town government

The relationship between the county government and its subordinate authority, i.e. township/town government, is the reverse story of the relationship between the county and prefectural or provincial city authorities. The existing *tiao tiao* ((vertical) and *kuai kuai* (horizontal) inter-governmental system gives the county government significant authority over the township/town government. The *tiao tiao* section of the township/town government is primarily under the jurisdiction the higher governmental authorities while the *kuai kuai* section of the township/town government is directly under the administration of the township/town government. For this reason, the *tiao tiao* governmental offices at the township/town level are, strictly speaking, not part of the township/town government.

In the past two decades, there has been a dramatic increase in *tiao tiao* governmental offices at the township/town level. The average of *tiao tiao* governmental offices at the township/town level had reached 30 in the early 1990s and employed 500 people.[37] A study of township/town government organization in a Hebei county found that 82 percent of township/town governmental organizations were *tiao tiao* offices from higher administrations.[38] The *tiao tiao* section of the township/town administrative apparatus is mainly under the jurisdiction of the corresponding offices of the higher authority (mostly at the county level) while the *kuai kuai* section is fully under the jurisdiction of the township/town government. The main *tiao tiao* offices (see Table 8.4) usually include industry and commerce, state tax, local tax, finance, agricultural equipment, bank

Table 8.4 Tiao Tiao offices at township/town level

State tax post (*guoshui suo*)	Public security post (*gongan paichu suo*)
Local tax post (*dishui suo*)	People's court (*renmin fayuan*)
Judicial post (*sifa suo*)	Transportation post (*jiatong yunshu suo*)
Power management post (*dianguan suo*)	Post office branch (*youdian suo*)
Industry and commerce post (*gongsheng suo*)	Finance post (*caizheng suo*)
	Price post (*wujia suo*)
Economic management station (*jingguan zhan*)	Measurement post (*jiliang suo*)
	Water management post (*shuiguan suo*)
Land management post (*tudi guanli suo*)	Agricultural science station (*nongke zhan*)
Agricultural technology station (*nongji zhan*)	Agricultural equipment station (*nongji zhan*)
	Public health station (*weisheng zhan*)
Irrigation station (*shuili zhan*)	Animal husbandry station (*xumu zhan*)
Forrest station (*linye zhan*)	Broadcasting and TV station (*guangbo dianshi zhan*)
Veterinary station (*shouyi zhan*)	
Cultural station (*wenhua zhan*)	Hospitals (*weishengyuan*)
Theater (*dianyingyuan*)	Credit union (*xinyong she*)
Plant protection station (*zhibao zhan*)	Food administration post (*shipin suo*)
Education office (*jiaoyu zhu*)	Agricultural crops post (*liangguan suo*)
Supplies and sales cooperative (*gongxiao she*)	Family planning management office (*jihua shengyu guanli bangong shi*)
Agricultural seed station (*zhongzi zhan*)	Middle schools (*zhongxue*)
Agricultural bank branch (*nonghang Banshichu*)	Chinese people's insurance company post (*baoxian gongsi banshichu*)
Industrial and commerce bank branch (*gongshang yinhang banshichu*)	

branches, Chinese People's Insurance Company, credit union, food administration, branch post office, supplies and sales cooperative, power management, public health station and clinics, public security, people's court, cultural station, irrigation station, transportation, radio and TV, middle schools and hospitals.

Three specific factors have contributed to the increase in *tiao tiao* governmental offices at the township/town level. The first factor is the higher authorities' attempt to prevent a concentration of power by the township/town government and a fear of loss of control by the county government. The fear is that if the township/town government officials, who are suspected of putting local interests or their own interests above the regional and national interest, are given too much power they would have the capacity to torpedo policies from above. The second factor is concern over township/town government officials' professional ability to take charge of affairs at the township/town level. Township/town government officials in China, most of whom are from rural areas, tend to have fairly low levels of education and professional training and skills. The third factor and probably the most important factor is the strong desire of the various agencies and bureaus of higher authorities to maintain and to expand their own sectoral interests and influence, especially their financial interests. It is no coincidence that money-making and fee-collecting township/town government offices have been "verticalized" agencies subject to the jurisdiction of higher authorities. This has caused a major loss of revenue for township/town governments in China. The "verticalization" of money-making agencies and organizations has also created disharmony and animosity between *kuai kuai* officials and *tiao tiao* officials due to the fact that the latter tend to make more money than the former.

Officially, *tiao tiao* governmental offices at the township/town level are under the dual jurisdiction and administration of the county government and the township/town government, as reflected in the following relationships:

1   the township/town Communist Party committee is in charge of the Party affairs of the *tiao tiao* governmental offices at the township/town level;
2   the professional and technical affairs of the *tiao tiao* governmental offices at the township/town level are the responsibility of the corresponding county government bureaus;
3   the county government, in consultation with the township/town government, has authority over personnel matters of the *tiao tiao* governmental offices at the township/town level;
4   the *tiao tiao* governmental offices at the township/town level should conduct their work in cooperation with the township/town government.

But in reality, the current *tiao kuai* system at the township/town level is seen as "*tiao tiao* dictatorship." The *tiao tiao* governmental offices at the township/town level are simply out of the reach of the township/town government. Such a relationship between the township/town government and the *tiao tiao* governmental offices at the township/town level significantly reduces the authority and effectiveness of the township/town government as a policy-implementation body. If the township/town government needs the cooperation of the *tiao tiao* governmental offices at the township/town level, it either has to directly beg the *tiao tiao* governmental offices or has to ask for help from the county government, which may direct the request to the appropriate county bureau(s) for action. As a result, township/town government officials have to spend much time and energy in dealing with the various *tiao tiao* governmental offices at the township/town level and the bureaus at the county level. Township/town government officials often complain that on the one hand they have to implement unpopular policies made by the *tiao tiao* and rarely get credit for doing so, while on the other hand, they themselves are blamed and criticized should the policies fail or if the policies are unpopular among the peasants.[39] Conversely, *tiao tiao* governmental offices at the township/town level also need the cooperation and goodwill of the township/town government in carrying out their work in the township or town. If they fail to obtain the cooperation of the township/town government, they can only go to the county government through the county government bureaus to influence the township/town government.

Another drawback of the *tiao tiao* and *kuai kuai* governmental system at the township/town level is the conflicting policies formulated and carried out by the various *tiao tiao* governmental offices due to the fact that these policies are often based on narrow departmental interests and with little or no coordination among the various agencies at the county level. The township/town government is supposed to be the chief policy coordinator at the township/town level. But due to its lack of authority, the township/town government often fails in fulfilling that role. This contributes further to the bureaucratic bickering and red tape at township/ town level. In addition, the current *tiao tiao* and *kuai kuai* governmental system at the township/town level weakens the policy-monitoring ability by the township/ town government over the *tiao tiao* governmental offices for two reasons. First, the township/town government does not have formal and real controlling authority over the *tiao tiao* governmental offices at the township/town level. Second, the township/town government is often reluctant to report any irregularities by the *tiao tiao* governmental offices to the county government for fear of retaliation by the latter in the form of non-cooperation in the future. As a result, the *tiao tiao* governmental offices at the township/town level tend to become independent "kingdoms" since the county government finds it impossible to monitor them closely due to the large number of these offices and their physical distance from the county government.

County government finance

Fiscal relations are a major aspect of the relationship and a thorny issue between the central government and local governments and between various levels of local governments in China. Financial and fiscal relations between different governmental authorities in China are not easy to follow. Much has been written on the declining ability of the central government to collect taxes and the decreasing fiscal power of the center over localities in China during the reform period.[40] Using their newly found financial and economic power, local authorities in China are said to have built a "dukedom economy" (*zhuhou jingji*).[41] However, fiscal and financial relations at the local level, including county and township/town level, have not been written widely about by Western scholars.[42] But financial relations between the central government and local authorities and the financial situation at county and township/town levels are key factors in explaining county and township/town Party and government officials' behavior and policies.

County governments are financed primarily comes from two sources: intra-budgetary and extra-budgetary revenues.[43] The former refers to state-allocated or state-approved funds for the county government, while extra-budgetary revenues consist of additional income accrued to the county government. Prior to the reform era, the county government each year negotiated a packet of revenue and expenditure targets with the higher authorities. After the targets were set, the county government was left with little autonomy to make changes to the budget or to decide how the money was spent. In the early 1980s, a financial contract system (*caizheng baogan*) was introduced, in which each county, depending on its level of economic development, was contracted to hand over a fixed amount of revenue to the higher authorities. Any additional revenues generated by the county government was kept and spent by the county government. This new system produced mixed results for the central and local governments. On the one hand, it provided strong incentives for the county government to generate more revenue and to spend it on local economic development. On the other hand, however, this financial contract system prevented the central government from maximizing its benefits from the rapid economic growth at local level and contributed to the budget shortfalls of the central government.

To strengthen its fiscal capability, the central government changed the financial rules of the game once again in 1994 by the adoption of a new separate tax system or *fen shui zi* for the central government and the local government. Under the new system, which is often referred to as "eating in separate kitchens" (*fen zao chi feng*), the central government is responsible for collecting state taxes (*guo shui*) and the local government is authorized to collect local taxes (*di shui*). State taxes primarily consist of value-added tax on industrial products and consumption tax. To provide an incentive for the county government to help collect state taxes, the county is allowed to retain 25 percent of the state taxes for itself. County local taxes, which the county government is entitled to keep, include sales tax, local enterprise income tax, contract tax, animal slaughter tax, agricultural tax, special agricultural produce tax, etc.[44]

This change in the tax system has had a significant negative impact on the finances of most county governments in China.[45] A major source of income for the county government has been the county-run state-owned industrial enterprises (*xianji guoying* or *difang guoying*). Under the new separate tax system, value-added tax, which is a state tax, is guaranteed as long as the industrial enterprise continues to exist regardless of its profitability, while the collection of enterprises' income tax by the county government is not guaranteed and depends heavily on the profitability of the enterprise. County government officials often are reluctant to levy too heavy a tax on enterprise incomes for fear of reducing incentives. Also, profitability of county-run state enterprises has declined sharply since the 1990s.[46] As a result, county government revenues in many places slid in the 1990s.

The other important source of county government income comes from extra-budgetary revenues composed primarily of ad hoc fees of various kinds and forced collection of funds (*ji zi*) for specific projects. Partly due to the decline of county governments' intra-budgetary revenues, county governments have intensified their efforts since 1994 to expand their extra-budgetary revenues, which has been a main reason for the widespread practice of excessive fee collection (*luan shoufei*) in rural China. A specific fee collection quota is often assigned to each county bureau. If the quota is met, the bureau chief and deputy chiefs are awarded a generous bonus (out of their own bureau budget). If they fail to meet the quota, the bureau chief and deputy chiefs are punished by a fine.

Table 8.5 illustrates one county's tax and fee collection system with monetary rewards and fines. Several points are worth noting. First of all, as Table 8.5 indicates, the assigned amounts of money to the county bureaus vary significantly depending upon their ability to raise money or fees. Profitable and economic-oriented bureaus such as the Economic and Trade bureau and the Enterprise Management bureau were apparently given much larger quotas. But even purely service-oriented bureaus such as Education and Culture and Civil Affairs could not escape their responsibility. Second, the monetary reward also differed significantly. The highest monetary reward (3,200 yuan for the Agricultural Equipment bureau chief) was more than ten times of that of the lowest (300 yuan for deputy bureau chiefs of the Investment Bureau). There seem to be two factors in determining the size of the reward for county bureau cadres. The first is the absolute amount they handed over to the county government and the second is how much more they collected over their assigned quota. For example, the chief of the Education and Culture bureau was given a bigger bonus than his counterparts in some comparable bureaus because he handed over 218,000 yuan, more than nine times of his assigned amount. Third, a number of bureaus failed to fulfill their quota. As a result, their chiefs and deputy chiefs had to pay a sizeable amount in fines.

Conclusion

Local Chinese officials' behavior and policy implementation at the county level are significantly affected by the institutional arrangements of county government and relationships between the county government and its superior and subordinate authorities, i.e. the dominance of the local Party committee and its secretary, the "hollowing out" of the local government and the disadvantageous financial position of the county government. The exclusive Communist Party rule personified in the dominant rule of the Party secretary and the lack of func-

Table 8.5 Rewards and penalties for tax/fee collection in S County, Hebei Province (1997)

County government bureaus	Assigned amount	Completed amount	Reward for bureau chief	Reward for vice bureau chiefs	Penalty for bureau chief	Penalty for vice bureau chiefs
Education/culture	24,000[a]	218,000	800	600		
Investment	13,000	87,000	500	300		
Construction	94,000	252,000	1,100	800		
Material supplies	230,000	567,300	2,000	1,400		
Agricultural equipment	500,000	1,030,000	3,200	2,200		
Agriculture	15,000	26,700	500	400		
Food	121,000	193,100	800	600		
Transportation	640,000	763,300	2,600	1,800		
Civil affairs	20,000	23,000	500	400		
Fertilizer supplies	102,000	103,000	700	400		
Commerce	206,000	205,400			500	300
Economics/trade	3,084,000	1,830,000			2,600	1,700
Enterprise management	1,749,000	838,200			2,000	1,900
Planning	132,000	60,000			500	200
Fuel supplies	315,000	270,700			2,000	1,300
Management Co.	224,000	119,000			500	200

Source: Adapted from Zhang Jing, Jiceng zhengquan: xiangcun zhidu zhuwenti (Grassroots Government: Problems in Towns and Villages) (Hengzhou, China: Zhejiang People's Press, 2000), pp. 152–153.

Note
a All in Chinese yuan.

tional differences among the various branches of governmental authority at the county and township/town levels make it easier for the Party secretary to establish an "independent kingdom" which leads to policy neglect and distortion, corruption and cheating by local officials due to lack of effective supervision. However, the power of the Party secretary has been reduced in recent years by the increasing number of local governmental units being turned into *tiao tiao* organizations administered by higher governmental authorities. The "hollowing out" of the local governments leads to lack of policy coordination and ineffective and incoherent policy implementation. The recent experiment of putting the county government under the administration of the provincial government, though promising, is fraught with challenges and problems.

The most pressing issue facing Chinese local governments is a lack of funding due to the increasingly bloated local bureaucracy, the financial relationship between the central and local governments and arbitrary mandates from Beijing. Local officials at county and township/town levels are being forced to find the resources to support their increasingly bloated bureaucracies while at the same time having to meet the central government's demand that they reduce taxation and fees levied on the rural population. Due to the lack of effective supervision and sanction by higher authorities, county and township/town officials often opt for increasing taxes and fees. Currently over 80 percent of county and township/town budgets goes to employees' salaries and benefits. The lack of financial resources has seriously undermined the local governments' ability to promote economic development and social welfare caretaker for the local population. Excessive fee collection has also become the most direct factor in sparking rural resentment and protests, a major form of social instability in the PRC.

Notes

1 See *Zhonguo tongji nianjian 2000* [*China Statistical Yearbook 2000*] (Beijing, China: China Statistics Press, 2000), p. 3.
2 See Diao Tianding, *Zhongguo difang guojia jigou gaiyao* [*An Overview of China's Local Government Organs*] (Beijing, China: China Law Press, 1989), p. 259.
3 See Zhao Baoxu, Cao Wenguang, Zhu Changnian and Song Lijuan, eds, *Xingzheng jigou gaige toushi* [*An Analysis of Administrative Organizational Reform*] (Suzhou, China: Suzhou University Press, 1998), p. 68.
4 See Wu Peilun and Qian Qizhi, eds, *Difang jigou gaige sikao* [*Reflections of Local Administrative Reform*] (Beijing, China: Reform Press, 1992), p. 120.
5 Due to a mutual agreement, I should keep the county's name anonymous.
6 Ren Jie and Liang Ling, *Gongheguo jigou gaige yu bianqian* [*Reform and Evolution of the Republic's Organs*] (Beijing, China: Huawen Press, 1998), p. 142.
7 Baoxu *et al.*, *Xingzheng jigou gaige toushi*, p. 65.
8 Ibid.
9 Bai Yihua, *Zhongguo jicheng zhengquan de gaige yu tansuo* [*Reform and Exploration of China's Governance at Grassroots Level*] (Beijing, China: China Social Press, 1995), p. 782.
10 Baoxu *et al.*, *Xingzheng jigou gaige toushi*, p. 65.
11 See Yihua, *Zhongguo jicheng zhengquan de gaige yu tansuo*, p. 791.
12 On the three meetings, see Tianding, *Zhongguo difang guojia jigou gaiyao*, pp. 289–290.

13 Wang Guoyi, *Xianji dangzheng lingdao banzi jianshi jianlun* [*A Brief Discussion of Development of County Party and Government Leadership Group*] (Hangzhou, China: Hangzhou People's Press, 1996), p. 42.

14 A new CCP Central Party Committee's circular in 2006 requires significant reduction of number of deputy party secretaries. Some provinces such as Hebei, Anhui, Fujian, Ningxi and Hainan have decided to appoint only three deputy party secretaries. See http://news.tom.com, accessed April 10, 2006.

15 Deng Xiaoping, "On the Reform of the System of Party and State Leadership," in *Selected Works of Deng Xiaoping (1975–1982)* (Beijing, China: Foreign Language Press, 1984), p. 302.

16 See Jean Oi, *Rural China Takes Off* (Berkeley: University of California Press, 1999), pp. 11–14.

17 See Suisheng Zhao, "China's Central–Local Relationship: A Historical Perspective," in Jia Hao and Lin Zhimin, eds, *Changing Central–Local Relations in China* (Boulder, CO: Westview Press, 1994), pp. 19–34.

18 During the trial, the county officials were also found guilty of committing bribery to the tune of millions of yuan. This further highlights the breakdown of the oversight and supervision system over local officials in China. See www.duoweinews.com, accessed June 5, 2002.

19 See *Zhonghua renmin gongheguo difang geji renmin daibiao dahui he difang geji renmin zhengfu zuzhifa* [*Organic Laws of Local People's Congresses and Local People's Governments of the People's Republic of China*] (Beijing, China: Law Press, 1995), pp. 45–47.

20 For a comprehensive overview of local election regulations and procedures, see *Difang xuanju chaozuo guicheng* [*Local Election Procedures*] (Beijing, China: Law Press, 1992).

21 Tianding, *Zhongguo difang guojia jigou gaiyao*, p. 276.

22 On the problems of local people's congresses in China, see Zhao Baoxu, *Zhongguo zhengzhi tizhi gaige wenti yanju: mingzhu zhengzhi yu difang renda* [*Reform of Chinese Political System: Democracy and Local People's Congresses*] (Xian, China: Shanxi People's Publishing House, 1990). On some of the changes in the power and authority of the National People's Congress and provincial people's congresses in China, see Kevin O'Brien, "China's National People's Congress: Reform and its Limits," *Legislative Studies Quarterly*, Vol. 13, No. 3 (August 1988), pp. 343–374; and Ming Xia, "China's National People's Congress: Institutional Transformation in the Process of Regime Transition (1978–98)," *Journal of Legislative Politics*, Vol. 4, No. 4 (Winter 1998), pp. 103–130, and "Political Contestation and the Emergence of the Provincial People's Congress as Power Players in Chinese Politics: A Network Explanation," *Journal of Contemporary China*, No. 24 (2000), pp. 185–214.

23 Personal Interview File 9806041.

24 See Baoxu, *Zhongguo zhengzhi tizhi gaige wenti yanju: mingzhu zhengzhi yu difang renda*, p. 177.

25 Ibid., p. 277.

26 See Yang Zhong, "Political Culture in the Chinese Countryside: Some Empirical Evidence," conference paper delivered at the 97th American Political Science Association Annual Meeting, San Francisco, CA, August 30–September 2, 2001, p. 4.

27 Only the three centrally administered cities at the time, i.e. Beijing, Shanghai and Tianjin, and five provinces, Liaoning, Jiangsu, Guangdong, Fujian and Hainan, did not have prefectural administrative offices. See *Zhongguo tongji nianjian 2000*, p. 3, and Wu Peilun and Qian Qizhi, *Difang jigou gaige sikao* [*Understanding Local Administrative Reforms*] (Beijing, China: Gaige Press, 1992), pp. 95–96.

28 Wu Yue, *Lun diqu xingzheng jigou de yanbian qushi* [*On the Evolution of Prefecture Administration*], in Diao Tianding, Chen Jialing and Zhang Houan, eds, *Zhongguo*

difang guojia jigou yanjiu [*An Study of Chinese Local Governing Organs*] (Beijing, China: Qunzhong Press, 1985), p. 127.

29 See Peilun and Qizhi, *Difang jigou gaige sikao*, p. 91.

30 On the expansion of the prefecture office between the 1950s and 1980s, see Yue, *Lun diqu xingzheng jigou de yanbian qushi*, pp. 133–136.

31 Ren Xiao, *Zhongguo xingzheng gaige* [*China's Administrative Reform*] (Hangzhou, China: Zhejiang People's Press, 1998), p. 292.

32 See Xie Qingkuei, Xiao Yang and Yan Jirong, *Dangdai zhongguo zhengfu* [*The Contemporary Government of the People's Republic of China*] (Shenyang, China: Liaoning People's Press, 1996), p. 301, and Peilun and Qizhi, *Difang jigou gaige sikao*, p. 97.

33 See *Xinjingbao*, March 11, 2006, p. A10.

34 Ibid.

35 Ibid.

36 www.chinesenewsnet.com/MainNews'Forums/BackStage/2006_3_29_3_8.

37 See Li Xueju, Wang Zhenyao and Tang Jinsu, *Xiang zhen zhengquan de xiangshi yu gaige* [*The Reality and Reform of Township and Town Governments*] (Beijing, China: China Social Press, 1994), p. 39.

38 See Li Kang, *Zhongguo nongcun jiceng shequ zuzhi jianshe xin tansuo* [*A New Investigation of China's Basic Rural Level Organizational Developments*] (Beijing, China: China Science and Technology Press, 1992), pp. 136–137.

39 Ibid., pp. 177–178.

40 See, for example, Wang Shaoguang and Hu Angang, *Report on China's State Capacity* (Hong Kong: Oxford University Press, 1994).

41 Shen Liren and Dai Yuanchen, "Formation of 'Dukedom Economics' and their Causes and Effects," *Chinese Economic Studies*, Vol. 25, No. 4 (Summer 1992), pp. 6–24.

42 Excellent discussions of fiscal and financial relations between the central government and local governments and between local governments are found in Marc Blecher and Vivienne Shue, *Tethered Deer: Government and Economy in a Chinese County* (Stanford, CA: Stanford University Press, 1996), pp. 46–91; and Jean Oi, *Rural China Takes Off: Institutional Foundations of Economic Reform* (Berkeley: University of California Press, 1999), pp. 17–57.

43 I do not include the fiscal relationships between *tiao tiao* units in the county and township/town governments since their finances are largely out of the control of the county and township/town governments.

44 For a complete list of central and local taxes, see Oi, *Rural China Takes Off: Institutional Foundations of Economic Reform*, p. 217.

45 See Zhao Yang and Zhou Feizhou, *Nongmin fudan he caishuo tizhi* [*Peasants' Burdens and Rural Finance*], *Hong Kong Journal of Social Sciences*, No. 17 (Autumn 2000), pp. 74–76.

46 Ibid., p. 75.

9 Institutional barriers to the development of civil society in China

Zengke He

The formal and informal rules which dictate citizens' activities when they are creating and running a civil organization make up the institutional environment of civil society. These rules have both positive and negative effects; the latter can be described as institutional barriers. In contemporary China, these institutional barriers include the dual approval requirement in the registration of civil organizations; the dual responsibility system for supervising and managing civil organizations; annual checks and examinations; and report requirements. These institutional barriers create many problems for civil organizations throughout the whole process of their development. They affect the role civil organizations can play, the financial resources available to them, their access to skills and knowledge, their access to skilled and talented people, and their ability to gain the trust of society. The institutional requirements for civil society are designed with the aim of controlling and restricting civil organizations, with a view to maintaining the political regime and political stability.

Furthermore, the "civil society versus the state" mindset of party cadres and officials, and even of many ordinary citizens, contributes to the existence of such institutional barriers. In order to reach the goal of a harmonious socialist society, it will be necessary to change the old political attitudes and orientations. In this sense, the development of civil society in China depends on a shift toward a view which sees the relationship between the state and society as a partnership. An "empowering state" is needed to improve the institutional environment of civil society, to encourage the development of the non-state sector through empowering civil organizations and paying more attention to the latter's capacity building.

The institutional environment of civil society plays a key role in the development of civil society: a suitable institutional environment can promote the smooth development of civil society, while an unsuitable one can hamper it and lead quickly to confrontation between the state and civil organizations. The institutional barriers of civil society are those negative factors within the institutional environment that impede the development of civil society and its organizations. The purpose of this chapter is to discuss the improvement of the institutional environment and the ways in which it can promote the smooth development of civil society in China. It also looks at ways in which an improved institutional environment could help to promote harmony and cooperation between the state and civil society.

The structural weaknesses of China's civil society

Generally speaking, the institutional environment has become more favorable to the development of China's civil society since 1978, when China implemented the policy of reform and opening up to the outside world. Market-oriented economic reform and the transformation of government functions have provided the social space necessary for the development of civil organizations. At the same time, the development of the private sector and a new interest in China from transnational corporations and international NGOs provide enormous resources for the development of civil organizations. As a result, the number of civil organizations in China has grown rapidly. According to the official statistics, there were only 4,446 registered civil organizations in 1989, but by 2003 the number had reached 266,612, showing an annual growth rate of 34 percent during this period.[1]

According to more recent statistics, by the end of 2005 there were 168,000 various social associations, 146,000 private non-enterprise organizations, and 999 foundations.[2] Scholars have pointed out that a large number of associations are left uncounted if we just look at those associations which are officially registered and private non-enterprise organizations. According to their interpretation of the statistics, by 2003, there were 142,000 registered social organizations; 250,000 registered private non-enterprise organizations; 40,000 non-registered associations; 25,000 non-registered private non-enterprise organizations; 5,378,424 grassroots-level Trade Union branches, Communist Youth Leagues, and Women's Federations; 1,338,220 quasi-governmental organizations such as the China Disabled Federation, the China Association of Family Planning, and the China Federation of Literature and Arts; and 758,700 various grassroots-level organizations such as student associations, community entertainment associations, house owner committees, and associations formed through the Internet. Based on the above data, they concluded that the total number of various civil associations came to 8,031,344.[3] Other scholars suggest counting various urban and rural mass self-governance organizations as community organizations and including them in this total. According to statistics from the Ministry of Civil Affairs, by the end of 2004 there were 78,000 neighborhood committees and 644,000 villager committees, totaling an extra 722,000 civil organizations.[4] After adding the above types of organization to the total number of registered associations and private non-enterprise organizations, Wang Shaoguang believed that the total number of various civil associations had reached 8,802,343 by 2003. Although a variety of different methods have been used to achieve the statistics above, which are as such not completely reliable, it is clear that the number of civil organizations in China is rising rapidly and that, just as Wang pointed out, "China is indeed a part of global associational revolution."[5]

On the other hand, there are still a lot of factors within the institutional environment of civil society that are detrimental to the development of civil organizations. These negative institutional functions cause structural weaknesses within China's civil organizations, such as an inability to grow and expand, a shortage of funds, low capacity, low efficiency, and poor internal management. These civil organizations have not been able to fully develop the five basic features of a civil organization. A civil organization must be: organizational, non-governmental, non-profit, autonomous, and voluntary. Thus, many civil associations in China have only managed to achieve the status of transitional organizations.

We will now look at the five attributes of a civil organization, beginning with the organizational function. The stringent requirements for registration have limited the development of civil organizations. The number of civil organizations owned per 10,000 people in China is 1.45, but the same number in France own 110.45. This figure is 51.79 in the United States, 12.66 in Brazil, 10.21 in India, and 2.44 in Egypt,[6] all of which, as you can see, are higher than in China. The number of civil organizations per head in China is too low, and most of those existing organizations are local and grassroots, and their activities have only a narrow scope. According to one report by the NGO Institute of Tsinghua University, among those civil organizations investigated, 68.7 percent of them engage in activities within the limitation of one county, county-level city, or district, 8.6 percent of them within the border of one province, and only 1.1 percent of them have engaged in activities within the limitation of two or more provinces.[7] This could be due to the strict limitations on the regional scope of civil organizations in China. Most civil organizations are very small. One inquiry by the Center of China's Associations of Peking University on Zhejiang and Beijing finds that 60 percent of civil organizations have fewer than 1,000 members.[8] Another investigation by Tsinghua University finds that in 1998 more than 90 percent of civil non-profit organizations had an annual expenditure of less than 500,000RMB Yuan, and 5 percent less than 1,000RMB Yuan, while only 2 percent had an annual expenditure of more than 1,000,000RMB Yuan.[9] This reflects the current weakness of civil organizations in China.

Second, we will consider the non-governmental aspect of civil organizations. Most civil organizations in China depend on the government and various affiliated organizations for the necessary personnel, funds, and offices, and thus they have much in common with government-run organizations. The investigation by Tsinghua University indicated that 46.6 percent of civil non-profit organizations in China are provided with office space by their affiliated organizations, 31.9 percent of them have their own office space, 8 percent of them have to rent office space, and 1.7 percent of them have to work in their leader's home or a member's apartment. The same investigation finds that there are only 4.6 percent non-profit organizations with full-time staff, and the rest of them have 1–40 part-time members of staff. Even those non-profit organizations without full-time staff have their own part-time staff, which reflects the fact that many civil organizations are closely associated with government agencies.[10] The same investigation also finds that, of the total income of non-profit organizations in

1998, financial appropriation and subsidy by the government accounted for 49.97 percent, project funds from the government accounted for 3.58 percent, membership fees accounted for 21.18 percent, and business income accounted for 6.0 percent. Overall, civil organizations' income depends heavily on financial appropriation and subsidy from the government.[11]

Third, we will consider the non-profit and public benefit functions of civil organizations. Scholars have categorized the national associations according to their functions and found that academic associations account for 48 percent, industrial management associations for 28 percent, entertainment and sports associations for 11 percent, various interest-representing associations for 6 percent, while public welfare and service associations only account for 6 percent.[12] Among 48 interest-representing national associations, there are 27 associations serving "superior groups" (socially and financially powerful people), 17 associations serving "medium groups" (the middle classes), and only four associations serving disadvantaged groups of people. This is largely due to the very strict registration requirements for associations (there are political requirements, financial requirements, and a required minimum number of members), and only financially and politically powerful groups can meet these requirements.[13] According to the latest statistics from the Ministry of Civil Affairs, within 142,121 associations, there are 41,722 trade unions, 40,325 professional associations, 37,401 academic associations, 19,640 cooperative associations, and 2,079 miscellaneous associations.[14] All of the above types of association are "mutually beneficial" associations, while public welfare and service associations account for only a small percentage. As regards private non-enterprise units, within 124,000 registered units, there are 62,776 educational organizations, 26,795 health organizations, 9,037 labor organizations, 7,792 civil affairs organizations, 4,522 science and technological organizations, 2,811 cultural organizations, 2,682 sports organizations, 1,777 social service organizations, 728 legal service organizations, and 5,571 other organizations. Though private non-enterprise units are defined as non-profit organizations engaging in public service, the Act to Promote Private Education by the Chinese government publicly encourages the capital providers of privately run educational institutes to gain reasonable investment returns, while they enjoy preferential treatment in tax and some other aspects for public service industries. Other industrial statutes have had similar articles. Private non-enterprise units have a strong tendency to profit-seek, while they enjoy more preferential treatment in tax than other enterprises. The result is that, even if the government liquidates private non-enterprise units several times, they still continue to grow very fast. This reflects to some extent the weakness of the existing institutional arrangements and policies for the management of civil organizations.

Fourth, we will consider the degree to which civil organizations are autonomous. Many case studies find that civil organizations in China are not very autonomous at all. Based on questionnaire data covering associational organizations in Beijing, Zhejiang and Heilongjiang, scholars have carried out a quantitative analysis of the influence of the Chinese Communist Party and government on civil organizations.[15] The study indicates that most associations are sponsored by their affiliated authorities, and their purpose is to let these associations assist the affiliated organizations in fulfilling management tasks; that the laws and policies of the ruling party and government have a strong constraining force; and that the affiliated organizations play a larger part than the associations themselves in managing the daily operation of the associations. These affiliated organizations influence associations in various ways: by recommending association leaders, attending association meetings, taking part in association activities, examining and approving the annual work and financial reports of associations, and by dispatching staff to the associations, who usually fill important positions. The ruling party and government also influence associations by building party branches and appointing party or government officials as association leaders. As a result, the degree of associational autonomy is very low, and many associations have the bureaucratic characteristics of pursuit administrative ranks and treatment and seeking for administrative power. One study by the NGO Institute of Tsinghua University indicates that, among all the investigated non-profit organizations, less than 30 percent were non-profit organizations who elected their leaders democratically, while nearly two-thirds of cadres are either appointed by an affiliated organization or nominated by their leaders and then approved by an affiliated organization. Power over the appointment of personnel is the main way in which affiliated organizations control non-profit organizations,[16] and thus weaken the latter's autonomy. Private non-enterprise units have gained more control over internal affairs, such as personnel appointment, than associations and foundations.

Fifth, we will consider the degree to which voluntary work contributes to civil organizations. Many investigations have indicated that donations and volunteer workers, essential for the daily operation of civil organizations, are lacking in China. According to one study, there are only just over 100 charities in the country, charitable contributions account for less than 1 percent of GDP, and the total funds controlled by these charities account for less than 0.1 percent of GDP. Contributions are usually made in response to calls from the government and very rarely are voluntary contributions made regularly.[17] In addition, according to the same study by NGO Institute of Tsinghua University, when the revenues of non-profit organizations are broken down into their component parts, 5.63 percent of the income comes from enterprise contributions and project funds (ranked as the fourth income source) and income from donations accounts for only 2.18 percent (ranked as the seventh income source). Meanwhile, among the non-profit organizations that answered the questionnaire, 34.4 percent of them said that they have no volunteers, 17.5 percent of them have one to four volunteers, and only 18.3 percent of them have more than 40 volunteers. On average, each volunteer contributes 4.45 days per month.[18] This indicates that donations and volunteer work are still at very low levels in China. This is caused by the lack of incentives from institutions and policies for civil organization administration which might attract voluntary donations and workers. It also reflects the limitations of the current Act of Public Welfare Donation.

Institutional barriers faced by Chinese civil organizations

The development of civil society in China faces serious institutional barriers due to a highly restrictive administrative system. Specifically, the current institutional environment presents eight distinct problems for the development of civil organizations in China. It is worth highlighting these problems.

First, there is the problem of registration. The large number of requirements to be met by civil organizations seeking registration keeps costs high, making a huge number of civil organizations unwilling to register. They then lack legitimacy and exist outside the legal supervision system. Scholars carried out small field studies in Anhui province and Shenzhen city based on samples of towns and townships, and they found that registered civil organizations only account for one-twelfth to one-twentieth of the total number of associations, while registered private non-enterprise units only account for one-tenth to one-twelfth of the total number. These figures are much lower than those identified by the local officials.[19] Taking the example of rural professional economic associations, when the Ministry of Civil Affairs held the "National Conference for Developing Rural Professional Economic Associations" in 2004, there were 100,000 rural professional economic associations nationwide, but there were only 10,000 registered in civil affairs departments at different levels of government. It should be pointed out that this was the situation one year after civil affairs departments in these places simplified the registration procedures and lowered the requirements. Those civil organizations that fail to register face a problem with legitimacy, because they do not have approval and belong to "illegal" organizations. On the other hand, civil affairs departments also face the problem of administration. It would be a difficult task to ban so many non-registered civil organizations. However, it will also have a negative impact on legal civil organizations if the government allows "illegal" civil organizations to exist beyond the supervision of the rules and policies of civil organization management. Needless to say, the situation weakens the authority of civil organization management bodies.

Second, there is the question of the role played by civil organizations. Many civil organizations such as academic societies and trade societies have a strong tendency toward bureaucratization, and some of them even become like "second governments". There are private non-enterprise organizations which seek profits and evade tax. They often become a kind of enterprise or business. The role civil organizations should play in China is still not defined and no boundary yet exists between civil and other organizations.

Third, civil organizations have minimal access to talented personnel. They are not able to attract talented staff due to various factors such as low salaries, bad office conditions, and a lack of potential for career development. This lack of talent greatly limits the capacity and influence of civil organizations.

Fourth, there is the problem of funding. Funding from the government, enterprises, and international foundations is insufficient. The government procurement system focuses mainly on enterprises rather than non-profit organizations.

There are also no well-defined tax-exemption regulations for enterprise donations, and it is notoriously difficult to establish and operate private foundations.

Fifth, knowledge and skills are in short supply for civil organizations. They lack the capacity for proper professional training, feasible development strategies, and professional knowledge. There is a lack of support from the government in this area also.

Sixth, there is the problem of trust. The public does not trust civil organizations since some organizations lack self-disciplinary mechanisms, have low social credit and poor transparency. Many civil organizations engage in activities such as graft and embezzlement, and their leaders abscond with money. Local government officials often distrust civil organizations, and they often believe that civil organizations are against the ruling party and the state and that a strong civil society will lead to a weak state. Therefore, they tend to restrain the development of civil organizations. Even members of civil organizations sometimes distrust their leaders as their internal affairs are not democratically managed.

Seventh, there is the problem of participation. Civil organizations and their members are enthusiastic about participating in political life, but they only have one major channel through which to voice their opinions and suggestions, their affiliated authorities. Since civil organizations often depend on their affiliated organizations, the latter pays no serious attention to opinions and suggestions from the organizations they control.

Finally, there is the question of supervision. Registering (administrative) agencies place an emphasis on entry administration and thus often overlook the process management of civil organizations' activities. Furthermore, the affiliated organizations like to intervene in the internal affairs of civil organizations. The dual leadership system often leads to a situation where no department is accountable. Taxation departments should play an important part in supervising civil organizations, but their role is still very limited. The judicial system plays no role in managing civil organizations. Consequently, although administrative regulations are very detailed, their actual effects are very limited. Meanwhile, civil organizations experience too much administrative intervention and thus find it difficult to operate.

If one compares international practice in the management of civil organizations with the management of civil organizations in China, it is not difficult to see where the institutional barriers that Chinese civil organizations face originate.

First, there is the dual permit system for registering civil organizations. The first permit is issued by affiliated organizations (supervision bodies) on approval of the organization and the second permit by registering administrative agencies. There are thus numerous entrance requirements from each permit-issuing body for the civil organizations. There is no judicial remedy when these supervision bodies refuse to perform their duties of examination and approval. It is undoubtedly unfair to force civil organizations to seek permits from supervision bodies while no criterion or time limit for the examination and approval procedure has been stipulated. Moreover, the many societies which are unable to get permits from their supervision bodies do not legally exist. This type of regulation goes against citizens' Constitutional right to freedom of association. Extremely stringent registration requirements are unfavorable to the development of civil organizations.

A second problem with the dual supervision system is that it wastes valuable government resources. Registering administrative agencies and supervision bodies often undertake identical tasks, such as the examination of registration applications, annual checks, and the investigation of illegal behavior. There is no division of labor or division of responsibilities between the two departments. Consequently, they often blame one another when responsibility needs to be allocated.

Third, the supervision bodies intervene directly and comprehensively with the internal affairs of civil associations, weakening their autonomy. Civil associations are dependent on their supervision bodies since the latter control all the important activities of the associations such as political education, personnel recommendation and management, financial management, and external activities. The power of supervision bodies to recommend leaders for civil associations is not conducive to the democratic management and self-governance of civil organizations.

Another major institutional barrier to the development of civil organizations in China is the non-competition principle. The principle of non-competition between civil organizations and the limitation of cross-regional activities works against the development of civil organizations because it prevents healthy competition. Based on the principle of non-competition, the registering administrative agency will not give a permit to associations and private non-enterprise units if there are already other organizations engaged in the same or similar businesses. There are also bans on civil organizations setting up regional branches or local representative offices. These regulations are against the competition principle of a market economy and artificially empower some associations and private non-enterprise organizations, putting them in a monopolistic position and reducing their incentive to improve efficiency.

The lack of a system of tax-exemption and a tax supervision system makes it difficult for civil organizations to work on a non-profit principle. The Chinese government focuses on preventing the existence of hostile civil organizations, and there is no effective supervision of civil organizations who engage in profit-seeking activities. Regulations require that civil organizations are audited. However, the organizations have to cover the cost themselves, putting the objectivity and authenticity of the audit in doubt, as they can seek favors from the auditing bodies. Due to the lack of effective supervision, tax-exemption for non-profit organizations, and an information sharing system between registering administrative agencies and taxation bureaus, profit-seeking activities are very common among non-profit organizations in China.

Unfortunately, some of the policies and regulations aimed at promoting the development of civil organizations are not effective. For example, in order to encourage the development of trade unions, government departments often delegate industrial management tasks to Industrial associations. This practice more often than not strengthens the Industrial associations' position as "second governments", preventing trade unions from operating as non-governmental organizations. There are inconsistencies in the regulations which need to be solved. The registration procedures need simplifying, as do the requirements for rural professional economic societies and administrative regulations such as the Registering Administrative Act of Associations. The proportion of pre-tax deduction for donations is too low, at only 3 percent for individuals and 30 percent for firms. Only 25 charities approved by the authorities have the privilege of being able to issue a certificate of tax deduction or exemption for donations. These regulations are preventing the income from donations to civil organizations from increasing. There is no unified taxation law in China. The laws and regulations that encourage and support the development of ten different categories of private non-enterprise units cover preferential tax treatments. Hence, there are too many preferential tax treatments and too many loopholes in the tax collection system. The legal rules that grant investors in non-profit organizations the right to gain investment returns go directly against international norms and conventions which do not allow civil organizations to distribute profits among investors. In addition, the practice that government-sponsored institutions receive more preferential treatments from the government than private non-enterprises is against the smoothly development of the non-profit sector as a whole. It is also against the original intention of the regulations, which was to encourage the development of private non-enterprise organizations.

The rule that civil organizations have to request instructions and submit a report before they engage in important activities and the required annual inspection also act against the development of civil organizations. The pre-review and approval regulations stem from the fact that the government continues to distrust civil organizations. It is common international practice for the judicial system to impose penalties after organizations are involved in illegal activities. This practice both strengthens the accountability and autonomy of civil organizations and reduces confrontation between the government and civil organizations. The annual inspection of private non-enterprise organizations, associations, and foundations in China by both supervision bodies and registering administrative agencies often becomes a formality without any substance. This required procedure takes a great deal of time and energy and has no significance. It could be replaced by evaluations and investigation reports published regularly by non-governmental performance evaluation bodies. Non-governmental performance evaluation bodies could compete with each other, and the competition could lead to the establishment of a scientific and objective evaluation system which could in turn become a strong incentivizing force for civil organizations to improve their performance.

Finally, registering administrative agencies and supervision bodies have too much power of discretion over issues related to the punishment and suspension of civil organizations. The relevant laws and rules are too vague and abstract, and the gap between the upper and lower limits is too big. This undoubtedly enhances the discretionary power of registering agencies and supervision bodies and their staff. In many countries, the decision to abolish or suspend civil organizations is made by the judicial system according to strict judicial procedures, and there are many types of judicial remedy. But in China these decisions are made by various departments of civil affairs, and administrative reconsideration is also performed by the same department. Those civil organizations facing abolishment or suspension have no way of requesting a judicial remedy.

The causes of institutional barriers

The existing policies and laws have the effect of controlling civil organizations through what is called "orientation management". The purpose of this kind of control and management is to prevent the existence of hostile civil organizations which could become a threat to the political order and state security. Faced with the fear that civil organizations could go against the state, the Chinese government tries to prevent civil organizations from engaging in political activities that could undermine social stability and state security. The government does not want to allow what happened in Eastern Europe and some former Soviet republics to take place in China. The maintenance of political stability is given the highest priority when the government designs regulations for civil organizations. The policies and rules aimed at controlling civil organizations are based on the theoretical assumption that a dichotomy exists between the state and civil society. The government's assumption that civil organizations are in opposition to the state often leads the government to regard civil organizations as the enemy. This largely eliminates the possibility that civil society and the state could form a partnership.

The political attitudes of party and government leaders at different levels toward civil organizations are gradually changing. In the 1980s, party and government leaders had largely negative attitudes toward civil organizations. This attitude was enhanced by the 1989 Tiananmen Square protests. After this event, control and containment became the theme of all policies related to civil organizations. After the mid-1990s, with the establishment of the market economy and the transformation of government functions, party, and government leaders began to have a more positive attitude toward civil organizations, and they began to recognize the role that intermediate social organizations played. Consequently, intermediate social organizations were able to develop in a more tolerant environment.

Since the sixteenth party congress in 2002, when the private economy gained legal protection, party and government leaders have had a more positive attitude toward private non-enterprise organizations than ever before, and the environment for the development of such organizations become increasingly friendly. The Fourth Plenary of the sixteenth party congress in 2004 saw the announcement of the goal to build a harmonious socialist society. The plenary defined the roles of the party and government, society and citizens as leadership, corporative partner and participants, respectively, and specified the three positive roles of associations, trade unions, and intermediate social organizations. These were to provide services, to make petitions, and to normalize behaviors. Thanks to this development, the recognition by party and government leaders of the role of civil organizations has deepened. Government policy has begun to move toward the supervision and development of civil organizations. Meanwhile, the party and government have adopted the strategy of treating different types of civil organization differently. The strategy combines selective support with selective restraints. Party and government leaders are more willing to affirm, support, and encourage non-profit and apolitical civil organizations, which include public welfare organizations, community service organizations, rural professional economic and technological associations, charities, and private non-enterprise organizations. Toward those grassroots-level organizations that are needed by society and are politically harmless, such as flower fairs, temple fairs, and elders societies, even when they are not registered with the departments of civil affairs, most local party and government leaders show greater tolerance – they are adopting a "green light" policy. Nevertheless, party and government leaders continue to express their political distrust and have a negative attitude toward those civil organizations with strong political and religious features, specifically those organizations concerned with issues of ethnic groups, religion, social sciences, interdisciplinary subjects of natural sciences, youth, women and children, citizens' rights, and also those with a close link with foreign non-governmental organizations and foundations.

In general, the official attitude toward civil organizations remains contradictory. On the one hand, the government expects civil organizations to play a positive role in helping and assisting the government. On the other hand, due to the influence of the color revolutions in Central Asia, the government fears that civil organizations will become an anti-regime force and eventually challenge the authority of the party and government. In this sense, the government's trust of civil organizations is still very low.

These are the underlying causes of the policies which impose restrictions on civil organizations. These factors could also explain why the government has adopted the strategy of supporting and supervising civil organizations at the same time, with a combination of selective support and selective restraint.

Party and government officials, and indeed many citizens, also lack confidence in civil organizations, and they remain suspicious of their functions. There are historical reasons for this mistrust. Traditionally, civil organizations in China were identical to secret societies, which were usually opposed to the government. This mindset still holds in contemporary China. People tend to trust the ruling party and government more than they trust civil organizations, and many people still think that because civil organizations are non-governmental they could become anti-governmental. For example, during the 2003 SARS crisis, the central government only granted two official charity organizations the right to accept donations. All the other non-profit organizations were forbidden to receive any donations in order to, according to the government, "regulate the donation market". This policy reflects government officials' deeply rooted distrust of non-profit private organizations. According to an investigation by the Center for Women Legal Study and Assistance of Law School at Peking University, many people think that civil organizations are identical to non-governmental organizations and associate them with anarchy, thus believing that such organizations should be prevented from engaging in certain activities. The research indicates that as long as this mindset holds with the Chinese people, they will not accept civil organizations.[20]

However, it is important to point out that as the economy and society develops, along with people's enthusiasm for voluntary associations, emerging civil society organizations are reshaping their images and gradually changing the traditional mindset. Consequently, the degree of public trust of civil organizations is increasing.

Concluding remarks

During the last few decades, the number of civil organizations in China has increased dramatically. There are still a huge number of civil organizations which are not registered with the departments of civil affairs. Civil organizations also have structural weaknesses caused by their small size, shortage of funds, low capacity, poor efficiency, and poor internal management. Both the achievements and weaknesses in the development of civil society are closely linked with the current institutional environment. The policies and administrative rules created to foster the development of civil organizations and a harmonious society are beginning to have a positive effect.

However, there are also factors working against the development of civil organizations. The main problem is that government regulations are often oriented toward containing and controlling civil organizations. These policy orientations are also impeding the realization of the goal to build a harmonious society. The establishment of an enabling and empowering management system[21] aimed at promoting harmony and cooperation between the state and civil society should become the new goal if the institutional environment for civil organizations in China is to be improved.

Notes

1 Administration of Civil Organizations of Ministration of Civil Affairs, "Information on the Development and Management of China's Civil Organizations", *Academic Society*, No. 1, 2005, p. 12.
2 "2005 Statistical Bulletin on the Development of Civil Affairs" on the website of Ministry of Civil Affairs: http://admin.mca.gov.cn/111/gongbao05.htm.
3 Wang Shaoguang and He Jianyu, "China's Associational Revolution: Associational Map of Chinese Citizens", *Zhejiang Academic Journal*, No. 6, 2004, p. 77.
4 "Report on the Statistics of the Development of Civil Affairs in 2004 published by Ministry of Civil Affairs" cited from the website of Ministry of Civil Affairs: www.mca.gov.cn/news/content/recent/2005510114517.html.
5 Shaoguang and Jianyu, "China's Associational Revolution", p. 77.
6 Wang Ming, Liu Guohan and He Jianyu, *Reform of China's Associations: From the*

Choice of Government to the Choice of Society, Beijing: Social Science Literature Press, 2001, p. 105.
7 Deng Guosheng, *Evaluation on the Non-Profit Organizations*, Beijing: Social Science Literature Press, 2001, pp. 43–44.
8 Li Jingpeng, *General Report on the Investigation of Beijing and Zhejiang*, working paper, Beijing: Center for Civil Society, Beijing University, 2005.
9 Deng, *Evaluation on the Non-Profit Organizations*, p. 59.
10 Ibid., pp. 53–54.
11 Ibid., pp. 57–58.
12 Fan Baojun, ed., *A Dictionary of Chinese Associations*, cited from Wang, Liu and He, *Reform of China's Associations*, Beijing: Social Science Academic Press, pp. 114–115.
13 Wang, Liu and He, *Reform of China's Associations*, p. 116.
14 Administration of Civil Organizations of Ministration of Civil Affairs, "Information on the Development and Management".
15 Shen Youjun, "Quantitative Analysis on the Influence of the Ruling Party and Government on Civil Organizations", *Journal of Qiusuo,* No. 1, 2005, pp. 74–75.
16 Deng, *Evaluation on the Non-Profit Organizations*, pp. 54 and 57–58.
17 Ge Daoshun, "Current Situation of and Policy Suggestions for the development of China Charity Course": www.southcn.com/nflr/llwz1/200505250861.html.
18 Deng, *Evaluation on the Non-Profit Organizations*, pp. 54 and 57–58.
19 Xie Haiding, "Legitimacy Dilemma of Chinese Civil Organizations", *Journal of Legal Study*, No. 2, 2004, p. 20.
20 Guo Jianmei, "The Survival and Development of China's Civil Organizations: A Case Study by the Center of Women's Legal Study and Assistance of Beijing University", *Women Study Tribune*, No. 5, 2000, p. 34.
21 Gu Xin, "The Role of the Enabling State: Reform of Government-Sponsored Institutions and Transformation of the Non-Profit Sector", *Academic Journal of Hebei*, Vol. 25, No. 1, 2005, pp. 11–17.

10 Chambers of commerce in Wenzhou

Toward civil society?

Joseph Fewsmith

Throughout the 1980s and 1990s, Wenzhou, the once poor city in southeastern Zhejiang province, spearheaded the development of the private economy.[1] The "Wenzhou model" of family-owned enterprises was widely contrasted with the "Sunan model" (based in southern Jiangsu) of collective enterprises and the "Guangzhou model" of export processing. Given the illegitimacy of the private economy for much of this period, Wenzhou's development was controversial and given little support at the national level. But Wenzhou was a highly populated area with little arable land and that dictated that they find their own path to prosperity.

Local history was an important part in the development of the Wenzhou model. In the revolution, Wenzhou was not taken over by northern armies, as were the cities of southern Jiangsu, but rather by an indigenous Communist movement that had fought in the mountains near the city. The leaders of Wenzhou were thus more sympathetic to private business than leaders elsewhere in China. Given Wenzhou's "front-line" position in any battle in the Taiwan Straits, the central government invested little in the city, contributing to a smaller public sector than in most places. And then there was the very deep local pride in Wenzhou's unique language and culture. Cut off by mountains, Wenzhou dialect developed as a distinct and virtually unintelligible language, incomprehensible even to those living in cities not far away. The uniqueness of Wenzhou's dialect has helped the people together and to cultivate a certain "us against the world" mentality has led those from Wenzhou to form communities when they are away from the city. Finally, Wenzhou has had a long history of entrepreneurship and the export of talent, and these were never completely extinguished. Even during the Cultural Revolution, when others were "cutting off the tails of capitalism," risk-takers from Wenzhou were buying and selling. Contemporary Wenzhou has built on these historical legacies.

Based on these distinct local traditions and the development of private business, Wenzhou, over the past two decades, also pioneered the development of chambers of commerce and other trade associations. The development of business associations both reflect changing state–society relations and raise new questions about the development of "civil society" in China. Wenzhou's associational history has been livelier than anywhere else in China and is therefore worth examining, but one has to be very cautious in generalizing the results. The unique history of the area in the growth of business associations suggests that Wenzhou, rather than being on the forefront of developments likely to spread throughout China, it is an instance of a city that is nearly unique in its social development. Examination of "outliers" is useful because they tend to define the likely limits to the development of "civil society" in China, and it is in that spirit that this chapter looks at the development of business associations in Wenzhou.

Early development

Historically, the first chamber of commerce appeared in Wenzhou in 1906, three years after the Qing dynasty's newly established Ministry of Commerce promulgated regulations encouraging such organizations to exist. Business organization played a prominent role in Wenzhou's economic development, and by 1931, 106 industry associations had joined the chamber. This history remains relevant both as a source of local pride and as a repository of experience that later people have drawn upon. But building on this legacy had to wait. After 1949, and particularly after the Anti-Rightist Movement of 1957, the Wenzhou chamber, like other chambers throughout China, was basically silenced.[2] It was only after reform was inaugurated in late 1978 that this experience became relevant again.

In January 1979, Deng Xiaoping had dinner with five aging members of the former Industrial and Commercial Federation (*gongshanglian*, hereafter ICF) and suggested that they revive the organization. This meeting gave a push to industrial organization, re-establishing the legitimacy of the ICF, both nationally and locally. Wenzhou revived its ICF in 1980. In December 1987, the Secretariat declared that the ICF was a societal (*minjian*) chamber of commerce, and the following year, the National ICF held its sixth annual meeting and revised its bylaws. The new bylaws stated that the Association is a civil group representing people from industry and commerce and handled their internal and external business affairs. The bylaws permitted non-state owned enterprises to join and thus injected a new energy into the federations. In this new atmosphere, the Wenzhou ICF began to revive its subordinate industry associations.

These changes at the national level and the energy apparent at the local level were necessary to establish the legitimacy and policy framework on which the later chambers of commerce would be based. Without them, the chambers could not have emerged. But there was also a desire for organization growing up from below. By the mid-1980s, the city's business leaders had developed good personal relations with Wenzhou political leaders. The groups quickly convinced local government officials that Wenzhou's continued economic development depended on improving quality control, introducing new designs and technologies quickly, and developing a core of skilled workers. In particular, Wenzhou's ICF was convinced that steps had to be taken to reform local industry.

This point was driven home by a famous incident from 1987 when some 5,000 Wenzhou-made shoes were burned in Hangzhou.[3] The incident was a logical outcome of Wenzhou's pattern of development. Wenzhou had developed a reputation not only for hard work and inexpensive goods but also for cheap and fake goods. The scattered nature of Wenzhou's production meant that Wenzhou merchants inevitably tried to out compete with each other, the smaller producers often copying the designs, but not necessarily the quality, of their larger counterparts. The growing reputation for shoddy production threatened the profits of the larger merchants and, at least indirectly, the economic future of Wenzhou. Accordingly, it was the large manufacturers who took the lead in pressing for the organization of the shoe industry.

There is one other point evident in this incident that is important for understanding the development of business association in Wenzhou, namely that the very scattered nature of production meant that policing the industry was beyond the means of government. Either it would be done by the industry itself or it would not be done. So both the government, which had an interest in promoting Wenzhou's economy, but not the means to ensure product quality, and the industry (or at least the industrial leaders), which had an interest in not allowing a reputation for poor quality undermine its profits, looked to industrial organization as a way to promote economic progress.

Accordingly, the shoe industry, directly affected by the 1987 incident, became one of the first industries to organize. In 1988, the Lucheng District Shoe Industry Association (*Lucheng qu xieye xiehui*) came into being. The new association worked closely with the government to draft two regulations – the "Management Regulations on the Rectification of Quality of the Lucheng District Shoe Industry" and the "Provisional Regulations on After Sales Service of the Shoe Industry" – that set standards for quality in the industry. Enforcement became an important task of the new association, and their efforts quickly paid off. Before long Wenzhou-made shoes were once again selling well.[4]

From such modest beginnings, chambers of commerce and trade associations grew quickly. By August 2002, there were 104 such non-governmental business associations at the city level. In addition, there were another 321 associations at the county, county-level municipality, and district levels, with some 42,624 members covering most of Wenzhou's industrial enterprises.[5] Not only has the number of associations grown quickly, the number of enterprises participating in a given association has increased apace. For instance, the Apparel Industry Chamber of Commerce, founded in 1994, originally had only ten members. In 1998, it had 156 members, in 2000 it had 287 members, and at the beginning of 2003 it had 423 members. In the first half of 2003, its membership suddenly jumped to 1,025 enterprises. This jump was due to efforts to reach out to manufacturers of women's and children's clothing; the chamber had originally been organized around older, larger, and more established makers of men's clothing. As membership expanded, the number of leaders grew. In 1994, when the group was established, there was one chairman, two vice chairmen, and seven board members; by 2003, there was one chairman, 22 vice chairmen, 45 members of the board of directors' standing committee, and 121 board members. Obviously, the expansion of the group spurred an effort to include more voices in the chamber's leadership.[6]

Organization and structure

As mentioned above, trade associations and chambers of commerce in Wenzhou were originally nurtured by the Association of Industry and Commerce, also known as the Wenzhou General Chamber of Commerce, and were subordinate to the party's United Front Work Bureau. But at least some of Wenzhou's chambers of commerce – including the Lighting Chamber of Commerce, the Shoe Industry Chamber of Commerce, and the Apparel Chamber of Commerce – were initiated by the enterprises themselves. In this sense, they grew up "outside the system" (*tizhiwai*), though they quickly developed good relations with the ICF.[7] This felicitous arrangement in which the ICF promoted the interests of the chambers of commerce and encouraged their autonomy was dealt a setback in February 2002 when the Ministry of Civil Affairs promulgated the "Notice Re-Confirming the Management Units for Social Groups" (*Guanyu chongxin queren shehui tuanti yewu guanli danwei de tongzhi*). This regulation gave the authority to supervise social groups to 22 departments – but not the ICF.[8] The ostensible reason is that ICFs are societal organizations, not government departments, though the employees of ICFs are cadres on the government's payroll. It seems likely, however, that there was bureaucratic envy and lobbying involved in this decision.

In any event, this regulation caused considerable confusion in Wenzhou. To remedy the situation, local authorities decided that henceforth, newly organized industry associations would be supervised by the city's Economic and Trade Commission and other departments, but allowed those organizations already under the ICF to remain there. This has led to the odd situation in which the Federation of Industry and Commerce supervises 22 "chambers of commerce," the Economic and Trade Commission supervises 31 "trade associations," and other departments supervise still other trade associations.[9]

Relations between chambers of commerce and government

As the above account of the early history of business association in Wenzhou suggests, the relationship between the associations and the government has been close, to the point of collaborating on important regulations. Moreover, as with the shoe association, the ICF has generally worked with the largest manufacturers in establishing associations. For instance, in the case of the Apparel Industry Chamber of Commerce (*Wenzhou fuzhuang shanghui*), perhaps the largest and most successful of the various industry associations in Wenzhou, began with only ten enterprises in the early stages. The lead was taken by Liu Songfu, head of Golden Triangle Enterprise (*Jin sanjiao gongchang*). Although the ICF supported the establishment of the association, it provided no funds; the entire cost of running the association over the first years – some 100,000 rmb – was borne by Liu and a small number of other leaders.[10]

Like other industrial associations, the Apparel Chamber of Commerce maintained very close relationships with political leaders. The deputy head of the

ICF, Wu Ziqin, chaired the first congress of the chamber of commerce, and a number of political leaders were named either honorary board members or senior advisors. The support of the ICF, which became the sponsoring unit (*guakao danwei*) of the new chamber of commerce, was necessary for the chamber's registration, its ability to secure office space, and ability to convince other enterprises to join.[11] The authority of the ICF also supported the chamber's efforts to enhance quality control. Over time, however, relations between trade associations and government have become more (but not completely) institutionalized. Personal relations between association leaders and government leaders remain close, but there has been a tendency for government officials to be less involved in the internal affairs of trade associations. Although the government still appoints a few trade association heads, 77 percent report that they freely elect their chairmen in accordance with their own rules of operation.[12]

Moreover, the internal organization of trade associations – how many directors they have, how many committees they set up, and whether to organize training and consulting activities to raise funds for the association – seems to be free of government interference. Indeed, the fact that Wenzhou's trade associations receive no government funding makes them quite entrepreneurial. In addition to imposing membership dues, trade associations organize training classes to impart technical expertise and provide consulting services to raise funds. They also organize trade group trips abroad so members can learn about industry trends and relay the latest information and technical standards to colleagues back home.

The changing relationship between industry associations and the government may be symbolized by the Apparel Industry Chamber of Commerce. The chamber amended its charter in 2003 to specify that government officials should not be named as advisors. The reorganized Advisory Commission was composed of five prestigious entrepreneurs who had previously served as vice chairmen of the chamber.[13] This change was not an assertion of chamber independence from government supervision so much as a reflection of the government's growing trust that this non-governmental organization (NGO) could run its own affairs without running afoul of government concerns. Elections for leadership roles in chambers are becoming more competitive. The Apparel Industry Chamber of Commerce was the first to introduce *cha'e* elections (in which the number of candidates exceed the number of positions), and others have emulated the practice. Some have borrowed the practice of "sea elections" (*hai xuan*) from village elections, allowing nominations for association head to be nominated freely by members. In 2000, Liu Songfu, who spearheaded the establishment of the Apparel Industry Chamber of Commerce, was defeated by Chen Min, the leader of a new generation of entrepreneurs who have expanded the scope of chamber activities as well as its membership.

As previously noted, Wenzhou's chambers of commerce even have a degree of influence over government policy. For instance, the regulations governing Wenzhou's shoe industry, mentioned above, were a collaborative effort between the government and industry representatives. Similarly, the "10th Five-Year Development Plan of the Wenzhou Apparel Industry" was worked out by the Wenzhou Apparel Chamber of Commerce in coordination with the city's Economic Commission. During sessions of the local people's congress and Chinese People's Political Consultative Conference, Wenzhou's chambers of commerce recommended 141 entrepreneurs to join those two bodies and raised 54 proposals. The general Chamber of Commerce (Association of Industry and Commerce) also organized members of the Chinese People's Political Consultative Congress (CPPCC) to draft a proposal to create an industrial park.[14]

Trade associations have clearly given Wenzhou entrepreneurs a voice that they would not have had individually. Nevertheless, studies indicate that the influence of trade associations remains limited.[15] Although government officials have withdrawn, at least to some extent, from participation in trade associations, entrepreneurs are increasingly participating in politics, particularly in the people's congresses and CPPCCs at various levels. By 2003, a total of 421 members of 64 chambers of commerce participated in People's Congresses or CPPCCs, including three in the National People's Congress and 13 in the provincial people's congress.[16]

Geographic reach

A fascinating aspect of the development of Wenzhou's trade associations has been their rapid expansion throughout China (and, indeed, the world), forming in Wenzhou business communities wherever they can be found. For any student of Chinese history, this pattern is a familiar recreation of the sort of *lansmanschaften* associations (*huiguan*) that could be found throughout late imperial China. Since 1995, when Wenzhou businesspeople organized the first such association in Kunming, over 130 chambers of commerce have been established in cities throughout the country. Although other cities have established small numbers of *yidi shanghui* (chambers of commerce in other places), no other place has been anywhere as active and as successful as Wenzhou. Indeed, sometimes chambers of commerce from Wenzhou have an advantage over associations in their own native local. For instance, in Tianjin there is a chamber of commerce in the apparel industry that evolved from the government office that previously oversaw that industry and it continues to bear the hallmarks of that governmental past – unresponsive and unrepresentative. Private entrepreneurs, who dominate the apparel industry in Tianjin, have an informal organization – one that is quite active – but it has not been allowed to register with the government because of the "one industry, one location, one association" rule of the Ministry of Civil Affairs. But merchants from Wenzhou have been able to establish a chamber of commerce.

In Tianjin and in other cities around China, the Wenzhou government maintains a small representative office that serves as the sponsoring office (*guanli bumen*) for the association, which is then able to register with the local Civil Affairs Office. There is an office in the Wenzhou government that was established specifically to support such efforts.

Of course, the reason other cities have been willing and even eager to allow Wenzhou merchants to organize is because they bring investment. Sometimes these groups can apply pressure on Wenzhou by comparing its government unfavorably to other urban administrations. For instance, the head of the Wenzhou chamber of commerce in Shenyang, Liaoning province, said at a conference in Wenzhou:

> Last year [2003] people from Wenzhou invested over 6 billion rmb in Shenyang and this year the figure will reach 10 billion. Why? The government there plays the role of the nursemaid.
>
> Every day somebody specially goes to the enterprises to ask what they can do. So the CEOs can concentrate all their energies on building their businesses. In comparison, the service provided by the Wenzhou government has a ways to go.[17]

Wenzhou chambers of commerce have not only influenced governments throughout China, but also defended the interests of otherwise scattered producers against foreign actions. The most famous example occurred in 2002–2003, when the Wenzhou Tobacco Implements Trade Association (*yanju hangye xiehui*) successfully defended the interests of manufacturers of lighters against the European Union. This incident began in late 2001, when the trade association heard that the EU Commission on Standardization was drawing up regulations requiring lighters costing less than two Euros to have safety mechanisms to protect children from accidents. As the vast majority of lighters fitting this description were made in Wenzhou (the 500 or so Wenzhou industries that produce these lighters turn out some 600 million of them a year – 90 percent of the world's production), this EU action posed a serious threat to the industry. This was the sort of trade requirement (or sanction) that Wenzhou manufacturers, almost all of which were small, family operated operations, could never have fought on their own. But the Wenzhou Tobacco Implements Trade Association met and decided to resist this EU action by collecting relevant materials, raising funds, and hiring a lawyer.[18]

Wenzhou manufacturers viewed their reusable cigarette lighters encased in metal as fundamentally different than the plastic, disposable lighters that would also be affected by the regulation. Moreover, supporting materials provided by the EU to Wenzhou manufacturers indicated that the sanction was based on only one recorded case of a malfunctioning Wenzhou lighter – underscoring the overwhelming safety of Wenzhou lighters. Wenzhou manufacturers realized that the EU was using safety standards to erect trade barriers in violation of WTO rules.

In March 2003, representatives from the Wenzhou Tobacco Implements Trade Association traveled to Europe with specialists from MOFTEC (Ministry of Foreign Trade and Economic Cooperation) and the lawyer they had employed. After 17 days of negotiations with various parties, the EU indicated that it would revise the regulations accordingly. The trade association became an overnight sensation. This dispute had hardly gotten under way when the European Association of Lighter Producers accused China of dumping lighters on the European market. In response, in July 2003, the Wenzhou Tobacco Implements Trade Association took the lead in convening a meeting with its counterparts in Guangzhou and Ningbo. Again the associations decided to fight the charges, combining to raise funds to hire an international lawyer. Faced with the Chinese reaction – and dissension in their own ranks – the EU quickly dropped its action. An association of private enterprises – with government support (but no funding) – had managed to defend the interests of an industry composed of countless small producers who could never have prevailed on their own.[19]

Civil society or corporatism?

Does the growth of local business associations suggest the rise of civil society in China? And does the increasing participation of business leaders in political institutions suggest the possibility of society leading the state? While it is tempting to jump to such conclusions, it is quite premature to make such judgments even with regard to Wenzhou, much less the rest of China.[20]

In a system where "development is the last word," it is not surprising that local (and national) business leaders are gaining recognition and participating more in the political process. This was the import of Jiang's "Three Represents" and the decision to admit private entrepreneurs into the party. (Even though many "red capitalists" had already joined the party before the ban on their participation was formally lifted, reversing the ban imposed in 1989 was symbolically important.) Quite a few private entrepreneurs attended the sixteenth Party Congress in 2002 as delegates, and one, Zhang Ruimin, head of Haier Corporation, was named an alternate member of the Central Committee.

The increasing participation of business leaders in politics, however, suggests more an alliance of interests than broad-based political participation. Chinese researchers often speak of the "quasi-institutionalized" relationship that exists between trade associations and local government. By using the term "quasi-institutionalized," they are suggesting that the relationship is based more on informal understandings that have evolved than on a legally based lobbying system or legislative hearing system. As noted above, there is still no national chamber of commerce law, though one has been under discussion for some years. Even if one is promulgated, it will take a long time for it to be implemented in an impartial manner.

Legislation, though desirable, inevitably raises questions about the legitimacy of chambers of commerce. These bodies have acquired a certain legitimacy in part because they have taken over certain government functions, such as supervising trades with regard to quality control and "excessive" competition. But if the role of chambers of commerce were defined legislatively they might define them as a "second government," that is, endow them with certain enforcement functions that the government cannot itself undertake. Doing so would end questions about the political legitimacy of chambers, but it would likely undermine the vitality that has made them important.[21]

The quasi-institutionalized status of chambers of commerce suggests that what we are witnessing is more the accumulation of social capital than the development of civil society. There is no doubt that the business community of Wenzhou has developed that density of personal relations that defines social capital, but civil society requires a more formal apparatus, including legal institutions, that make institutions more than "quasi-institutions." Formal institutions require third party enforcement, and China, even in Wenzhou, is far from that standard.

Indeed, it might be suggested that the sort of quasi-institutionalized arrangements developing in Wenzhou and perhaps elsewhere will actually delay the development of a more robust civil society. Entrepreneurs have organized themselves as a way of presenting their concerns to government (they do not make demands), and the personal relations they develop are a way of making a very uncertain environment somewhat more predictable. But precisely because these informal relationships are ways of ensuring greater predictability for the entrepreneur (and giving the official greater confidence in the activities of merchants), they tend to limit competition and retard the development of a more level playing field. Wenzhou merchants have been very successful in developing chambers of commerce throughout China, but their very presence, and perhaps the not so subtle lobbying of Wenzhou merchants, appears to delay if not prevent other communities from doing the same things. If opportunities are not monopolized, they are certainly seized to a great extent by Wenzhou entrepreneurs. Interests grow up around these relations, and to the extent they do, there is less reason to open up the same opportunities to others. Perhaps market forces will gradually force open the halls of government, making law more effective, but it will take a long time.

The organization of Wenzhou business associations also raises questions about the corporatist structure that the Chinese government has been developing for dealing with NGOs. Current regulations limit associations to a single group, dealing with one industry, in only one locality, though it is evident that in practice China has been more flexible than its regulations suggest. Although on paper associations in Wenzhou uphold this corporatist structure, there are already many informal linkages across political boundaries. Moreover, classic corporatist structure requires all businesses to participate in one and only one association, but Wenzhou's associations are quite clearly voluntary (though there are advantages, including access to information, that come with joining) and many Wenzhou entrepreneurs join more than one association, sometimes in different locations. And then there are the Wenzhou chambers of commerce that have been established outside of Wenzhou. These cannot be regarded as branch associations, but they clearly maintain close contact with each other, including biannual meetings to share experiences and information. This is more horizontal organization than normally associated with either corporatism or Leninist organization.

If Wenzhou does not adhere to our understandings of corporatist organization, it seems far from adopting pluralist models. Some opening up of the

NGO system may be allowed; for instance, some places have discussed allowing the organization of business associations without having to register with the Civil Affairs Office. But China seems to have a natural tendency toward corporatism – the regulations governing business associations in the 1930s were classic in this regard – and it is difficult to imagine competing associations of apparel manufactures, for instance. The informal understandings between government and industry seem likely to prevent such a development. So, if we can understand the relationship between chambers of commerce as semi-institutionalized, perhaps we can also characterize their position in Chinese society as embodying social capital and structured in a semi-corporatist manner.

Conclusion

The emergence of chambers of commerce and other trade associations in Wenzhou marks a further evolution in state–society relations in China as the growing importance of the private economy generates pressures to readjust interests. Conservatives in China feared that the emergence of the private economy and the emergence of non-governmental associations would threaten the Chinese Communist Party (CCP). Indeed, the growth of chambers of commerce stalled in Wenzhou after Tiananmen. Deng Xiaoping's journey to the south in 1992 touched off a new upsurge in the private economy as well as the organization of business.

Ironically, the fears of conservatives have proven misplaced. The CCP has learned to accommodate this most capitalist of institutions, using chambers of commerce to promote the local economy and bring order to an unruly sector. For their part, chambers of commerce in Wenzhou have learned how to promote their business interests without threatening the ultimate authority of the party. Indeed, for better or worse, a new ruling elite composed of both party officials and private entrepreneurs seems to be emerging in Wenzhou.

Many people in China look to the emergence of chambers of commerce as one step along a long road to democracy. They reflect an increasing accommodation between the political system and the interests of an increasingly diverse society. Thanks to trade groups, policymaking is more consultative and better reflects the needs of industry. Relations between state and society are placed on at least a quasi-institutional foundation and thus regularized. Associational affairs are increasingly managed democratically and without governmental interference. But if this is a step toward democracy, it is only a very preliminary step. Indeed, political authority remains central to the operation of the system. The growth of chambers of commerce can help regularize state–society relations, but ultimately the very existence of trade associations is based on the legitimacy bestowed by government.[22]

Indeed, to the extent that the Chinese government can develop a consultative policy-making process and accommodate the interests of society, it may well delay the implementation of political democracy. The test will come when the accommodation between the state and business is challenged by other groups, ranging from environmentalists to workers.

184 J. Fewsmith

Notes

1 Wenzhou has drawn considerable scholarly attention. See Alan P.L. Liu, "The 'Wenzhou Model' of Development and China's Modernization," *Asian Survey*, 32, No. 8 (August 1992): 696–711; Kristen Parris, "Local Initiative and Local Reform: The Wenzhou Model of Reform," *The China Quarterly*, 134 (June 1993): 242–263; and Yia-Ling Liu, "Reform from Below: The Private Economy and Local Politics in the Rural Industrialization of Wenzhou," *The China Quarterly*, 130 (June 1992): 293–316.

2 Yu Jianxing, *Zai zhengfu yu qiye zhi jian: Yi Wenzhou shanghui wei yanjiu duixiang (Between government and enterprise – Wenzhou chambers of commerce as a topic of study)* (Hangzhou: Zhejiang renmin chubanshe, 2004), pp. 52–64.

3 Chen Shengyong, Wang Jinjun, and Ma Bin, *Zuzhihua, zizhu zhili yu minzhu (Organized, self governance and democracy)* (Beijing: Zhongguo shehui kexue chubanshe, 2004), p. 38.

4 Ibid.

5 Ibid., p. 228.

6 Ibid., p. 286.

7 Yu Hui, *Hangye xiehui jiqi zai Zhongguo zhuanqi de fazhan (Trade associations and their development in China's period of transition)*, accessed from www.usc.cuhk.hk/wk_wzdetails.asp?id=4164.

8 Shenggyong *et al.*, *Zuzhihua, zizhu zhili yu minzhu*, p. 301.

9 See chart on ibid, p. 196.

10 Ibid., p. 285.

11 Ibid., p. 293.

12 Jianxing *et al.*, *Zai zhengfu yu qiye zhi jian*, p. 286.

13 Shenggyong *et al.*, *Zuzhihua, zizhu zhili yu minzhu*, p. 294.

14 Jianxing *et al.*, *Zai zhengfu yu qiye zhi jian*, p. 80.

15 Shenggyong *et al.*, *Zuzhihua, zizhu zhili yu minzhu*, p. 263.

16 Ibid., pp. 229–230.

17 Ibid., p. 241.

18 *Shenfang Wenzhoushi yanju xiehui (Interview with the Tobacco Implements Trade Association of Wenzhou)*, accessed from www.wzgcc.cn/ReadNews.asp?NewsID=2413.

19 Shenggyong *et al.*, *Zuzhihua, zizhu zhili yu minzhu*, pp. 49–51.

20 See, for instance, Kenneth W. Foster, "Embedded within State Agencies: Business Associations in Yantai," *The China Journal*, No. 47 (January 2002): 41–65.

21 Jianxing *et al.*, *Zai zhengfu yu qiye zhi jian*, p. 48.

22 Zengke He, *Zhongguo zhengzhi tizhi gaige yanjiu (Study of China's political structural reform)* (Beijing: Zhongyang bianyiju chubanshe, 2004), p. 254.

11 How can deliberative institutions be sustainable in China?

Baogang He[1]

In recent years, China has witnessed the development of consultative and deliberative institutions.[2] An increasing number of public hearings have provided people with opportunities to express their opinions on a wide range of issues such as the price of water and electricity, park entry fees, the relocation of farmers, the conservation of historical landmarks, and even the relocation of the famous Beijing Zoo, to name a few.[3] Participatory and deliberative institutions in China can be seen as a deliberative way of democratising China, and they are helping to develop deliberative Chinese citizens.[4] As T.V. Smith and Eduard C. Lindeman pointed out, "Genuine consent, a vital ingredient of the democratic way of life, is the end-product of discussion or conference. Citizens of democratic societies are equipped for their role when they have acquired the skills and the arts of conferring."[5]

Chinese intellectuals have recently studied and advocated deliberative democracy. Lin Shangli at Fudan University has argued that the deliberative model of democracy is more suitable to China's local conditions.[6] Chen Jiagang has taken the lead in translating, introducing, and advocating deliberative theories of democracy in China.[7] Li Junru, the Vice President of the Central Party School, has advocated consultative and deliberative institutions. He has called for the development of deliberative institutions in China by drawing on the Chinese political tradition of consultation and improving the Chinese People's Political Consultative Committee ("CPPCC").[8]

The key question is whether these deliberative institutions will make a substantial contribution to Chinese democratisation. Before one can answer this question, one has to answer the question of whether these deliberative institutions will continue to develop. This chapter will focus on this question. The structure of the chapter is as follows. Section 1 describes briefly recent experiments in developing deliberative institutions. Section 2 identifies the sustainable problem. Section 3 then offers an explanation of three key determinants of the Chinese style of deliberation. Section 4 outlines four approaches to the sustainable development of deliberative institutions.

Development of participatory and deliberative institutions

China has a long-standing tradition of discussion and deliberation on community-related issues at the local community level. Confucian scholars established public forums in which they debated and deliberated national affairs centuries ago.[9] During Mao's time, the "mass line" emphasised the need for public consultation to give value to the voice of the people in the political process. Indeed, the socialist tradition of political participation generally might be a useful resource in developing deliberative and participatory institutions.

The introduction of *village* elections and the establishment of participatory and deliberative institutions, such as village representative assemblies since the 1980s, and in particular since the late 1990s, has changed the structure of village politics and the political behaviour of some 3.2 million "village officials" in the 734,700 villages in China. Since the middle and late 1990s, some villages have developed village representative meetings wherein major decisions on village affairs are discussed, debated, and deliberated upon by village representatives.

Local *urban* communities have also developed a number of new participatory and deliberative institutions. The Chinese consultative meeting or public hearing is designed to get people's support for local projects and to be a forum for people's opinions. The popular conciliation or mediation meeting is designed to solve various local problems and conflicts. For example, in the Shangcheng district of Hangzhou, a consensus conference or consultation meeting is held once a month. Citizen evaluation, first introduced in Shandong and Shenyang, and then in Shanghai and Hangzhou, is designed to give the ordinary people an opportunity to rate and evaluate the performance of local cadres.[10] The rating seriously affects the political career or the level of performance bonus of local cadres.

The practice of holding public hearings has also developed at the national level. In 1996, the first national law on administrative punishment introduced an article stipulating that a public hearing must be held before any punishment is given.[11] Another famous article 23 of the Law on Price passed by China's National Congress in December 1997 specified that the price of public goods must be decided through public hearing. This was followed by the Law on Legislature, passed in 2000, which requires public hearings to be an integral part of the decision-making process for all legal regulations and laws.[12] More than 50 cities have now held legislative public hearings. On 29 September 2005, a public hearing was held by the National People's Congress (NPC) Standing Committee to decide whether the central government should raise the personal income-tax threshold.

The progress in Wenling City, Zhejiang Province is a good example of successful integration of deliberative institutions. It is a county-level city with a vibrant private economy. In 2004, it was awarded the national prize for Innovations and Excellence in Local Chinese Governance. From 1996 to 2000, more than 1,190 deliberative and consultative meetings were held at the village level, 190 at the township level, and 150 in governmental organisations, schools, and business sectors.[13] Such meetings are called *kentan,* meaning "sincere heart-to-heart discussion". Some meetings were "one shot" discussions; that is, sessions dealing with only one topic that meet only once. Others were continuing discussions about more complex matters or a series of matters. For example, five deliberative meetings were held to deal with the relocation of the fishery industry. Some meetings were just consultative without connecting with decision-making directly, while others were well connected to policy decision-making through the local people's congresses.

The development of participatory and deliberative institutions in Wenling City has involved four stages.[14] In the first stage, local leaders found that traditional ideological mobilisation did not work as a mode of persuasion. In 1996, a democratic "heart-to-heart" forum was therefore invented to give villagers a genuine opportunity to express their grief and complaints. However, the villagers who experienced this democratic forum soon discovered that it was only a forum for discussion, not decision-making. Their political enthusiasm decreased, the turn-out rate dropped, and disillusionment followed. In the second stage, in order to continue to attract people, the local officials turned this discussion forum into a decision-making mechanism. By 2000, local leaders would respond to questions of participants, and make decisions on the spot.

The third development, in 2004, was a democratic discussion forum attended by the deputies of the local People's Congress. Local leaders had discovered that if the issue being considered was controversial, decisions made in deliberative meetings gained support from some, but faced opposition from others. In order to defuse its responsibility and gain legitimacy for the policy on any controversial issue, the local party organisation decided that deputies of the local People's Congress should vote on certain difficult issues in a deliberative meeting – and the result of voting constituted a final decision that overrode the authority of the local party secretary. Leaders held the view that the only reliable and indisputable source of legitimacy is democratic voting, which generates a basis for public will on certain disputable issues. This is an institutional innovation that combines deliberative institutions with the empowerment so sorely lacking in much experimental deliberative democracy in the West.

In the fourth stage, in 2005, Wenling introduced China's first experiment in Deliberative Polling on a budget issue, adopting methods of social sciences to deliver a scientific basis for public policy. Wenling officials realised the deficiencies of their deliberative meetings, such as unscientific representation and insufficient time for a full discussion. Accordingly, they accepted advice from James Fishkin and myself to use a random sampling method to select the participants to avoid selection bias and to provide well-balanced information to all the participants, who would spend an entire day deliberating over the town's budget issue.

Posing the problem

These deliberative institutions discussed above have serious deficiencies. The Chinese saying goes, "when the man leaves, the tea cools off". When it comes to developing deliberative democratic institutions, once leaders go their ways, institutions slacken off. The place of origin of democratic deliberations – the township of Songmen in Wenling – is a case in point. With changes to the township party committee, the outcomes of the original discussions on fishery were shelved. With the departure of the party secretary of a municipal party committee, the driving force of democratic deliberation was reduced. The original secretary regarded it as his "baby", nurturing it lovingly and actively promoting it. But the incoming secretary held no such positive attitude. While not negating it, he puts no great effort into promoting it, so the party secretaries at the city level do not earnestly support it, nor is any enthusiasm shown by leaders lower down at the township level. Alternatively, a leader would be promoted due to his innovations, but once in high office he or she would become conservative and cautious, unwilling to run risks with further innovative experiments.

These phenomena are by no means unique to China. In Perth, Western Australia, Janette Hartz-Karp organised some extremely successful deliberative experiment in recent years. A twenty-first-century Town Meeting on the city's development that she organised was attended by over a 1,000 people. But as soon as her superior leader left the leadership, she became "unemployed". She set up her own non-government organisation (NGO), which continues to drive the development of deliberative democracy in Australia.

It can be seen from this that deliberative democracy is driven by elites. Its survival and key aspects of its development are determined by their will and determination. Can it continue to develop without the support of the governing elite? Can it develop into a widespread daily practice of democratic movement?

The criterion for institutions of deliberative democracy being developed is that at least 50 per cent villages and towns should adopt such procedures to solve problems in practical life. Only then can they have true value. While instructive, the cases that have been successful so far have in terms of this criterion played a very minor role. Economic development in China in recent years has taken place at a rate of 9 per cent per annum. In places like Shenzhen civil associations have grown by over 20 per cent. But the development of institutions of deliberative democracy has been restricted to isolated individual cases with very small size and scale.

This is a worrying problem. The speed of development of institutions of deliberative democracy now lags behind that of the economy and of civil associations. Most local officials still seek solutions to the various social and political issues caused by economic development through coercive mechanisms. When deliberative institutions are absent, people look to non-institutional methods, with deleterious consequences for social stability.

The problem of the sustainable development of deliberative democracy institutions is a major one which cannot be neglected. If such institutions were to develop at a rate of 5 per cent per annum, it would be possible to seek a harmonious society.

Three determinants of deliberative institutions

Before we discuss the sustainability of these institutions, we first need to discuss the conditions under which they occur. Deliberative meetings or roundtables at first were regarded as outside the official system. Transforming them into an institution within the official system is determined by the following three factors:

1 an approving attitude on the part of higher levels;
2 a democratic attitude on the part of the local government;
3 the degree to which the populace need such institutions.

To find acceptance from the higher leadership, deliberative democracy has to be consistent with the existing system and match the mentality of Beijing leaders. And still more important, the Beijing leadership has to see it as useful in solving social problems. In facing the pressures associated with the rapid democratisation in Eastern Europe and Asia, Beijing has tried to develop a new art of ruling that combines administrative order with a consultative mechanism that will bring governments and people together, improve the relations between cadres and the masses, and achieve good governance in local politics. To be sure, Beijing has used deliberative institutions as a form of moderate democracy to avoid a radical and substantial political reform that would directly challenge the political power of the Chinese Communist Party (CCP). It is believed that deliberative institutions are peripheral and marginal, so they do not undermine the power of the CCP. And, accordingly, the national government has encouraged the development of the mild form of democracy. As a result, mobilised, consultative, and deliberative institutions have developed even faster than the competitive electoral institutions at the township level and beyond. Still, the inherent logic of deliberative institutions may push China past the moderate form of democracy that was intended by Beijing.

Local leaders have various motivations and incentives to push the development of deliberative institutions. Some officials aim to achieve a genuine consensus so as to gain legitimacy for certain policies, to reduce social conflicts, and even to win personal honour. Others see deliberative institutions as an effective tool to bring about democratic management and monitoring. Still others, however, are under great pressure to introduce these institutions to ease the tension between cadres and the masses. Pressure also comes from the private sector. In some local counties or townships in Zhejiang, private tax contributions constitute more than 70 per cent of the local budget. Private businesspersons and interest groups desire to express their voices about public policies that affect their economic life. As a result, consultation meetings and other institutions are organised in response to the demand from the private sector.

Key to the willingness of grassroots governments to attempt deliberative democratic procedures is their attitude to deliberative democracy. Certain officials in economically developed areas of Zhejiang are starting to be more intelligent as politicians, fully aware that administrative methods of coercive suppression and harsh control are incapable of solving sharp social conflicts. Deliberative democracy is quite a good mechanism for harmonising conflicts of interests. In 1990, for example, one town leadership used administrative methods to abolish an old market and set aside some new land to open a new market. They encountered widespread popular resistance and protest, with the result that the old market carried on as usual, and the new one was a waste of money. The township leaders learned from this event that they should have convened a democratic roundtable beforehand, soliciting suggestions from the people, and so avoid making a wrong decision.

Some villages and town leaders in Zhejiang have adopted transparent deliberative democratic means to prioritise capital construction projects. In this way avoiding, first, charges of "siphoning off cash", and second, using the public opinion produced by deliberative democracy to convince these not to willing to move from their homes. Third, if there are problems in selecting capital construction projects, these are not the mistaken choices of the leadership, but of the people.

The leaders of the Bianyu village in the Zheguo Township, Wenling City, Zhejiang, were more astute. They held a village-level deliberative democracy conference to discuss the major issues of whether to build housing for migrant workers (whom they called the "new people"). After the village-level deliberative democracy conference decided they should do so, they use this public opinion as an indicator to apply to the higher-level leadership for land to use. Moreover, the village deliberative democracy conference discussed how much the rental of village land and how long the term should be. The village leaders then used the villagers' opinion to negotiate with bosses of the enterprises which were to become their tenants. The greatest advantage of so doing was that the need for the enterprise bosses to treat village leaders a banquet, or bribe them to keep the rent down, was avoided, so the village leaders could be spotless in the villagers' eyes.

These cases show the driving forces for deliberative democracy to be pluralistic and complex, but the main thread is clear: intelligent grassroots politicians have learned to reduce the pressure and responsibility on them by means of deliberative democracy. They avoid the opprobrium associated with corrupt officials and resolving various social conflicts in their localities, and use public opinion to fend off various unreasonable demands. When more grassroots leaders learn the benefits of adopting deliberative democracy, it will develop more quickly and become more widespread.

Many local leaders are unwilling to attempt deliberative democracy. There are all sorts of reasons. First, some leaders regard decision-making as a matter for the leadership; the common people cannot be allowed to join discussions of community policy. Second, some worry that the outcomes of democratic consultation may conflict with the views of the government, and it might be difficult to come to a conclusion. Third, grassroots leaders depend on their own superiors for promotion. Democratic consultation institutions are not included in assessments of merit, so carrying them out provides no grounds for promotion. A scholar once announced a project when giving a class. She stepped down to find a group of grassroots leaders surrounding her, all bidding to get the project for themselves. When they heard it was a democratic consultation pilot project, however, all but one lost interest and turned to leave. This story vividly illustrates the attitude of current grassroots leaders to democratic consultation. It shows why, without the pressure of direct elections at the township level, the grassroots leaders have no incentive to positively promote such institutions.

Popular demand for deliberative democracy is a third important condition. When the majority of the populace demands deliberative democracy conferences be convened to make decisions that accord with public opinion and safeguard their interests, the grassroots local authorities are forced to introduce these mechanisms. What "forces" this is public pressure. When social conflicts and contradictions become extremely sharp, and the existing administrative method are unable to solve them, or can do so only at a very high price, local authorities are forced to adopt deliberative democracy institutions. This is an inherent, deep-seated origin of sustainable development of deliberative democracy. Its motive force originates from the people and from the needs for civilised, transparent, equitable solutions to modern social contradictions and conflict. History teaches us that sustained institutional development must be based on people's needs. Take an example of Mao Zedong who tried every possible way such as waging campaigns through revolutionary songs and handing everything over to Huang Guofeng whom he trusted to institutionalise the Cultural Revolution. But no sooner had he passed away than all his revolutionary effort disappeared. Sustainable development of the Cultural Revolution was a pipedream. The reason was simple: people did not revolution forever, and they were tied of daily "revolution".

Four approaches to sustainable development of deliberative democracy

Institutionalisation

Institutional solutions to these problems have been adopted in every region in the country. In 2004, Fujian ruled that all villages must hold four village-level democratic hearings a year. As early as 2002, Wenling City ruled that townships must hold four democratic roundtables per annum. The requirements of Document No. 7 for 2004 were to promote the institutionalisation of democratic roundtables and to get real results in making the roundtable conferences, decision-making, management, and supervision democratic. There were to be no less than four per annum at the township/street committee level and two at the village/community level. They were to be awarded four merit points. Responsibility for carrying it out would be shared between the Party's Departments of Organisation and Propaganda. They, moreover, actively carried out collective wages negotiations in non-state enterprises and trades. Various towns (street) were to develop at least one collective negotiation in a trade, with real results obtained. This would be worth three merit points. The task was taken on by the Department of Propaganda. Chen Yimin, an officer of Wenling City Propaganda Department, devised an examination and assessment system to actively promote the deliberative democracy system. Purely ceremonial or empty shows, such as those concerned with cultural development, would not score points. Because it held no roundtables in 2005, the Taiping Street Committee was docked three points, whereas the Zheguo Township, which that year set up a high grade democratic consultation system, gained four points.

Such institutional methods may to a certain extent solve the problem of the development of the institutions of democratic deliberation stagnating as soon as a leader moves on, but on the other hand they lead to another problem – that of formalism. In order to pass inspections by the city Propaganda Department, the townships under it randomly find a couple of minor issues and call some people to meetings to make up the numbers. This is passive "deliberative democracy"!

Habituation to democracy

The promotion and repeated practice of discussion in Wenling's deliberative democracy led officials and the peasants in certain regions to come to like this procedure and feel attracted to it. Now, as soon as a major issue appears, they may want to use deliberative democracy methods to solve it. The Zheguo Township in the township of Wenling is a case in point. Party secretary Jiang Zhaohua and Mayor Wang Xiaoyu twice adopted methods of deliberation and public opinion poll in discussing questions of choice in significant public construction projects in the town. When they encountered major issues of land and migration, they also thought of using democratic deliberation methods to set public policy that would be both scientific and based on public opinion.

In some villages in Wenling, democratic discussion has become customary. When village leaders fail to hold democratic roundtable, they ask why not. They jointly demanded that democratic roundtables be held. Not holding the democratic roundtable leads the peasants to complain. This is a new culture and a new pressure. Fujian Province has ruled that one-fifth of villagers or one-third of the villagers representatives may jointly request that a village-level democratic hearing meeting be held. When I myself went down to the countryside to carry out political experiments in recent years, I was delighted to find that the peasants naturally have the very high latent rationality, and given any opportunity for deliberative discussion, their communication ability will develop very quickly. This is the most important resource and source of sustainable development of deliberative institutions.

The significant propelling force of sustainable development of deliberative institutions comes from citizens. When peasants become modern citizens, they seek to safeguard their rights.[15] They demand that deliberative democracy system be put into practice. Sustainable development of democratic institutions is possible only when citizens strive and struggle. Depending only on enlightened leadership without citizens participating, it is placed in question.

The practice of New England town meeting has been an amazing aspect of American democratic tradition. Needing no push from government, such a grassroots institution of deliberative democracy still goes on as before. Only when institutions of democratic consultation become a lifestyle of the people, only when they become a new tradition of the Chinese culture, can they take roots. When Deng Yuwen, a senior reporter of the Central Party School's *Xuexi shibao* [*Study Times*] came to the Zheguo Township to inspect its deliberative democratic institutions, he grasped the key issue: the adaptation and habituation of deliberative democracy.[16]

Political competition

In recent years, something interesting has happened in local political reform in China: while leadership changes may lead to stagnation of deliberative institutions, better democratic hearing institutions have been emerging elsewhere. Mechanisms of competitive political reform may reduce concerns about the sustainable development of these institutions. In some localities, deliberative democracy comes to an end when the leadership changes. But it doesn't matter, other regions take the opportunity promote their unique institutional innovations for political reform. In many localities, public hearings are fraudulent, formalistic, or the speakers are nominated beforehand. Again, it doesn't matter – such formalistic institutions will eventually be eliminated. People do not attend such meetings and even if they do they give no credence to the outcomes. Cai Dingjian at the Central University of Politics and Law has stated that people are not too happy when legislation hearings are held nowadays, because they are merely "hearings". In a commercial society at an earlier period, fake products could make money for a while. But only genuine goods at reasonable prices are truly a hit with people. The same logic also applies in political sphere slowly. Only genuine deliberative democracy, it can gain the common people's support and trust. In 2005, the Zheguo Township adopted the deliberation polling method to advance deliberative democratic institutions for the first time. That year some 70 per cent of a random sample of over 260 people thought the government would implement the results of the deliberative public opinion poll. In 2006 the Zheguo Township once again adopted this method, some 80 per cent of people thought the government would respect public opinion and carry out its outcomes – an increase of 10 per cent over the previous year. This 10 per cent is the result of genuine deliberative experiments.

We should of course be quite clear that political competition in the area of the institutional innovations takes place in the absence of direct elections of township leaders. This implies a limitation of such current political competition: it is restricted to competition between people who want to promote political reform, and the common people are unable to eliminate corrupt officials through the election mechanism.

Intellectual impulse

NGOs play a very big role in pushing sustainable development of deliberative democracy in Western advanced democracies. They can maintain its independence and advance and perfect it. But in China, "NGOs" are politically controlled, their roles in promoting deliberative democracy are limited. Private enterprise association is inherently against deliberation; the chairman or manager often exercises total dominance. On the level of values, it is very difficult to accept and promote institutions of deliberative democracy. The founder of America's Marriot hotels said, he always disliked deliberation and discussion as a waste of time and missed opportunity.

The potential role of Chinese scholars is huge. In modern history, Liang Shuming, the last Confucius, formulated the idea of communicative rationality, the philosophical foundation of deliberative democracy, 50 years earlier than Jugen Habermas.[17] He devoted himself to rural reconstruction project which aims to develop peasants' communicative rationality capabilities. Perhaps today the development of deliberative institutions in rural China is a historical return to this Chinese tradition. One may alternatively say that it stimulates a historical gene, restores or continues what Liang Shuming was unable to complete in the past – through developing folk communicative rationality to construct a new countryside. Deliberative democracy is an advance of Liang Shuming's idea of communicative rationality and is to complete the historical mission Liang Shuming began.

Scholars are a force that can guarantee sustainable development of institutions of deliberative democracy. Intellectuals help local authorities to practically carry out each deliberative democracy conference and may directly help enrich specific villages, townships, and towns. This is more valuable than publishing one or two academic articles which a handful of people may want to know about. Their mission lies in uncovering grassroots problems, and researching and comparing various methods of solving them. The further down Chinese deliberative and democratic institution goes, the greater the demand for it, the greater its vitality. The further downward intellectuals go, the greater is society's demand for them, and the higher the value of their life. Intellectuals are another significant power and resource for promoting and safeguarding the sustainable development of regional institutions of deliberative democracy.

Notes

1 I would like to thank the participants for their comments and suggestions on the early version of this chapter presented at the International Symposium on the Development of the Non-State Sector, Local Governance, and Sustainable Development in China, 24–25 June 2006, Hangzhou, China, co-organised by Department of Political Science, Zhejiang University and China Policy Institute, The University of Nottingham, and David Kelly for his translation of the early version of Sections 2–4 from Chinese into English, but later I have made substantial revision and addition.
2 Baogang He, "Participatory and Deliberative Institutions in China", in *The Search for Deliberative Democracy in China*, eds, Ethan Leib and Baogang He (New York: Palgrave, 2006), pp. 176–196.

3 Peng Zhongzhao, Xue Lan and Kan Ke, *Public Hearing System in China* (Beijing: Qinghua University Press, 2004).

4 Baognag He, "Western Theories of Deliberative Democracy and the Chinese Practice of Complex Deliberative Governance", in *The Search for Deliberative Democracy in China*, pp. 133–148.

5 T.V. Smith and Eduard C. Lindeman, *The Democratic Way of Life: An American Interpretation* (New York: New American Library of World Literature, Inc., 1951), p. 130.

6 Lin Shangli, "Deliberative Politics: A Reflection on the Democratic Development of China", *Academic Monthly* (Shanghai), no. 4 (2003), pp. 19–25.

7 Chen Jiagang, ed. and trans., *Deliberative Democracy* (Shanghai: Shanghai Sanlian Publishers, 2004).

8 Li Junru, "What Kind of Democracy Should China Establish?" *Beijing Daily*, 26 September 2005.

9 Chen Shengyong, "The Native Resources of Deliberative Politics in China", in *The Search for Deliberative Democracy in China*, pp. 161–174.

10 Baogang He, "The Theory and Practice of Chinese Grassroots Governance: Five Models", *Japanese Journal of Political Science*, vol. 4, no. 2 (2003), pp. 293–314.

11 Zhu Mang, *Multiple Dimensions of Administrative Law* (Beijing: Beijing University Press, 2004). Chapter 1 is devoted to the topic of public hearing on administrative punishment.

12 Wang Quansheng, *A Study of Legislative Hearing* (Beijing: Beijing University Press, 2003).

13 See the official document, *Democratic Sincerely Talk: The Innovation from Wenling*, compiled by the Department of Propaganda, Wenling city, 2003, p. 98.

14 Mo Yifei and Chen Yiming, *Democratic Deliberation: The Innovation from Wenling* (Beijing: The Central Compliance and Translation Press, 2005).

15 See David Kelly, "Citizen Movements and China's Public Intellectuals in the Hu-Wen Era", *Pacific Affairs,* vol. 79, no. 2 (Summer 2006), pp. 183–204.

16 Deng Yuwen, "When Democracy Becomes Habit and Custom", *Xuexi shibao*, 9 May 2006.

17 Liang Shuming (1893–1990), social activist and professor at Beijing University, cultural theorist, and later a noted rural reformer. See Guy S. Alitto, *The Last Confucian: Liang Shu-ming and the Chinese Dilemma of Modernity* (Berkeley: University of California Press, 1979).

12 Foreign NGOs' role in local governance in China

Qingshan Tan

In the history of village election and self-government, foreign non-governmental organizations (NGOs) have played an important role in publicizing and contributing to the development of rural political reform and governance.[1] NGOs have made funds available to sponsor publications of foreign books and training materials on elections and international conferences on village elections. Moreover, they have provided trainings for electoral officials and conducted training courses for elected members of villagers' committees from all over the country.

In this chapter, I argue that foreign NGOs' involvement in village election and governance has made important and positive impact on the process of village elections and has contributed to building and improving the village electoral institution in China. I first examine the initial consideration of Chinese officials in obtaining foreign involvement and the avenue with which various cooperation and agreements were explored and reached between Chinese and foreign counterparts. Then I assess foreign contribution to and influence on village elections and evaluate how the interaction between central and local election officials and various foreign individuals and groups affects policy implementation and innovation and the development of the village electoral institution.

Chinese effort to seek out foreign input

Chinese village election from the start was an indigenous growth out of the initiative by villagers to fill in the vacuum of village power and the government desire to solve the crisis in village authority after de-communization. It was later affirmed and expanded by the government in an attempt to re-establish a grassroots political system of governance. There was little foreign coverage on village self-government movement in the 1980s and the earlier part of 1990s. Much of the focus was on Chinese economic reform in the 1980s, the Tiananmen crackdown, and the ensuring collapse of the Soviet Union. The Chinese government initially did not publicize it since village self-government was a controversial issue itself in domestic politics. The Ministry of Civil Affairs (MoCA), which was responsible for implementing village elections, was initially more discreet about implementation of the experimental Organic Law,[2] and was trying hard to avoid publicity that may cause visible opposition. In the words of MoCA officials, "we just do it by working with friends, quietly of course. We try to avoid criticizing those who did not carry out village elections. There was no need to attract more opposition."[3]

In 1992, the China Basic-Level Governance Research Institute, which was under the leadership of the Department of Basic-Level Government of MoCA, decided to invite ten scholars from seven countries to visit Liaoning and Fujian for a study of village self-government.[4] Through this invitation, MoCA opened the door to foreign observers interested in village elections. It was the first time that foreign observers cast a glimpse on what had happened in village governance in the Chinese countryside. Starting in 1993, MoCA held three consecutive international conferences on election systems, village representative assembly systems, and legal systems of village elections.[5]

The MoCA decision to invite foreign observers to study village self-government and election was a quite bold move, given MoCA's past quiet approach to village election implementation. What factors were responsible for making MoCA change the course? One line of explanation was that self-government could be a good publicity material for promoting human rights image in the arena of international public opinion. This argument came clearly as an afterthought, since it had nothing to do with solving the problem of village governance and could not possibly have been a motivation for establishing village self-government.[6] Could the central government desire to improve China's international image in the aftermath of the Tiananmen event prompted MoCA to invite foreign scholars to the countryside? It could, certainly given the fact that the Chinese government increasingly became aware of importance of public relations and the fact that MoCA held jointly media conferences with the Ministry of Foreign Affairs on village self-governance.[7] The other evidence to support this argument was the description of foreigners' appraisal on self-government made by Li Xueju, then Director of MoCA's Department of Basic-level Governance:

> Some arguments took place among several western journalists in a hotel in Beijing. American Newsweek journalist Frank Gipney was vividly describing his coverage on village self-government in Lishu County of Jilin. He was talking about village elections and the way village democracy.... Then other western journalists present gibed him that he was deceived and it was impossible to have basic-level democracy in the Chinese countryside. Gipney repeatedly assured "it is true, it is true. I saw it with my own eyes." He then discretely told our staff to hold them off when other journalists requested for field coverage, and that he wanted to be the first one to report Chinese village self-government.[8]

However, the afterthought argument does not explain the timing of and the immediate reason for the MoCA decision to open up village elections to foreign observers in 1992 and the ensuing three international conferences on village self-government. Another possible explanation was that MoCA officials realized the importance of building an electoral institution to standardize and improve village elections. Yet, election inexperience and lack of electoral rules and procedures had resulted in variations in implementation of village elections and in election outcomes, which led to more disputes and controversies. Election needs operational rules and procedures. To achieve this end, MoCA decided to invite foreign experts and scholars to study village self-government with an emphasis on village election.[9] Furthermore, MoCA officials recognized the insufficiency of the 1987 Organic Law that only outlined village self-government in principle, but neglected procedural rules to guarantee the implementation of self-government.[10] MoCA was ready to revise the 1987 Organic Law. According to one of the participants in the 1992 field trip, the primary purpose of MoCA's invitation was to seek foreign assessments and suggestions that could help MoCA revise and improve the Organic Law.[11]

To better understand international legal systems and practices of grassroots governance and facilitate exchanges with foreign scholars and practitioners, MoCA created a Research Society of Basic-Level Governance in 1989, consisting of MoCA high ranking and middle- and lower-middle-level officials who were responsible for rural development and for implementing the Organic Law.[12] This Research Society, acting as a "non-governmental organization" (NGO) for MoCA, enabled MoCA to solicit foreign assistance in improving and promoting village self-government. The Ford Foundation, which has a Beijing Office, quickly came to offer financial support and helped MoCA establish international contacts.[13] The Society won a Ford grant for promoting self-government. The grant made it possible for MoCA to invite the first group of foreign sinologists and grassroots governance experts to observe and study village self-government. The Ford Foundation Beijing Officer, Jonathan Hecht, was instrumental in successfully assembling this foreign delegation, much to the delight of MoCA officials. Hecht's role in introducing village self-government to the outside world was acknowledged in a 1993 research report of village self-government by the Research Society.[14]

The first foreign non-governmental delegation, consisting of scholars and practitioners from Bangladesh, Britain, India, Indonesia, Japan, the Philippines, and the United States, gained some rare access to observing first-hand village self-government practices and election. The delegation was divided into two groups, one visited Fujian and the other Liaoning. The delegates conducted meetings with members of villagers' committees, discussed election issues with local officials and participated in a three-day study conference in Beijing on village self-government, with provincial civil affairs officials from 15 provinces. MoCA gave the foreign visit a very high evaluation in the summary report filed by the Research Society.[15] The report pointed out that the visit achieved the objective of introducing and publicizing village self-government and learning from foreign experience and advice. It specifically cited the article published by George Mathew of India praising the practice of village self-government. The report also noted the contribution of foreign input on improving village electoral rules and procedures in candidate nomination, selection, secret ballots, and election training. MoCA officials were especially pleased that the visit helped establish international channels through which MoCA later sent several village self-government delegations to Japan, India, and the United States.

Using the Ford grant, MoCA also started to introduce foreign grassroots governance practices through a series of translation projects. Two books that MoCA officials selected for translation had something to do with the delegation members. Kamal Siddiqui, a member of the 1992 delegation, wrote one book on comparative studies on local government in South Asia. When MoCA officials were invited by George Mathew, also a member of the 1992 delegation, to visit India to study local governance in 1993, they chose a book on local governance in Western Bangladesh. The translation project aimed at gaining a comparative perspective and studying foreign experiences in local governance. According to the project leader, then the MoCA Rural Division Chief of the Basic-level Governance, Wang Zhenyao, an energetic advocate of village self-governance, believed that local experiences in India and South Asia offered some lessons for China. First, China needs to find her own way in building grassroots governance, given her history and local tradition. At the same time, innovations should be encouraged for developing local self-government. Second, local democracy is an incremental process. China needs to adopt a gradual approach to implementation of village self-government. Third, creation of a legal framework for local governance was an important part of this incremental process. China should also learn to develop an electoral institution based on rule of law and legal systems. Last, but not least, there should be a greater role for central and local governments to educate and train local officials and people by publishing training materials and offering training courses.[16]

MoCA's experiment with the initial foreign exchange proved to be successful judged by the perception of MoCA officials on the 1992 field trip. The official response to the trip feedback was positive and many comments made by the participants were reported and quoted in various officials publications. *Township Forum*, a weekly magazine affiliated with MoCA published an article entitled "Village self-government in the eyes of foreigners," which reported the delegation trip to Fujian and Liaoning. While it mentioned delegation members' suggestions and recommendations, the article profusely quoted positive comments made by the members of the delegation.[17] In his book on the study of basic-level governance, Li Xueju also reflected on the encouraging reaction of delegation members to what they saw in the countryside. Li quoted George Mathew's article on the trip:

> The reason we paid attention to Chinese village self-governance is because they have been determined to give the power to villagers, but do not neglect the Chinese Communist Party (CCP) leadership in the meantime. This institution of basic-level governance with Chinese characteristics will be a surprise to the world.[18]

It was still risky for Li Xueju and MoCA officials to make an initiative in seeking foreign engagement in village governance in the wake of the Tiananmen crackdown. Even though the overall trend was not to close the door to foreign exchanges, the political atmosphere was still tense. There was a risk of facing conservative political backlash. However, risk is always associated with potential rewards. The positive foreign reaction and contribution gave a boost to promotion of village governance and helped careers of MoCA officials along the way.

Foreign NGO players in village self-government

The Ford Foundation

The Ford Foundation office was opened in Beijing in 1988, it initially concentrated its activities in three fields: economics, law, and international relations. It gradually expanded lines of work in other fields, such as civic society, educational reform, social justice, cultural diversity, gender and environmental study, governance and public policy, in response to China's evolving needs and changing priorities.[19]

The Ford Foundation was one of the earlier, if not the earliest, foreign NGOs involved in village self-government. The Foundation's Beijing office through its program officer, Johnathan Hecht, established a working relationship with MoCA officials in charge of implementing village self-government. It assisted MoCA in establishing communication with foreign grassroots governance experts and practitioners and in sponsoring exchanges between MoCA and foreign counterparts. The most noticeable involvement of the Foundation in grassroots governance was Hecht's liaison and participation in organizing the first foreign observation visit and the Beijing conference in 1992. In addition, Hecht was recognized his role in assisting several provincial legislation of the implementation methods of the 1987 Organic Law.

Although it later expanded activities to many other areas, the Foundation continued its involvement and sponsorship in building grassroots governance. In recent years, the Foundation funded a program that aimed at increasing women participation in rural governance and village election. The program, implemented through cooperation with MoCA and local governments, provided training and consultation and facilitated exchanges of information on women activism through conference and visits. The program helped encourage women running for positions in villagers' committees in several provinces, such as Hebei, Shaanxi, and Hunan. Particularly in Qianxi, Hebei Province, the Foundation helped fund the Center for Women Legal Service, one of the first centers in the countryside exclusively devoting to women legal rights and political participation. The Center directly involved in promoting women rights participating in rural political life, particularly in village elections. The effort yielded noticeable increases in numbers of women elected as members of villagers' committees in Qianxi. According to an edited book by the Center that referenced the Foundation's support for the Center, in the fifth village election of 1999–2000, the county turnout rate among women was above 85 percent. Three hundred and one women were elected to 287 out of the total 417 villagers' committees in the country, of which three women were elected committee chairs, 18 vice chairs, a recognizable increase from the past.[20]

In 2003, The Foundation working with MoCA's Rural Division of the Department of Basic-level Governance funded a program seeking a policy innovation to raise the ratio of women elected to villagers' committees. The program selected Tanggu of Tianjin as a demonstration model. The program experimented on a range of policy innovations aiming at increases of women participation in the electoral process: from promoting woman candidates in local election methods to writing open letters to raise women conscience and to call on women to fulfill their duties.[21] The program enabled the participants to conduct policy research and field investigation, published election handbooks and materials, provided training and filed observation, and organized conferences that attracted women and practitioners from all over the country. According to a program review and summary commissioned by MoCA, the experiment on policy innovation produced a positive effect on boosting women participation in the demonstration area. In the fifth village election in Tanggu from 2003 to 2004, women participation rate was 71 percent; 34 women were elected to villagers' committees, amounting to 27.6 percent of the total elected; and one woman was elected as chair. The ratio of women elected to villagers' committees was increased by 6.6 percent, compared to the fourth election.[22] The review pointed out that women representation in Tanggu fared better than the national average of 16 percent of women holding committee positions.

The Ford Foundation involvement in village governance generally tended to be program-specific and was confined to policy networks. The grant selection and distribution were limited to certain people from the policy circle. The project-focused approach worked well for selected model activities and could be significant if the demonstration model became nationally known and spread. The drawback also arises from its project-specific approach if grantees just wanted to use the project to get funding and did nothing beyond the completion of the project.

The International Republican Institute

The positive perception of foreign experts and observers made it possible for MoCA to expand its foreign exchange programs and cooperation. In 1994, MoCA invited the International Republican Institute (IRI) to send a delegation to observe village elections. IRI became the first foreign NGO to observe village elections in China. Earlier in 1993, IRI under the leadership of Senator John McCain decided to explore IRI programming possibilities in China due to her strategic importance. IRI called on a variety of China experts including Chinese dissidents to give their advice on how to engage China. Instead of working with Chinese dissidents, IRI took the advice of many experts who believed that it would be more meaningful for IRI to support and enhance reforms underway in China that would "result in a more positive future relationship in line with our interests."[23]

The 1994 IRI observation mission led by Lorraine Spiess yielded an extensive report on village elections in Fujian. The report, while recognizing problems and errors, found that village elections had some minimally sound technical quality and that, given proper advice, they could be improved to provide village voters with an opportunity to choose their leaders in a direct and competitive electoral process. The report recommended 12 specific ways to improve the electoral process, among which, the single most important one is the institution of secret voting booths so that voters can exercise their rights to a secret ballot. The report also suggested the provision of civic education programs and training courses for both voters and election officials.[24] IRI continued its observations of village election until 1996 when Spiess left IRI to work for UNDP and did not resume its activity in village election until 2000. Since 1994, IRI has observed more than 50 village elections in ten provinces and has made detailed recommendations on election rules and procedures.[25]

Another area of IRI activities in China is election training. As its 1994 report pointed out that civic education was the key to promotion of democratic awareness of both voters and election officials, IRI sponsored workshops and training seminars for grassroots election officials. Workshops focused on the core elements of democratic elections and trained attendees on election rules and procedures, such as voter registration, proper polling place, the use of secret ballots, and vote tabulation. Training programs also included mock elections in which participants acted as poll workers, candidates, and voters. In 1996, IRI worked with MoCA officials to design a how-to-vote poster for demonstration at polling stations and voting centers on election days. The poster displayed a simple and clear voting procedure; it was widely used in village elections throughout China. In 2000, IRI sponsored a "regional networking conferences" for 30 election officials and scholars from southern and eastern China and a similar conference in 2001 for eight provinces in northern and central China. In December 2002, IRI held a conference on fairness in election campaigning; the conference introduced American experiences running and regulating competitive grassroots election campaigns. Participants of these conferences were able to exchange experiences and strategies for improving electoral rules and procedures in future elections; they presented written reports discussing issues in their provinces such as criteria for nomination, campaigning methods, election and polling station administration, prevention of election fraud, recalls, and the relationship between village committees and local party branches.

In sum, IRI, through cooperating with rural reformers at the central and local levels, carried out a variety of programs on monitoring rural elections, providing expertise and advice on the electoral process, and training government officials, election workers, election monitors, and newly elected village officials at the national, provincial, county, township, and village levels. IRI took a different approach to village election by working directly with provincial and local organizations. This approach enabled IRI to bypass the central bureaucracy and develop location-specific projects for election observations and training at the provincial and local levels. Pending on cooperative spirits of local officials, this approach could be time-saving and effective in making a difference in local village election.

The Carter Center China Program

Prior to its involvement in Chinese village self-government, The Carter Center had some programs in China in the area of public health but did not have any ongoing programs. However, when the China project began in July 1996, the project founder, Robert Pastor, had developed a program for monitoring and mediating elections over a ten-year period. Due to his international reputation, Pastor was invited to China and visited Zouping County of Shandong with Michel Oksenberg, a China expert, to look at village election in July 1996. While in Beijing, Pastor conducted three long meetings with Mr Wang Zhenyao, MoCA's chief official in charge of village election, and Wang asked Pastor to organize a mission to advise them in the electoral process. On September 1 and 11, Pastor received invitation letters from Wang and Ambassador Zhou Wenzhong, respectively, asking him to organize a delegation to "assess the election process and to advise us on ways it could be improved."[26]

After receiving the letter from Wang, Pastor invited a number of scholars, including Oksenberg, Harry Harding, and foundation representatives to meet with Carter and him to look into the possibility of developing a China project. The center held a China orientation seminar on possible areas of cooperation with the Chinese government. A consensus was reached that the center should identify village election as the possible project. This project was consistent to the center's focus on global elections and the center has established reputation and expertise on election-related issues. Pastor suggested to Jimmy Carter that a China project was warranted given the growing transformation in China.

Shortly after the decision to go ahead with Chinese village election, Pastor started to assemble a Carter Center team to observe Chinese village election. I joined Pastor in exploring project possibilities and preparing the China trip at this time. I wrote a memo to Pastor, underlining some issues on village election we needed to consider on our trip. First, we needed to see if the vague election laws and nomination procedures were widely posted and made known to villagers. I was concerned that lack of knowledge of laws and procedures could make the election process take on "local colors." I was also concerned that nomination procedures may not be plainly spelled out and followed. Second, we needed to look at campaign issues, such as methods and financing. Third, we wanted to observe voting-related issues, such as accessibility of ballet boxes, how villagers voted, and how votes were counted. In addition, I also suggested another issue to be explored, namely possible setup of a local election data center. This data-collecting or training center could be a vehicle for better monitoring local elections.[27]

In March 1997, the Carter Center delegation, consisting of seven members (I was one of the seven members), at the invitation of the MoCA, visited and observed village elections in Fujian and Hebei. The composition of the delegation, as one scholar observed, was a mix of independent scholars, a management consultant, and the director of Program Development for the Asian Foundation.[28] The inclusion of Ian McKinnon, a former aid to Prime Minister Joe Clark, was to use his Canadian connection to get Canadian government support for and involvement in our effort to develop cooperation with Chinese counterparts. Apart from observing village elections, Pastor's mission also included negotiations with MoCA officials regarding longer-term cooperation between the Carter Center and the ministry. The visit paved the way for President Carter to visit China in July.

From the very beginning, the Center's strategy was to use President Carter's personal reputation and his contacts with Chinese leaders to set up cooperation with MoCA. It happened that Carter met with Minister Doje Cering when he visited Tibet in 1987. When Carter wrote to him expressing his interest in village election project, Doje Cering invited him to visit China in July 1997. Carter visited China and related his positive comments to the Chinese leaders on village elections. Carter also held a specific talk with Doje Cering at the US embassy regarding future cooperation with MoCA. At the meeting, Pastor asked the Minister how many village elections were conducted with standards like those of Fujian.[29] Doje Cering was candidate with his question saying he did not know and then offered an estimation of perhaps 50 percent.[30] Pastor proposed to set up a national data collection system, to which the Minister agreed. Subsequently, Pastor negotiated an agreement with Xu Rongxin, the Vice Minister, to develop a national system for collecting election results and assessing the election procedures and process. This data collecting system would enable MoCA to better improve civil education programs, identify problem areas, and target the areas most in need.

Despite the top ministerial support in principle for cooperation, MoCA middle-level bureaucrats in charge of foreign exchange proved to be fussy about diplomatic etiquettes and specific programming. Pastor had an extensive agenda, but he realized that his Chinese counterparts wanted to move much more slowly, and so he negotiated a more modest, incremental setup steps.

- An exchange of visits between representative of the Carter Center and the Ministry.
- Development of a computer system for collecting information and results on village elections.
- Training of village election officials.
- Development of uniform election procedures.
- Special training of senior election officials, perhaps in the United States
- Civic education and publicizing elections.

In his invitation letter to Doje Cering to visit the United States, Carter reiterated these cooperation items to the Minister and urged him to conclude a formal agreement earliest possible.[31] The formal agreement of cooperation between the Carter Center and MoCA was reached during the second Carter Center delegation to observe village elections led by Pastor in March 1998. The agreement included all the points raised in Carter's letter. The focal point of the cooperation was the development of a computer system that would enable MoCA to collect village election data directly from county civil affairs offices vie internet. This national system of collecting data on village election would permit MoCA and provincial officials to answer the question as to where elections are being implemented properly and where they are not. It would assist the Ministry to measure and explain the rate of re-election of village committee chairs, the fairness of the nomination process, and which areas do not have competitive election. The center team worked for three months on nearly 100 drafts to perfect two survey forms that would be used to report at each village the electoral process and results. The survey results would then be sent to township civil affairs officers who would take the surveys to county civil affairs offices to be input into the election database.

In order to implement the agreement, Pastor decided to hire an internet company to develop software to be used for collecting and transmitting village election data between MoCA and pilot provinces. The basic idea was to collect election data at village and township levels and send the data to county civil affairs bureaus where computer staff will input the data. Upon finishing the data, staff will upload it to the internet and transmit it to the MoCA. Once the software was designed, there was need to train local civil affairs bureau staff to use the software. The Carter Center and the MoCA jointly set up training programs and the Carter Center conducted training section in 1998 for 22 local civil affairs staff from Fujian, Hunan, and Jilin provinces. The training focused on the use of the software, data collection and entry, and data transmission and reception.[32]

There are two reasons for establishing a national data system. First, no one had any idea of how many competitive and fair elections were held in China. Until this project, the only data were anecdotal. No one could speak with any authority on how well the elections were doing without a comprehensive data collection system, which would begin by providing a good sample. Second, once the pilot project was done, one could use the system for the entire country, and that system, in turn, could become the spine of a national election commission. The data collection system could be used not just to do a survey of each election but to communicate the full results. It would be a short step from that to having the capacity to conduct national elections. Once the database was created and training was done, what was left was the implementation.

According to the agreement, the national trial was to be implemented in nine pilot counties in three pilot provinces. The trial project, later joined by another 40 counties in Hunan, was completed in 2000, with the data transmitted to MoCA. MoCA officials believed that the project would help enhance election data gathering at provincial and national levels. It would aid MoCA officials with an electronic eye in identifying where election implementation has problems and how election rules and procedures can be improved and standardized. In the past, according to Zhan Chenfu, then the Division chief of Rural Basic-level Governance, the MoCA had to rely on three methods of monitoring national village elections: occasional visits by MoCA officials, reports or newsletters from local civil affairs bureaus, and selective official statistics.[33]

Despite the initial success of the pilot data gathering system, the continuation and the expansion of the project faced uncertainty, due to the leadership change at the Carter Center resulting in the different orientation of the Carter Center and MoCA toward the data-gathering project. Initially, the Carter Center wanted to introduce the concept and help fund the pilot project. Then, it expected MoCA to take over and build up the system based on the pilot project. MoCA, on the other hand, wanted the Carter Center to raise funds to equip local civil affairs bureaus, at least down to the county level, with computers and other hardware. MoCA initially was hoping that the Carter Center could equip all the villages in the three pilot counties with computers estimated at 3,000. The divergence of the objectives dampened the initial enthusiasm of MoCA officials and the project was carried out to terms only after the Carter Center promised to try to obtain as many computers as possible. After the completion of the pilot data gathering system, the Carter Center initiated another three-year cooperative project with MoCA that included the expansion of computerized election data gathering in four provinces and upgrading the data gathering software in 2000. The Carter Center committed $1.2 million to the three-year cooperation. By 2002, 162 counties in Fujian and Jilin were equipped with the software and hardware and MoCA gathered 2000 and 2001 election data of Fujian and Jilin.[34] In 2003, Jimmy Carter persuaded Michael Dell to donate 1.3 million yuan worth of computers to be used for gathering village election data in Hunan, Chongqing, and Shaanxi, a number far short of 3,000 computers of what was initially discussed and understood.[35] However, depending on how many resources that could be made available to MoCA through this cooperation, the actual implementation of the moderately expanded project could be in question. Even today, there is little evidence that MoCA officials actually utilized the national village election data gathered in the pilot project to improve and standardize election rules and procedures as MoCA has shifted the emphasis from election to management, decision-making, and supervision of village self-government.

The difference between the Carter Center and other international NGOs in their involvement in village election lies in the Center's utilization of high-profile contacts with high-level Chinese officials – a top-down approach to setting up village election programs in China. Jimmy Carters' personal involvement and the endorsement he received from top Chinese leaders opened up the door to cooperation. The initial masterful planning and execution of the Center's village election project under the leadership of Robert Pastor resulted in the Center's international reputation for promoting and improving village election and won the Chinese good will and appreciation for the Center's contribution to raising domestic and international awareness of village election and self-government.

Assessing the impact of foreign participation

With an exception in the area of economic development, foreign involvement in village election and governance is the most extensive and its influence widely spread in social and political development in China. Foreign NGOs, inter-governmental organizations (IGOs), and individuals alike have participated through various channels of cooperation with Chinese central and local partners in the process of building a village electoral institution. Through such coopera-tion, foreign participants have gained unprecedented accesses and reached mil-lions of villagers in so many different locations including some most remote and backwards areas in Guangxi, Yunnan, Gansu, Shaanxi, and the northeast region. Despite some uneasiness, the Chinese government endorsed and even encour-aged cooperation with foreign participants, which resulted in dynamic interac-tions and exchanges between Chinese and foreign observers, scholars, policy makers, and practitioners in the field of village self-government and election. To what extent have foreign involvements made an impact on Chinese village elec-tion and governance? Chinese and foreign scholars have tried to assess the role of foreign organizations played in developing village elections.[36] While it is dif-ficult to assess the actual foreign impact on the real life of villagers, there are signs and evidence to show that foreign advice, expertise, and funding have helped improve village electoral institutionalization, electoral processes, local participation, and public management of village affairs.

Impact on raising public awareness of village elections

Village elections had been held long before foreign participation, it was virtually unnoticed and ignored by the outside world. Initially, the Chinese government did not fanfare the practice, but quietly observed and limitedly endorsed vil-lagers' initiative, because this rural political reform was controversial from the start, and also because the government did not know if villagers' initiatives would work to improve rural governability. The initial foreign participation by scholars and IRI did not generate much publicity abroad, but did arouse the awareness of government officials, especially MoCA officials who believed that this was something they could explore to the advantage of their cause. Often than not in Chinese politics, experimental practices like village election may not get an immediate official acknowledge and public endorsement, simply because they have not been proven or their consequences are unknown. More often than not, when foreign press or opinion affirms the practices, it can become a selling point to gain domestic support as top leaders pay close attention to foreign opinion. Positive foreign feedback boosts practitioners' confidence. Then using foreign publicity to promote the cause is a logic afterthought and reinforces the experimental resolve. Deng Xiaoping's reform policy in the late 1970s and earlier 1980s was a good case to illustrate this point.

Village election was not initially set up for foreign consumption; it was an experiment to deal with emerging rural problems. When foreign affirmation and praise became apparent, MoCA officials artfully used it to advocate further implementation and boost their reform status. The observation and comments made by the first foreign delegation members were received positively by MoCA officials. Li Xueju, then Director of the Department of Basic-Level Government, cited extensively those comments in his book to show that MoCA was doing the right thing in implementing village elections.[37] There was little doubt that MoCA officials used the newly generated foreign publicity to silence the opposition and further promote village self-government.[38]

This is not to say that the Chinese government always embraces foreign media coverage on Chinese affairs. Often, the government reaction to foreign reports is cautious, with a suspicious eye. The initial reaction of the government to foreign involvement and media coverage on village election was rather guarded. The Chinese government, while accepting Jimmy Carter's proposal, was very precautious in receiving the first Carter Center delegation to observe village election. The immediate question facing government officials was how to make of the Center's intention and purpose. But there was also an issue of diplomatic formality: who would be an appropriate host for the Center? The government initially did not know how to receive the delegation, since the government considered the Carter Center as a non-official entity. It was then decided that the Intercontinental Communication Center, a semi-official media corporation under the Information Office of the State Council, and MoCA would jointly host the delegation.[39] During the whole trip observing village elections, officials from both institutions accompanied the delegation members. It was not until 1998 when the Carter Center delegation made the second visit that the government began to feel comfortable in dropping the Intercontinental Communication Center and letting MoCA officials directly host the delegation.[40]

Chinese official media initially had limited coverage on the Carter Center delegation activities. In contrast, the second Carter Center delegation was well covered by Chinese media: *People's Daily*, *China Daily*, *Youth Daily*, and Beijing TV all sent out reporters to cover the delegation activities.[41] According to a study on the foreign media coverage, the 1997 Carter Center delegation received no coverage in the official English paper China Daily. On the second delegation mission in March 1998, however, the China Daily published two articles on the delegation activities, and four more articles on the Carter Center's July visit.[42]

The 1997 Carter Center delegation mission generated international interest in and coverage on Chinese village election, which must have attracted Chinese leaders' attention. Jimmy Carter endorsed village election by publishing an Op-Ed article in the New York Time.[43] The Atlanta Journal and Constitution ran a series of articles on the Carter Center China mission and the Reuters covered the delegation activities. The Christian Science Monitor and Associated Press published articles with titles like "China's Village Elections Hint at Democracy" and "Village Elections Provide First Seed of Democracy in China."[44] The Atlanta Journal and Constitution published Pastor's article "Village Elections a Sign of Progress."[45] Perhaps more importantly, the Chinese government took a special notice of Vice President Al Gore's comment on the March 26 during his visit in China, citing the Carter Center's participation in observing village elections. In answering reporter's question of human rights during a press conference, Gore revealed that he discussed village elections and the Carter Center's role in observing village elections with the Chinese leaders.[46]

The media effect resulting from the Carter Center 1997 and 1998 observation missions could be largely attributed to Robert Pastor's adept assembly of delegation members that included well-known scholars, educators, a journalist, a photographer, and a documentary file maker who were able to report and assess village elections as well as communicate their opinion with western audiences. But more importantly, the Carter Center's international reputation and Pastor's masterful use of publicity to report the Center's field observation and activities attracted world attention. Pastor was perhaps the first NGO delegation leader who held press conferences in Beijing Jian Guo Hotel that were well attended by Chinese and foreign press corps. At the press conferences, Pastor discussed the delegation reports that assessed village elections, and delegation members answered the questions from the audiences. The efficiency and transparency of the delegation work gave Chinese officials very deep impression on the Center's missions.[47]

The positive international reaction to Chinese village election that the Carter Center brought about was a catalyst for changing the attitudes of high-ranking officials toward the Carter Center in particular and the international coverage of village elections in general. The government specifically granted Pastor's request to include Tom Friedman, a columnist from the New York Times, in the 1998 delegation, a rare treatment for a foreign journalist without going through the approval procedures administered by the Ministry of Foreign Affairs. When Minister Zeng Jianhui of the Information Office of the State Council met with the delegation members the first time in 1997, he was cordial, welcoming, and listening. By the second time, he hosted Pastor and his team, he was just as welcoming, but much at ease and very thankful for what Pastor and the Carter Center delegation did on the 1997 mission. He was instrumental in getting the State Council approval of Friedman's participation in the Center's mission.

Another minor incident also demonstrated that the government was determined to give Pastor and his delegation as less trouble as possible in the Carter Center's second observation mission in March 1998. Due to the high profile of the delegation, many foreign journalists stationed within China wanted to come along with the delegation to observe village election. However, the state regulation required foreign journalists to apply to the Ministry of Foreign Affairs for their travel permit; most of journalists could not make it in time to go with the delegation. There was one journalist from Columbia Broadcast Service, a Chinese national, whose husband is a dissident living in the United States. With her background and her profession, this person's profile made her a perfect candidate to be monitored by the State Security. She appealed to Pastor to take her along. When Pastor recommended her to MoCA officials, they were obviously concerned and not accommodating. With Pastor's insistence, she did make the trip and the Chinese government did not make an open issue with Pastor. Instead, State security officials had her followed during the trip. A case like this on other occasions could have given Pastor a hard time and could have had adverse effect on the mission.

The involvement of foreign NGOs, particularly the 1997 and 1998 Carter Center observation missions generated international and domestic high-ranking officials' interest in village elections. Pastor personally briefed White House and State Department officials as well as Newt Gingrich, who was from Georgia and participated in many Carter Center activities. It was not surprising that President Bill Clinton and Vice President Al Gore and the US House Speaker Newt Gingrich discussed village elections during their trips to China. Clinton even visited one village to experience village self-government in Shaanxi during his official trip to China in 1998.[48] Many officials from the European Union and Japan came to China and asked to observe village elections. All the major western media had coverage on the rural participation and electoral development.

Not all foreign attention could have gone without notice of top Chinese leaders. In a way, top officials were caught off guard by the amount of foreign interest and attention and the questions raised by foreign dignities in village election.[49] Nevertheless, it was certainly a pleasant surprise to them, given the positive response from and coverage by foreign visitors and journalists. Premier Zhu Rongji was the first to tune to village elections. In his answer to Jimi ForCruz, the Beijing Bureau Chief of Time Magazine, who traveled with the Carter Center delegation observing elections in March 1998, Zhu commented that:

> Of course I am in favor of democratic elections. One of the U.S. foundations (the Carter Center, author added) organized a mission to China to look into these elections in China, and they issued a very affirmative report on that.... So I think these are all very good ways and also a good direction for development.[50]

Li Peng, Chairman of the Standing Committee of the NPC, after stepping down from the premier post, began to show his own interest in village election. Right after he took over the NPC, he asked for the revision draft of the Organic Law that had been pending in the Legislative Office of the State Council for a number of years. He was responsible for pushing the legislative process in approving the newly revised legislation. He went out of the way to open up the legislative process on the draft law for national review and input. During his field trip to Lishu of Jilin, the birthplace of *haixuan*, where the Carter Center delegation just visited on 8 March 1998, Li made the following comment on village self-government:

> I believe three issues are important: the first one is election. The direct exercise of democratic rights by villagers and the election of cadres who have the trust of people must be guaranteed though the revision of the 1987

Organic Law on Villagers' Committees. Election is also supervision on cadres[51]

President Jiang Zemin also broke the silence and openly spoke on village election during his field trip to Anhui before the fifteenth party congress in September 1998. His speech was more "dialectical"; while supporting village election, it emphasized the party leadership in dealing with rural affairs at the same time. Jiang said that:

> expanding rural grassroots democracy and guaranteeing direct exercise of democratic rights by peasants are the most widely-spread practice of socialist democracy in the countryside.... It is also of fundamental importance to encourage peasants' initiative and ensure long-term governance and stability in the countryside.

Jiang emphasized that while "the main task is to conduct direct election of villagers' committees, expansion of rural grassroots democracy must be under the party leadership, based on rule of law, orderly, and step by step."[52]

1998 was a watershed year for village election and self-government as the result of increasing international interest and coverage. Most of the top leadership's speech and comment on village self-government were made in that year as far as the available and published government documents and Chinese press reports showed. It was also the year in which the long-awaited revision of the 1987 Organic Law was adopted and the top leadership openly, albeit with various qualifications, endorsed village election. A new wave of implementation of village elections began immediately after the promulgation of the 1998 Organic Law. Even Guangdong Province, the last stronghold in resisting village election, rode on the wave by conducting its provincial village election in 1998. 1998 also saw the first controversial township head election was conducted in Buyun of Sichuan, which was hailed as an expansion of village election.[53]

Foreign influence in building an electoral institution

Foreign involvements and MoCA's openness have produced a dynamic interaction between foreign and Chinese participants and positive impact on the electoral development. Apart from publicity effect on the perception of Chinese top officials regarding village election, foreign participants have made an impact on the improvement of village election and on building the village electoral institution. While using foreign praises to shine the works of village self-government, MoCA officials was also trying to listen to expert suggestions and advices on how to improve village election and possibly to drum up domestic support for implementation effort. As a result, the village electoral institution has been improved and strengthened with better rules and procedures that reflect internationally accepted standards.

Foreign participation in conferences, observations, and training programs has helped improve village electoral rules and procedures. Both central and local officials greatly benefited from accessing to foreign advices, comments, suggestions, and criticism regarding the implementation of village elections. Chinese do not always openly acknowledge or admit their learning from foreign advice. In public, officials usually do not endorse any new ideas and advice, but in private, they often concede that such ideas and suggestions are actually good. In some instances, Chinese officials were polite in listening but non-committal in face-to-face talks. Then next thing you know they were quietly implementing the advice they received in the face-to-face conversation. Even today, Chinese officials have yet to give enough credit to international contribution to the institutional development of village elections, at least in official statement, even though they discreetly acknowledged that they have learned from foreign advice.[54]

In March 1998, the Carter Center observed elections in several villages in Jilin. In Gujialingzi Village, we noticed that each schoolroom had five desks dispersed throughout the room. Five voters entered into the room simultaneously, and often voters marked their ballots at the same desk in clear view of each other. Although voters were not bothered or uncomfortable, the lack of screening around each desk fell short of international standards for secret balloting. Pastor mentioned this to the companying officials who did not respond to his comment right on the spot. But at the next stop where we observed an election, to Pastor's surprise, secret voting booths were set up in a room with windows covered by curtains and voters entered into the room individually to vote.

The fact is that at the very beginning of implementing village elections, election officials were either lack of sufficient knowledge about voting rules and procedures or paid no adequate attention to such rules and procedures, for MoCA officials were more concerned about the opposition to implementing the Organic Law. It was the comments, criticism, and suggestions made by foreign observers that boosted the confidence of supporters of village election and attracted Chinese officials' attention to the issue.[55]

At the conference held in Fujian in 1992, Kevin O'Brien, a member of the delegation, noted that the revised provincial implementation method, which was under the review of Fujian people's congress, contained the same indirect voting by household representatives as the 1990 version. He pointed out that this indirect voting requirement was far short of international standard of one person one vote. MoCA officials who had been working with Fujian officials to revise the regulation quickly used this comment to persuade Fujian in adopting the direct election standard and to encourage other provincial officials at the conference to do the same.[56] Other members, for example, Tyrene White, also stressed the important principle of direct individual voting.[57] The role of foreign individuals and the Ford Foundation in influencing Fujian electoral institutional building was also recognized in the IRI 1995 report after an IRI delegation observed elections in Fujian in 1994.[58]

Both the IRI and the Carter Center observation delegations have produced extensive observation reports and those reports were given to central and local officials. In those reports, specific issues observed during the practice of village elections were raised for discussion. The reports then proposed recommendations as a way to solve the issues or improve the electoral rules and procedures. The IRI identified 12 issues areas in the election and made 40 specific recommendations in its 1994 report, which became the benchmark to evaluate elections for its subsequent visits and observations. The 1997 Carter Center report gave out 14 suggestions, and the 1998 report put forth 13 recommendations. Most of the suggestions and recommendations dealt with election rules and procedures, though the 1998 recommendation raised some medium to long-term issues such as creation of voter identification cards and an election commission. The subsequent reports followed and repeated the initial issues and recommendations.

To what extend have those suggestions and recommendations been heeded and implemented? According to the IRI own assessment of the 12 issue areas, 18 specific recommendations were implemented, 11 were partially implemented, and 11 were not implemented. From 1994 to 2003, the IRI adopted a time-series model of observation of the same locations over years. From its published reports of observations from 1994 to 2003, Fujian has adopted many recommendations from the IRI, which made Fujian among the best in terms of village elections in the country. These include the elimination of proxy voting, the strict control of the use of roving ballot boxes, the universal and mandatory use of secret voting rooms, and the elimination of negative voting. The IRI report calls on other provinces to learn from Fujian's experiences and put newly improved rules into the practices of their own village elections.[59]

The impact of foreign advice on election rules and procedures has also been documented in scholarly works and commented by Chinese election officials on various occasions. An important internationally recognized election principle is secret balloting. The incorporation of this principle in the Organic Law and election practices clearly demonstrated foreign influence. In the past, the Chinese adopted the concept of *wujiming*, a Chinese equivalent to secret ballot, in various elections. But the understanding of secret balloting was no more than "don't mark your name on the ballot." There were no procedural rules to ensure *wujiming*. The repeated foreign comments and emphasis on this important election principle eventually sank in with provincial and central officials. A good example was the exchanges taking place between Minister Zeng and Pastor during the 1997 and 1998 missions. Minister Zeng was initially very opposed to the idea of writing secret ballot into the law, but by the end, he completely agreed with the importance of a secret ballot and pledged to make the change in the law.[60]

Prior to the 1998 Organic Law, most of provincial implementation laws and methods did not have procedural rules guaranteeing secret ballots. The Election Handbook of Villagers' Committees compiled by MoCA officials in 1995 defined the term of *wujiming* explicitly as "the casting of votes in a secret environment without recording one's names."[61] However, the handbook did not prescribe procedural rules to create such a "secret environment." It was not until

1998 with the culmination of previous foreign advice and criticism, the high-profile Carter Center observation reports, and personal inputs,[62] all pertaining to this principle, that the new Organic Law set the procedural rule guaranteeing secret ballots. The Article 14 specifically requires secret booths to be set up for voting. The foreign influence on the 1998 Organic Law was positive and contributing, though was not publicly recognized by the Chinese government.[63]

As early as 1992 when the MoCA first invited foreign scholars and practitioners to observe village elections, foreign inputs were considered instrumental in making Fujian adopt one-person-one-vote principle in the implementing law. Until then, most of village elections in Fujian were conducted with each household casting one vote.[64] Another related practice is proxy voting. On this issue, foreign observers pointed out that this practice violates the individuality of the ballot and suggested the banning the use or limiting the number of proxy votes.[65] Fujian is the first province that took the advice of foreign observers and prohibited the use of proxy votes in the 1997–1998 election. In the subsequent update on the provincial implementation regulation, Fujian replaced proxy votes with absentee ballots.[66]

The Chinese government used to require a majority rule to determine the winner in village elections. The 1987 Organic Law mandated the "fifty plus one percent" rule stipulating that any candidate must receive the majority votes of the registered voters, short of which a run-off much be held between the two top vote getters. In the run-off election, half of the registered votes cast and winning at least 33 percent of the vote cast are needed for an election to be considered valid. The majority winning rule was set with the intent to ensure that the winner reflect popular will and support, thus can indisputably govern. This stringent requirement led to 28 percent of unsuccessful elections in Fujian and higher percentage and repeated failures of run-offs elsewhere.[67] While considering the merit and good points of the winning rule, the IRI suggested in the 1994 report to abandon the "fifty plus one percent rule" in favor of a direct primary election.[68] The Carter Center 1997 report also put forth a suggestion to reduce the run-off requirement to "a plurality of 40 percent." In revising the 1987 Organic Law, the NPC adopted some of the suggestions to revise the 50 percent rule; the new law now requires the majority of the total votes cast, instead of the total registered votes, to determine the winner, provided the majority of the total registered voters cast their vote. The new law leaves run-off election rules to be promulgated by provincial implementation regulations. Most of provincial regulations have adopted a plurality rule in determining the run-off winner as long as half of the registered voters cast their votes.[69]

Foreign effect on policy implementation and innovation

One of the most notable and recognizable contributions by international organizations and individuals to the development of the village electoral institution is in the area of training. Training in village election and governance was one of the major cooperative programs involved by foreign organizations and Chinese counterparts. Foreign NGOs such as the Ford Foundation, IRI, the Carter Center, and the Asian Foundation have all engaged in the provision of training materials and courses for electoral officials and elected village committee chairs and members. These training activities have helped spread local awareness of village election and improve electoral rules and procedures. Moreover, foreign involvements in exchange programs have enabled civil affairs and local government officials to acquire technical expertise and comparative knowledge in conducting village elections. Furthermore, foreign assistance reinforces MoCA commitment to policy implementation and innovation in village election and governance.

There are three characteristics of village election and governance training in which foreign organizations have involved. First, training programs are extensive, covering almost all the provinces. IRI, as one of the earliest foreign organizations that sponsored training, worked with local government officials to conduct training for election officials in eight provinces. The Carter Center, working with MoCA, held two training sections attended by civil affairs officials from 28 provinces except Beijing, Jilin, and Hainan in 2000 and 2001. In addition, the Center engaged in training elected villagers' committee chairs on procedures of village government in Shangdong provinces. The EU–China project carried out 34 training courses and seminars involving people from more than 20 provinces and hosted back-to-back central-level training and research conferences in 2002. Provincial and local civil affairs officials from 31 provinces attended the two-week long conferences.[70]

Second, training programs are populous. More people have participated in election training than in any known foreign sponsored projects in China. The Carter Center training project attracted 730 trainees in its various training sections offered at the central and local levels. Its Shandong training alone had 165 local participants.[71] The EU–China project has engaged in the largest training undertaking by far. By 2004, it recruited 3,202 "training trainees" who were county- and prefecture-level civil affairs officials and people who are already trainers from more than 20 provinces including Heilongjiang, Yunnan, and Xinjiang. MoCA estimated that by the end of the five-year cooperation, it would have 5,000 participants to be trained in Beijing and tens of thousands to receive training at local training centers.[72]

Third, training programs are diverse in content. The Ford Foundation had an innovative training program with an objective to raise women participation in village governance. IRI had seminars on regional networking where participants from southwestern, northeast, and central regions gathered to exchange information on their own village election experiences and discussed ways to further improve village elections. The Carter Center and The EU–China project sponsored international conferences focusing on village election and governance. The Carter Center also supported the development of village election handbook which has been distributed to provinces – an effort to standardize electoral rules and procedures. Based on the election handbook, the EU–China project developed an interactive teaching materials that include

"Overhead Transparencies on Village Elections," "Village Elections: A Polling and Counting Manual," and "Monitoring Manual for Village-Committee Elections." In addition, training courses were held on governance transparency and management of village affairs in Ningxia, Anhui, and Zhejiang in 2005.

Foreign participation in village election has further promoted exchange programs between China and foreign countries in the area of political development and local governance. A great number of civil affairs and county and township government officials who may not otherwise have the opportunities participated in foreign exchange programs and personally experienced elections and local governance in other countries. In the earlier 1990s, more foreign scholars and practitioners were invited to observe village elections and attend conferences. Most of them were individuals, not representing institutions, such as the ten experts and scholars from seven countries in 1992. Since 1994, MoCA began to work directly with foreign NGOs such as IRI, the Asian Foundation, and the Carter Center.

But more importantly, foreign contacts also enabled MoCA to send Chinese practitioners and policy implementers to visit and observe foreign elections and local governance. Through foreign exchanges, MoCA recruited and trained many civil affairs and township and county officials with an international outlook. For example, Lishu's Fei Yuncheng was among the earlier local officials to go to Japan to study local governance in 1993. Many central and local civil affairs officials visited India, Britain, Holland, Bangladesh, and Southeast Asian countries to experience first-hand local governance. In 1995, Wang Zhenyao, then the Deputy Director of Department of Basic-Level Governance of MoCA was invited to give a talk at a forum on Chinese rural development at Columbia University. With the establishment of institutional relations, MoCA had resources to send more central and local civil affairs officials to study foreign elections and governance. IRI, the Ford Foundation, and the Carter Center sponsored Chinese delegations to observe American elections; the most noticeable visits were NPC and MoCA delegations to observe 2000, and 2004 presidential elections in which delegation members were able to visit polling stations and electoral wards to talk directly to voters and polling officials.[73] In 2003, the Carter Center also invited MoCA officials to observe Nigeria presidential election. Since 2004, the EU–China project also sponsored four MoCA delegations to study European local elections, training, and governance in Sweden, Germany, and France.[74]

Foreign organizations' interaction with MoCA's in developing cooperative projects also produced innovative policies with regard to village elections and governance. The best example is the promotion of woman participation in villages' self-government. Women rights and participation in village self-government had been an issue since de-communization. In many places, women were discriminated in land contracts and allocation of village resources as well as in representation on villagers' committees.[75] Hunan was the first province that tried to address women representation at the provincial level.[76] In its village election method promulgated in 1996, it stipulates that at least one member on the villagers' committee must be a woman. Procedural measures have been established to ensure at least one woman candidate for the election.[77] In 2001, the State Council issued a platform to promote women rights; it specifically encourages women to participate in village election and raises ratio of women representation in villagers' committees.[78] Seizing the opportunity, the Ford Foundation funded several women programs to promote women participation. After Qianxi, The foundation worked with MoCA to initiate Tanggu demonstration project. The project gathered useful information and practices in training women participants and cadres and produced a number of results. It increased women representation as a result of greater numbers of women elected to villagers' committees. The project also turned out several publications pertaining to raise women participation rate in village governance such as "Practical Election Handbook for Women" and "Training Manual for Rural Women." The Tanggu demonstration project provided a positive lesson of using institutional arrangements to raise women status in rural governance.

Last but not least, foreign involvement has deepened Chinese own study and spending on village election and self-government. The publicity effect of the Carter Center visits in 1997 and 1998 not only attracted international attention, but also boosted up domestic interest in the academic and policy communities. There was a great surge in publications and PhD dissertations on village election and governance.[79] In a publication index compiled by Liu Xitang, an MoCA official involved in village election, books, and articles published since 1997 have increased quite noticeably.[80] Foreign involvement in funding various village projects also stimulated Chinese spending at the various levels on village election and self-government. In MoCA, for example, the office budget was 90,000 yuan for three departments in 1991, but by 2002, the Department of Basic-level Governance alone had an office budget of three million.[81] Rural divisions of provincial civil affairs departments have also increased their budgets in implementing the Organic Law.

Conclusion

In recent years, foreign involvements in village election and governance have been active, extensive, and influential. Major players include IGOs, NGOs, and individual scholars and practitioners. The forms of such involvement are also diversified; some work with central government institutions, others team up with local governments, still others cooperate with scholar and research communities. The effectiveness of foreign projects often is a function of project objectives, selection of partners, management philosophy, funding, and implementation methods. Through various collaborative projects, foreign participants have been able to observe and assess rural political development and provide advice and training to improve village election and governance.

Why did the Chinese government allow foreign IGOs and NGOs to get involved in rural political development in the first place? The answer to the question needs to take into account several factors. First, the Chinese state since economic reform has deliberately reduced its reach to society, especially in the areas of providing certain social services and grassroots governance. It has allowed the growth of native NGOs; most of them are cultural, recreational, social, and environmental in nature. But in rural areas, there was a great void in terms of government or other social organizations providing needed services and education. Second, foreign involvement was an incremental process; the initial approach was more discrete, subtle, and sensitive and specific to Chinese needs. Their work in China was generally viewed as positive by Chinese partners. Third, there are certain incentives and need for government institutions to work with foreign organizations; often such cooperation leads to additional institutional resources such as funding or foreign visits. In addition, real needs for technical advice, foreign lessons, and training also put pressure on the government. Fourth, as a Chinese observer pointed out, foreign NGOs operating in China are still very small in numbers and most of them tend to cooperate with the Chinese government in their activities. The government has so far felt confident in dealing with foreign NGOs and in mitigating the "side effects" that foreign organizations may bring about.[82]

While foreign involvement has helped promote village election and governance, the true impetus for building an effective electoral institution has come from Chinese reform-minded policy makers, central and local civil affairs officials, and various local practitioners. They have been facing the challenge of responding to popular dissatisfaction and deteriorating rural governance.[83] What foreign participants have brought to the table is the assistance in building the technical capacity of an electoral institution to meet the growing challenge from the countryside.

Notes

1 This chapter is based on an earlier paper presented at the International Conference on the Development of the Non-State Sector, Local Governance and Sustainable Development in China held in Hangzhou, Zhejiang, China on June 24–26, 2006.
2 The 1987 Organic Law was a trial law that called on elections of villagers' committees. Because of its trial nature, the law did not mandate village elections.
3 Author's conversation with MoCA officials, March 1997.
4 The plan to invite foreign experts and scholars was made in mid-1992. See, "On the issues of village self-government," in Minzhengbu jiceng zhengquan jianshesi, *Chengxiang jiceng zhengquan jianshe gongzuo jianbao 1992* (*Bulletin on the work of urban and rural basic-level government construction 1992*), www.chinavillage.org/readbook.asp?BookContentID={C5C44B0B-D9B1-4A78-B65E-4F42B3D8CDD9}.
5 Research Group on the System of Rural Villagers' Self-Government in China and China Research Society of Basic-Level Governance, *Legal System of Village Committees in China: Research Report on the System of Village Self-Government in China 1995* (Beijing: Zhongguo shehui chubanshe, 1996), p. 82.
6 Daniel Kelliher, "The Chinese Debate over Village Self-Government," *The China Journal* 37 (1997), pp. 63–86; 75–78.
7 Marcus W. Brauchli, "China Has Surly Image, but Part of the Reason Is Bad Public Relations," *Wall Street Journal*, June 18, 1996, pp. A1, A6; Elaine Sciolino, "China, Vying with Taiwan, Explores Public Relations," *New York Times*, February 2, 1996,

pp. A1, A4; Wu Guimin, "Zhongguo nongcun jiceng minzhu zai gaige zhong fayu chengzhang (China Rural Basic-Level Democracy Is Growing Mature in Reform)," *Zhongguo shehui bao*, July 13, 1995, p. 3.

8 Xueju Li, *Zhongguo Chengxiang Jiceng Zhengquan Jianshe Gongzuo Yanjiu* (*Work Study on the Construction of Basic-Level Governance in Urban and Rural China*) (Beijing: Zhongguo shehui chubanshe, 1994), pp. 81–82.

9 Research Group on the System of Rural Villagers' Self-Government in China and China Research Society of Basic-Level Governance, *Study on the Election of Villagers' Committees in Rural China: Research Report on Villagers Self-Government 1993* (Beijing: Zhongguo Shehui Chubanshe, 1994), Forward 1.

10 Research Group on the System of Rural Villagers' Self-Government in China and Governance, *Legal System of Village Committees in China*, p. 21.

11 Kevin J. O'Brien, "Implementing Political Reform in China's Villages," *The Australian Journal of Chinese Affairs* 32 (1994), pp. 33–59; 34.

12 One of the prominent members of the society, Li Xueju is now the minister of MoCA.

13 MoCA officials had tried very hard to get international academics interested in village election, without much success. Author correspondence with Kevin O'Biren, one of the ten field participants in the 1992 field trip.

14 Research Group on the System of Rural Villagers' Self-Government in China and Governance, *Study on the Election of Villagers' Committees in Rural China*, Preface.

15 See, Minzhengbu jiceng zhengquan jianshesi zhongguo jiceng zhengquan jianshe yanjiuhui, *guanyu jiedai qiguo xuezhe kaocha woguo cunmin zizhi zhuangkuang de zongjie* (Summary of the observation by scholars from seven countries on the conditions of village self-government in our country), Beijing, January 1993, in Minzhengbu jiceng zhengquan jianshesi, "Bulletin on the work of urban and rural basic-level government construction 1993," www.chinavillage.org/readbook.asp? BookContentID={96BCF34D-40D4-480F-9573-952F0E0D4F2D}.

16 Wang Chenyao, "Translator's Preface," in *Naya defang zhengfu bijiao yanjiu* (*Comparative studies of local governments in Southeast Asia*) (Beijing: zhongguo shehui chubanshe, 1994), p. I.

17 *Township Forum*, no. 11 (1992), p. 14.

18 Li, *Work Study on the Construction of Basic-Level Governance*, p. 83.

19 More information can be found in the Ford Foundation annual reports on www.fordfound.org/elibrary/search/advanced.cfm.

20 Wang Shuzhen, *cong cunweihui zhixuan kan funÜ canzheng* (*View women political participation through direct election of villager's committees*), in *FunÜ falÜ fuwu zhongxin, FunÜ yu fa* (*Women and law*), 2001, http://www.chinavillage.org.

21 Minzhengbu nongcunchu, *tigao nongcun funÜ dangxuan cunweihui chengyuan bili zhengce chuangxin shifan xiangmu* (*Demonstration activity on policy innovation for raising the ratio of women elected to villagers' committees*), 2004, www.chinarural.org/readnews.asp?newsid=%7BA47BF5C9-C78B-4D03-8E8F-C4386CD33A10%7D.

22 Liu Jiuhong, *tigao nongcun funÜ dangxuan cunweihui chengyuan shifan xiangmu pinggu* (*Evaluation of demonstration activity on raising the ratio of women elected to villagers' committees*), December 2004, www.chinainnovations.org/read.asp?type01= 2&type02=9&type03=4&articleid=2116.

23 IRI, Testimony of Lorne W. Graner, April 30, 1998.

24 For IRI reports, visit www.iri.org.

25 www.iri.org/countries.asp?id=1039578672.

26 The letter is in Carter Center Delegation Report, *The Carter center delegation to observe village elections in China* (Atlanta: The Carter Center, 1997).

27 Author's memo to Robert Pastor, February 11, 1997.

28 Becky Shelley, "Political Globalization and the Politics of International Non-Governmental Organizations: The Case of Village Democracy in China," *Australian Journal of Political Science* 35, no. 2 (2000), pp. 225–238; 232.

29 Fujian was recognized both by MoCA officials and by international observers as one of the best provinces in conducting village elections.
30 Author's note. This author was a participant at the meeting when the exchange was made.
31 Jimmy Carter's letter to Doje Cering, July 31, 1997.
32 The Carter Center Delegation Report, 1999, p. 18.
33 The Carter Center Delegation Report, 2000, p. 7.
34 Zhongguo nongcun jiceng minzhu zhengzhi jianshe nianjian bianweihui, ed., *Zhongguo Nongcun Jiceng Minzhu Zhengzhi Jianshe Nianjian* (*The 2001 Yearbook of Democratic and Political Grassroots Construction in China*) (Beijing: Zhongguo shehui chubanshe, 2001), p. 543.
35 "Daier diannao zhuangbei cunweihui xuanju (Equip Village Election with Dell Computers)," December 11, 2003, www.chinavillage.org.
36 Paul C. Grove, "The Roles of Foreign Non-Governmental Organizations in Development and Promotion of Village Elections in China," *American Asian Review* XVIII, no. 3 (2000), pp. 111–126; Zhenglin Guo, "Waiguo Xuezhe Shiyezhong De Cunmin Xuanju Yu Zhongguo Minzhu Fazhan Yanjiu Pingxu (Research Review of Village Election and Chinese Democratic Development in the Eyes of Foreign Academies)," *Zhonguo nongcun guancha* (*China rural survey*) 5 (2003), pp. 71–78; Youxin Lang, "Waiguo Feizhengfu Zuzhi Yu Zhongguo Cunmin Xuanju (Foreign Non-Governmental Organizations and Chinese Village Elections)," *Zhejiang Xuekan* (*Zhejiang Academic Journal*) 4 (2004), pp. 143–150; Shelley, "Political Globalization and the Politics of International Non-Governmental Organizations."
37 Li Xueju, *Zhongguo Chengxiang Jiceng Zhengquan Jianshe Gongzuo Yanjiu* (*Work Study on the Construction of Basic-Level Governance in Urban and Rural China*) (Beijing: Zhongguo shehui chubanshe, 1994), pp. 81–84.
38 Kelliher, "The Chinese Debate over Village Self-Government"; Shelley, "Political Globalization and the Politics of International Non-Governmental Organizations."
39 The official explanation of the 1997 Carter Center delegation visit was that the delegation was invited by the Information Office of the State Council, not MoCA. See, Zhongguo nongcun jiceng minzhu zhengzhi jianshe nianjian bianweihui, *The 2001 Yearbook*, p. 603.
40 Part of the reason in changing the government position was due to Carter himself directly negotiating with the Minister Doje Ceren in the summer of 1997.
41 Both Pastor and this author were interviewed on the spot by Beijing TV, and the interview was later incorporated into a television special on village elections.
42 Shelley, "Political Globalization and the Politics of International Non-Governmental Organizations."
43 *New York Times*, August 10, 1997.
44 *Associated Press*, Beijing, March 20, 1997; *The Christian Science Monitor*, March 26, 1997.
45 *The Atlanta Journal and Constitution*, March 1, 1997.
46 Press Conference, The Carter Center Delegation Report, 1997, Appendix H.
47 Several MoCA officials who worked with the delegation told author in private about their positive impression on Pastor's hard working habit and on the candid and objective reports that were submitted to MoCA at the end of the trips.
48 Jim Fish, "Clinton in China," *BBC News*, June 26, 1998
49 MoCA officials told author that since the Carter Center delegation visits in 1997 and 1998, they had received more than usual instructions from the State Council and the General Office of the Party Central Committee to prepare briefings and reports on village election and governance.
50 The Carter Center Delegation Report, March 1998, Appendix 8.
51 *People's Daily*, July 8, 1998, p. 1.
52 *People's Daily*, September 28, 1998, p. 1.

53 Vivien Pik-kwan Chan, "Town Poll Awaits Beijing Ruling," *South China Morning Post*, January 11, 1999.
54 Author's conversation with MoCA and local civil affairs officials. See also, Tianjian Shi, "Village Committee Elections in China: Institutionlist Tactics for Democracy," *World Politics* 51, no. 3 (1999), p. 408.
55 Zhenyao Wang, *Maixiang Fazhixing Xuanju De Lishi Luoji* (*The Historical Logic of Developing Legalized Election*) (Beijing: Zhongguo shehui chubanshe, 2002).
56 Shi, "Village Committee Elections in China," p. 408.
57 In a personal communication with author. See also, Shelley, "Political Globalization and the Politics of International Non-Governmental Organizations," p. 230.
58 IRI Delegation Report, 1995, p. 12.
59 IRI Delegation Report, 1995, p. 3.
60 Author's correspondence with Bob Pastor, March 12, 2006.
61 Minzhengbu jiceng zhengquan jianshesi (Ministry of Civil Affairs' Department of Basic-Level Government Construction), ed., *Zhonghua Renmin Gongheguo Cunmin Weiyuanhui Xuanju Guicheng* (*The Handbook of Villagers' Committee Election of People's Republic of China*) (Beijing: Zhongguo shehui chubanshe, 1995).
62 For example, Pastor, in answering the call to make inputs on revising the Organic Law, wrote a personal letter to the NPC suggesting various ways to improve village elections.
63 In private, Chinese officials did not hide their feelings about the positive influence by foreign scholars, observers, and various organizations. Interview with MoCA officials, Beijing, Summer 2003.
64 Usually, the head of the household, a male most of time, would represent the family to cast a vote in elections. This type of voting was quite widespread in earlier rounds of elections throughout China. Fujian was one of the earliest provinces that banned the household voting in the provincial implementation law.
65 See, IRI Report, 1994; The Carter Center Reports, 1997, 1998.
66 In the countryside, postal service is grossly inadequate, making it impossible for absentee ballots to be sent out and back in time for the election. Due to the impracticality of absentee ballot, most of the provinces do not adopt this method of voting. Eventually, Fujian also abandoned this requirement while upholding the ban on proxy votes in its new implementation regulation. See *The Compilation of Village Election Regulations*, The Rural Division of the Department of Basic-Level and Community Government, June 2002, Beijing, pp. 63–66.
67 The IRI Report, 1994, p. 24.
68 IRI proposed that in a direct primary, if a candidate wins the majority of votes, the candidate should be declared the winner and no more election is needed. However, if such a primary system is not adopted, the 50 percent rule should be retained to ensure that the election process will not be controlled or manipulated by a small percentage of voters. IRI Report, 1994, pp. 23–24.
69 Some provinces such as Fujian only requires a plurality votes while other provinces such as Anhui adopts a qualified plurality votes of minimum 33 percent.
70 The EU-China Training Programme on Village Governance, *Newsletter*, December 2003, p. 4.
71 www.cartercenter.com/activities/showdoc.asp?countryID=19&submenuname=activities#.
72 Zhongguo nongcun jiceng minzhu zhengzhi jianshe nianjian bianweihui, *The 2001 Yearbook*, p. 543.
73 Members of delegations told author that they learned more from first-hand experiences than from any textbooks.
74 For delegation reports, see www.chinavillage.org.
75 For a study on the problem women land rights, see Jinxin Wang, "Zhongguo Nongcun Funü Tudi Quanli (Land Rights of Rural Women in China)," *Zhongguo nongcun jingji* (*Chinese Rural Economy*) 6 (2003), pp. 12–22.

76 Author interview with Huang Peisheng, Division Chief, Basic-level Governance of Hunan Department of Civil Affairs, Changsha, March 13, 2003.

77 Zhongguo nongcun jiceng minzhu zhengzhi jianshe nianjian bianweihui, ed., *Zhongguo Nongcun Jiceng Minzhu Zhengzhi Jianshe Nianjian* (*The 2003 Yearbook of Grassroots Democratic Development in China*) (Beijing: Zhongguo shehui chubanshe, 2003), p. 16.

78 Zhongguo nongcun jiceng minzhu zhengzhi jianshe nianjian bianweihui, ed., *Zhongguo Nongcun Jiceng Minzhu Zhengzhi Jianshe Nianjian* (*The 2002 Yearbook of Grassroots Democratic Development in China*) (Beijing: Zhongguo shehui chubanshe, 2002), p. 90.

79 Author was told that there were more requests made on MoCA for interviews and materials relating to village election in the years between 1998 and 2002.

80 For the index of Chinese publications on rural political development, see Qingshan Tan, *Village Elections in China: Democratizing the Countryside* (New York: The Edwin Mellen Press, 2006).

81 Author interview with Zhan Chengfu, Deputy Director of the Department of Basic-Level Governance, Beijing, August 2003.

82 Lang, "Foreign Non-Governmental Organizations."

83 Robert Pastor and Qingshan Tan, "The Meaning of China's Village Elections," *The China Quarterly* 162 (2000), pp. 490–512.

13 External actors in process of village elections

Foreign NGOs and China

Youxing Lang[1]

Introduction

There are several theoretical approaches to the study of democratic transitions and democratization.[2] For example, structural or systemic factors, particularly pertaining to economic development and democratization, have been contrasted with actor-centered or elite-oriented approaches. A distinction has also been drawn between the domestic and international dimensions of democratization. Advocates from more advanced democracies, regional or global powers, as Di Palma argues, can help in the democratization of developing countries;[3] the process can also be facilitated by the presence of domestic conditions such as the level of socio-economic development, the socio-political culture, presence of civil societies and the quality of the political elite. So, while internal factors are generally acknowledged to be of primary importance in the promotion of rural democratization, external actors are also known to exert certain influence which domestic actors have not been able to. China is one such country that exhibits such a characteristic. This chapter focuses on the role of foreign actors, in particular non-governmental organizations (NGOs), in China in promoting village democracy.

China is a society transiting from authoritarian rule to democracy. To date, improvements in Chinese human rights records and its transition to more democratic rule have been attributed to many elements at home and abroad including the presence of foreign NGOs. China thus serves as a fitting case for one to examine the role of external actors in a country's transition to democracy. It is conceded that domestic factors (as mentioned, such as socio-economic level, culture, civil societies, presence of a political elite) are of primary importance in the promotion of rural democratization in China. Admittedly, unlike Eastern Europe, external factors have not had much influence on Chinese domestic political forces. However, it must be pointed out that the little influence exerted by external actors has been crucial, since domestic actors could not accomplish this influence.

Much has been written about the relationship between civil society and democratization. Works on Chinese civil society, including NGOs, are widely available. For example, Gordon White and Larry Diamond have summarized some democratic functions of civil society. At the very beginning of the article under the title of "*The Chinese Debate over Village Self-Government,*" Daniel Kelliher wrote, "Western interest in the prospect of village democracy in China is booming." According to him, journalists, diplomats, scholars and organizations took interest in village elections in China by different ways such as grant, fieldwork.[4] Shi Tianjian observed that foreign actors such as Western foundations, academics, politicians and journalists "participated in various stages of the political struggle over the implementation of the Organic Law" through "providing financial support, advice, and criticism."[5] In analyzing the roles of those who played in the spread of village elections, Kevin J. O'Brien and Lianjiang Li mentioned the international support to village elections.[6] In *The Making of a Nascent Civil Society in Contemporary China*, He Baogang specifically analyzes the cooperation in village elections between the Chinese government and one domestic-based-Beijing NGO, Tianze. He points out that, due to the nature of Chinese politics, the Chinese government has not established any direct cooperation with fully autonomous organizations, but such a partnership has great potential.[7] Two obvious limitations are inherent in these works. First, their focus is on domestic NGOs and not foreign ones. Second, these works do not keep track of the roles played by foreign NGOs in Chinese village democracy, even though the relationship between foreign NGOs and democratization in China has been a key issue. As Becky Shelley acknowledges, "Although there is a body of research regarding the development of village self-government in China, there is only limited research regarding the activities of international NGOs in relation to this development."[8] Her work has made a significant contribution toward filling this gap.

Shelley approaches the issue from a global political perspective. She argues that increasingly, activities promoting democracy are "a fertile area for NGO involvement." She believes that NGO involvement in rural democracy in China exemplifies a process she calls "political globalization," based on her case study of three American-based NGOs.[9] However, her article does not analyze the goals and strategies adopted by these NGOs; at the same time, there is a lack of detailed description of their activities. These shortcomings limit readers from fully grasping the roles played by foreign NGOs in village elections. This chapter tries to remedy these limitations.

Foreign NGOs have been involved in the development of village elections in China. Among these, the major ones are the International Republic Institute (IRI), Ford Foundation and the Carter Center. Of interest in this chapter are the Carter Center and IRI. The Carter Center is especially unique in that it has an international reputation as well as rich experience in observing elections. Additionally, its founder, former US President Jimmy Carter, enjoyed a cordial relationship with China during his presidency. Mr Carter has since been able to maintain friendly relations with the Chinese government.

The central question in this chapter is, What has been accomplished by the foreign NGOs and their partners in promoting village elections in China and how have they done it? What democratic ideals does the Carter Center, or the

IRI, have? This chapter will also describe in detail the NGOs' activities during village elections. Two different methodologies are used. First, I have scrutinized relevant documents and reports. Second, I have conducted some interviews with the local actors from the Ministry of Civil Affairs (MCA), which is in charge of village elections in China and the Fujian Bureau of Civil Affairs.

Foreign NGOs as international promoters of democracy

Di Palma argues that democracy does not take place in an international vacuum, one reason in that international factors do affect domestic behavior. To him, international factors can operate in a number of ways, of which two are noteworthy: the promotion of democracy exercised by foreign agents on specific dictatorships or fledgling democracies, and the impact international opinion and successful examples implicitly have on specific countries and regions.[10] Since the 1980s, international communities such as foreign governments, NGOs and intergovernmental organizations (IGOs) have become increasingly important in facilitating democratic transitions. Particularly, the collapse of former Eastern and Central European socialist countries and the transition and consolidation of democracy in these countries have further confirmed the belief of the importance of international factors in democratization.

Today, the contributions of the international dimension, including international NGOs, to the processes of democratic transition and consolidation are a given. However, the question is, Why are external actors, and particularly some western-based international communities, so keen about supporting democracy abroad? Theoretically, one could argue that defending democracy is the best way to secure human rights and peace. As the common refrain goes, "World peace and respect for human rights require the extension and preservation of democracy."[11]

As external actors, different organizations play different roles, and each maintains its own advantages in promoting democracy. Robert A. Pastor, former director of the Latin American and Caribbean Program at the Carter Center, thinks that "NGOs have begun to play a critical role in advising local actors on the techniques of democracy, providing equipment, and mediating the rules of an election," actions which few foreign governments have performed.[12]

International NGOs run a number of programs to assist developing countries with the establishment and stabilization of democratic regime. Some of the measures used by NGOs to support and promote democracies in non-democratic countries include: first, election observation, one field that has recently been given much attention, and which the Carter Center has rich experience in; second, encouraging and supporting their partners to create an environment conducive to the establishment and development of democratic institutions and laws; third, establishing networks; fourth, providing funds and information and expertise essential for drafting further programs and strategies.

How then does one assess the functions of foreign NGOs? How and why are they able to meet their goals? This chapter uses the interaction theory to answer these questions. This theory holds that internal causes are crucial to any change, while external causes become operative through the outworking of internal causes. In China's case, under its current political system, the internal causes are the fundamental dynamics driving the democratic transition; external elements such as foreign NGOs become operative only through the Chinese government, and these outside bodies then promote the progress of Chinese democratization.[13] However, with increasing interaction and communication among states in the age of globalization, the external causes of change and development in a country have become more and more important and obvious. Village democracy in China is a case in point, exemplifying the interaction between internal and external actors in the global trend toward democratization.

How IRI and Carter Center operate in China's village elections

In a report, "The roles of Foreign Non-Governmental Organizations in Development and Promotion of Village Elections in China," Paul C. Grove from IRI argues that foreign NGOs should support Chinese village elections based on IRI experiences in China. He summarizes the IRI experience and offers some roles that foreign NGOs can play in the development of village elections.[14] Experts from IRI believe that the current Chinese uncertainties present foreign NGOs with new opportunities for cooperation.

Actually, since the early 1990s, many international NGOs have studied and observed Chinese village elections. The Ford Foundation and the Asia Foundation played key roles in supporting studies of village elections. The Carter Center and IRI have undertaken major evaluations of the village electoral process. The IRI was the first international team invited to observe village elections, and did so in Fujian in 1994 and 1997.

Introducing IRI and the Carter Center

International Republican Institute, or IRI, is a non-partisan American NGO that has close links with the People's Republic of China (PRC). Established in 1984 as a private and non-profit organization, IRI is the first foreign actor involved in Chinese village elections. In 1994, IRI started negotiations with MCA, the official agency of the Chinese government assigned to oversee the nation-wide implementation of village elections, with regard to how IRI could play an appropriate role in supporting the development of village elections. The question arose as to why IRI was supporting village elections in China and launching its "China Program." What considerations lay behind their decision? Paul C. Grove offered three major reasons. First, IRI thought that the election process could be a building block for greater political reforms. Second, some younger and better-educated reformers had requested for assistance, from both domestic and foreign sources. Third, national and local leaders were willing to cooperate with foreign organizations. In sum, to the Institute, although old problems remain and new ones have appeared in Chinese village elections, it is "cautiously optimistic about the future of election reform in China."[15]

The Carter Center was founded in 1982 by former US President Jimmy Carter and is associated with Emory University. In June 1996 and March 1997, the Chinese MCA invited the Carter Center to send a delegation to observe village elections in Fujian and Hebei provinces. After these observations, Mr Carter visited China in July of the same year. During the visit, Mr Carter and MCA discussed the major areas of cooperation that aimed to improve village elections. One role that other NGOs could not play was the Center's access to top Chinese leaders. Mr Carter could meet Chinese leaders which others could not. It is through these meetings that Mr Carter was able to offer suggestions and influence Chinese leaders. On March 14, 1998, the Carter Center and MCA signed a Memorandum of Understanding (MOU). This MOU marked the official launch of the Carter Center's "China Village Elections Project." Since then the Center has become the most important foreign non-government organization promoting rural democracy in China.

Why the Chinese government welcomes foreign NGOs

Before examining in greater detail the role of these NGOs in China's village elections, it is fitting to examine why foreign NGOs are allowed to participate in village elections. Unless they have the Chinese government's approval, these NGOs would not be able to make any contribution to Chinese democratization. Why then has the Chinese government agreed to accept the NGOs' assistance?

There are at least three reasons. First, the age of globalization has forced the Chinese regime to make use of various kinds of social powers, including foreign NGOs, for building its legitimacy. Chinese President Jiang Zemin had himself been quoted as saying that village election was one example of the democratic development in China. Jiang's remark was of course aimed at the international community, to demonstrate that human rights in China have improved, and that the Chinese Communist Party (CCP) still has a wide legitimate base. Indeed, village election and self-government could be interpreted as the CCP's attempt to regain its legitimacy in rural China. Second, democratic elections held at the grassroots do not affect the fundamentals of the Chinese political system. Third, while recognizing that these NGOs may sometimes turn out to be "trouble-makers," the Chinese government is confident that it can control the activities of these NGOs in the country.

Goal setting

NGOs usually pursue a wide variety of goals, and different types of NGOs will have different goals. However, there is a difference between what they want to do and what they can do. Many, therefore, have to be ready to revise their goals and to quickly adapt to new or changing circumstances. In this chapter, I will point out that NGOs should hold a realistic view of what they can and what they cannot do, and the kind of constraints they face; in other words, I will explore the "normative versus actual role of NGOs."[16] An understanding of this is critical to how effectively NGOs can contribute to the democratic transition.

Overall, NGOs support democracy with the aim of establishing "a world order of law and justice" and securing "greater allegiance to the basic principles of freedom and democracy." For instance, the Carter Center states that it is "guided by a fundamental commitment to human rights and the alleviation of human suffering; it seeks to prevent and resolve conflicts, enhance freedom and democracy, and improve health."[17] As to the "China Village Elections Project" which it began in March 1997, the Carter Center identified four main areas of cooperation with the Chinese Ministry of Civil Affairs:

1   to develop a national computer system for collecting data on village elections;
2   to provide advice and assistance to the MCA on developing uniform election procedures;
3   to conduct exchanges of Chinese election officials with the United States;
4   to assist in the development of civic education programs and publicizing information on village elections in China.

As for the IRI, it was established with the goal of promoting and strengthening democratic ideals and institutions worldwide. IRI aims at meeting the needs of the participants in the host country, offering programs such as training on civic responsibility, the legislative process for newly elected government officials and the mechanics of organizing political parties and election campaigns.[18] As to its Chinese program, IRI wants to support the ability of local electoral institutions to conduct legitimate, competitive elections at village level; it also aims to provide technical assistance to legislative drafting committees of the National People's Congress (NPC) responsible for drafting new commercial laws. The fundamental goal of IRI's work in China is thus to support political and economic reform at both the grassroots and the national levels.[19]

Strategies

How does an NGO translate its goals or objectives into specific actions or activities? This largely depends on the strategies adopted by an NGO. Some strategies IRI and the Carter Center adopt are shared, while others are exclusive.

Networking. NGOs usually emphasize the significance of networking in the promotion of global democracy. "Networks allow NGOs to broaden their scope, as well as to enhance their impact."[20] The value and importance of networks have been abundantly demonstrated in many NGOs' activities. The Carter Center has for instance established a network to work with Chinese officials to strengthen the process by which some 930,000 Chinese villages elect local administrators. The Center seeks cooperation and assistance from other organizations, either government or non-government, whether in China or elsewhere.

The Center has further cemented its cooperative relationship with the MCA and increased the exchange of views with the NPC; such a cooperative effort has proved to be more beneficial in improving the quality of elections in China.

However, it is necessary to point out, because there are few Chinese-run NGOs and their influence is limited, foreign NGOs tend to collaborate more with the Chinese government and not their Chinese counterparts. Anyway, to foreign NGOs, the most effective, if not the only, way to influence the development of rural democracy in China is to find some agencies of the Chinese government and work directly with them.

More techniques, less ideology. Given the claims by the Chinese government that external actors are not allowed to interfere in Chinese internal affairs, in particular in areas such as human rights and democracy, the Carter Center and IRI have prudently resorted to less ideologically loaded tactics. They have focused instead on providing technical support rather than meddling with fundamental issues such as Chinese political pluralism, party rule, etc. Furthermore, they tend to highlight positive aspects of democratic development in their appraisals and reports. In fact, the foreign NGOs have more praise than criticism, in contrast to the negativism of Chinese scholars and officials. This tactic has won NGOs the approval of the Chinese government to enter China for village elections purposes. Understandably, the Chinese government does not take very kindly to "political" NGOs with an ideological inclination. Admittedly, the Carter Center was very frank in pointing out the problems and shortcomings in village elections, but most of its suggestions and criticisms were technical in nature and thus apolitical. The MCA officials were naturally pleased to accept them.

This strategy can be called a "by-pass" one. These NGOs do not overstep nor go beyond what they were there in the first place, i.e. to provide technical assistance. Often, they apply a "band-aid solution" to problems rather than challenging the Chinese government or pressuring it to introduce political reform. This is a dilemma, since the implementation of village election in China is itself a political move; at the same time, it is this very issue of political reform that the foreign actors try not to interfere.

These two major strategies adopted by the foreign NGOs are suitable in China's current social context. Only when they conduct their activities and play their roles within the parameters marked out in these strategies can foreign NGOs hope to attain any measure of success. Indeed, their adoption of these strategies is a reflection of how well they know and understand the Chinese socio-political conditions. The NGOs know that unless they cooperate with the Chinese government, which they see as a major partner, there is very little they can do to promote democracy in China.

Resources

NGOs need and rely on certain resources to implement their programs. One of these is financial resources, which are mainly donations from foundations and individuals. IRI is federally funded through the National Endowment for Democracy (NED) and the US Agency for International Development (USAID), as well as privately funded by donations from individuals, corporations and foundations. The Carter Center is financed by private donations from individuals, foundations and corporations. AT&T Foundation, Ford Foundation, United States–China Business Council, JP Morgan Chase Foundation and Loren W. Hersey Family Foundation also provide financial support to the Center.

Resources required are of course more than economic. Both IRI and the Carter Center also pay close attention to human resource and, in particular, to expertise on laws and elections. The Carter Center is also skilled in capitalizing on Jimmy Carter's prominent stature and reputation. It is this resource that makes the Carter Center an exceptional actor among the external promoters of rural democracy in China. For example, the former US President led a delegation to China from 2–6 September 2001. The visit was to promote The Carter Center's China Village Election Project and observe a village election in Zhouzhuang Town, Jiangsu Province. During the trip, the delegates also exchanged ideas with top Chinese leaders including Chinese President Jiang Zemin, NPC Standing Committee Chairman Li Peng, Chairman Zeng Jianhui and MCA Minister Duoji Cairang on issues of common concern. Mr Carter was able to raise the issue of applying the improved electoral procedures in village elections to elections at the next higher level, i.e. direct election of township/town people's congress deputies.[21]

Major activities and roles of IRI and Carter Center in village elections

Monitoring or observing

The observation of village elections is one of the major activities that NGOs have in village elections; it is also their first step in participating in these elections. Since the interviews with numerous officials and villagers on village elections by Dr Robert Pastor, a Carter Center fellow, during his visit to three villages in Shandong Province in July 1996, the Center has sent several delegations to observe village elections. Table 13.1 shows its observation activities in chronological order.

In May 1994, IRI became the first western organization to observe village elections in Fujian Province. Since then, IRI has observed more than 50 elections in many areas, such as Fujian, Hebei, Jilin, Henan, Guangxi, Shanxi, Sichuan and Yunnan. In July 2000, the IRI-initiated Chinese Program sent one small group to travel to Shanxi Province (6–8 July), Hebei Province (10 July), Henan Province (12–13 July), Guangxi Autonomous Region (13–16 July) and Yunnan Province (16–20 July) to assess the state of village election development and to get a sense of possible directions for further electoral reform.[22]

What have these observations contributed to the promotion of Chinese village elections? One observer Anne F. Thurston noted, "The presence of foreign

Table 13.1 Carter Center's observation of village elections in China

Dates	Investigation locations			Forms of investigation
	Provinces	County/city/township	Villages	
4–15 March, 1997	Fujian	Songjie, Hubing, Fengpu, Chengda Townships of Gutian county	Guanjiang Cun, etc. (three villages)	Focus groups, observation of elections
	Hebei	Chengde city	Fuyingzi, Qui Wo	
2–15 March, 1998	Jilin	Nong An county, Dong Feng county	Gui Jia ling Zi Cun, Heng Dao Cun, Hou Shi Cun	Focus groups, observation of elections
	Liaoning	Jin Zhou district	Cheng Zi, Hai Tou, Mi Tian	
23–26 June, 1998	Fujian	Heshan town of Huli district, Bangtou town, Laidian Town of Xianyou county	Xiangling Cun, etc. (three villages)	Focus groups, observation of elections
19–30 September, 1999	Hubei	Xiantao county	Liujiachang Cun	Observation of elections
4–9 January, 2000	Hebei	Saheqiao town of Qianxi county	San Cun, Daguan zhuang cun	Observation of primary election, official election
31 July– 5 August 2000	Fujian	Shuikou town of Dehua county	Qiuban Cun	Observation of primary election, and interviews
	Fujian	Laidian town of Xianyou county	Xiangling Cun, Liuxian Cun	Official election and interviews
9 January, 2001	Jiangsu	Zouzhuang town of Kunshan city	Quanwang Cun	Official election, and interviews
19 December, 2001	Hunan	Pingtang town of Wangcheng county	Shantang Cun	Official election, and interviews

Sources: *Fujian sheng shi nian cun min zi zhi cheng guo ji (Collection of Fujian Village Self-government Achievements in the Recent Ten Years)* (unpublished) and reports from the Carter Center.

observers during the election process is a strong incentive to organize elections well."[23] While reports by observers provide recommendations to MCA, the visits and investigations by these outside observers appear to have more immediate impact at the grassroots. For example, Fujian's officials have realized the important role that foreign NGOs such as IRI can play. The political elites in the province, such as Mr Zhang Xiaogan, regarded these visits as important resources to help them craft and implement democracy. All in all, the Fujian political elites received some 50 groups of foreign guests, mainly arranged by MCA. Their ideas have been changed and reshaped through their communication with these foreigners. Through their interaction with the guests, the elites have been able to craft their work more effectively.[24]

Providing suggestions for laws and procedures

Foreign scholars and experts from foreign NGOs have put forward suggestions on electoral procedures. IRI, which began observation of village elections in Fujian province in May 1994, has made 12 recommendations for improving the elections. For example, it highlighted that nominations of candidates by consultations or deliberations were not democratic.[25] Before 1994, no secret voting booth had been set up during elections. In view of this situation, the Institute suggested setting up ballot stations. They also recommended that candidates for village committee win election only if they receive more than 50 percent of the votes cast. The elites accepted these suggestions, which are now enshrined as important articles in the Organic Law.[26]

The Carter Center offered specific suggestions on ways to improve the election process. These include standardizing rule, abolishing proxy voting, opening the nomination process, synchronizing village elections within a county, making the election machinery impartial, punishing violations of the election law and encouraging campaigning. In June and July 1998, the China Village Elections Project of the Carter Center held several meetings to discuss the Chinese experts' suggestions for revising the PRC National Procedures on Village Committee Elections. In August, the Center offered proposals regarding the revision of the National Electoral Law for Village Committee Elections, implementation of the Organic Law and Punishment for violation of the Law, election period, secret ballot, eligibility of voters, ballot design and big differential method, proxy voting and roving ballot boxes, and appendices of Model Provincial Measures and Relevant Laws. Table 13.2 shows suggestions offered by the Carter Center and IRI to improve relevant laws and procedures.

Collecting information

The Carter Center provided support to MCA in developing a system for gathering village election results and assessing the implementation of election procedures as defined by relevant rules and laws of China. In a "Memorandum of Understanding Between the Ministry of Civil Affairs, People's Republic of China, and the Carter

Table 13.2 Suggestions made to modify laws and procedures

Items	Problems	Suggestions
Qualification for candidates	Too much specific qualification	Should not list specific qualification
Candidates' nomination	By consultations or deliberations	Formal candidates through a primary vote by all village citizens
Voting	Proxy voting, roving ballot boxes, no secret voting	Secret voting, abolishing proxy voting
Campaigning	Limits on campaigns	Encouraging campaigning, develop clear rules to govern campaigns, permit different kinds of campaigning
Election period	No united election day(s)	Synchronizing elections at least within a county
Voter eligibility	Empty household, non-permanent residents and the retired officials rights, etc.	Minimum residency requirement, etc.
Election fraud and enforcement	Vagueness	Modify election regulations, establish a commission in each province to investigate complaints of fraud
Electoral law for villager committee elections	Non-united National Electoral Law	Establishment of a National Electoral Law or Regulation

Sources: *Fujian sheng shi nian cun min zi zhi cheng guo ji* (Collection of Fujian Village Self-government Achievements in the Recent Ten Years) (unpublished), and reports from the Carter Center and IRI.

Center" (dated 14 March 1998), the Carter Center agreed to help in the establishment of a transparent and rapid national data gathering system.

Crucial election data include indications of the standardization of elections and the aspects of elections in need of improvement. More important, the election results collected can help strengthen faith in rural democracy when more qualified cadres are voted into office. Two forms, the "Assessment of the Village Electoral Process" and the "Report of Village Election Results," have been designed for collecting these two sets of data.

According to the MOU, the Village Elections Data System funded by the Carter Center envisages long-term cooperation in three main areas:

1   design and implementation of a national computer system to collect village data on elections;
2   standardization of electoral procedures and
3   exchanging and publicizing information about Chinese village elections.

Pilot projects were also planned for two or three provinces. MCA selected nine county-level districts from the 2,857 county-level districts in China as pilot districts: Linli, Shuangfeng and Xiangtan Counties of Hunan Province; Huli District (of Xiamen City) and Gutian and Xianyou Counties of Fujian Province; Huadian City and Dongfeng and Lishu Counties of Jilin Province. These places have been recognized as national models of village self-government.[27]

"The Co-operative Agreement between the Ministry of Civil Affairs and the Carter Center to Standardize Villager Committee Election Procedures" was signed on April 2000. This agreement is designed to develop model and replicable electoral practices through various activities including establishing a complete data collection system in Fujian and Jilin provinces and in one-third of the counties in Shaanxi province.[28]

Providing training programs

The training of election officials is very important to the success of any election. Proper training will ensure the efficiency of elections, including good organization, accurate counting of votes, etc. In fact, the highest consideration for all election officials should be "safeguarding the integrity of the election." In this regard, many foreign actors have been able to offer relevant training programs.

Since 1994, IRI has sponsored workshops and training seminars for local election leaders on good governance and national and provincial election regulations and procedures. Since 1996, IRI has sponsored election officials training workshops in eight provinces. Local officials have been trained in the fundamental elements of an election, including candidate voter registration, selection procedure, use of secret ballots and tabulation. For example, in May 2001, IRI sponsored a workshop in Anhui Province to review provincial regulations governing the administration of village elections in that province, which was a build-up to Anhui's fifth round of elections in 2002 (see IRI Website, IRI in China). After the initial training sessions, IRI then focused on training associated with budgeting and financial management and economic development; these areas, according to IRI, are the "natural progression of IRI's ongoing electoral reform program."

The Carter Center has likewise placed a heavy emphasis on training and has organized several training programs. One such program the Center is involved in is the China Rural Official Training Center (CROTC) under MCA. CROTC is a project jointly approved by the United Nations Development Program and the Chinese Government. The overall objective of this center is to promote rural democracy by providing training in villager's self-governance. According to MCA, there are three target groups: committee members elected by villagers who need to know how to manage public affairs; farmers who want to understand how to exercise their democratic rights and government officials who need to comprehend how to guide the villagers' self-governance. In this Program, the trainees include officials at provincial or county Bureau of Civil Affairs who are in charge of promoting villager self-governance and heads of town and township governments.

The Carter Center's involvement with the CROTC's training programs included two seminars. CROTC's first two training seminars on village committee elections were held in Beijing from 23–26 December 2000 and 3–6 March

2001, respectively. Both sessions emphasized resolving trainees' general and theoretical questions regarding village self-government. Speakers and training course leaders were mainly from the following departments: Ministry of Civil Affairs, the State Council, NPC, Central Commission for Discipline Inspection of the CCP and the Carter Center.[29]

The 113 trainees who attended the first seminar represented 29 provinces, municipalities and autonomous regions (Zhejiang and Xinjiang did not send trainees). Twenty-six trainees represented provincial Bureau of Civil Affairs, 41 prefecture-level Bureau of Civil Affairs, 45 county-level Bureau of Civil Affairs and one was a village-level Civil Affairs assistant. Twenty-two trainees were women (19.5 percent) and 91 were men (80.5 percent).

At the second seminar, 141 trainees represented 28 provinces, municipalities and autonomous regions (Beijing, Jilin, Hunan and Hainan did not send trainees). Ten trainees represented provincial Bureau of Civil Affairs, 34 prefecture-level Bureau of Civil Affairs, 94 county-level Bureau of Civil Affairs. One was a county-level Department of Organization assistant, and another a village-level Civil Affairs assistant. There were 22 female trainees (15.6 percent) and 119 male trainees (84.4 percent). It is estimated that 80 percent of the trainees attending both seminars had worked in village self-government for about a year or less.

Besides training programs, foreign NGOs have also helped established one website, organized specialized conferences on village elections and produced publications relating to the subject. The website is on village self-government and is sponsored by the Carter Center. As for conferences, the Carter Center and MCA coorganized an international symposium on villagers' self-government and the development of rural society in China in September 2001. In May 2000, IRI sponsored a regional network conference in Guangxi Zhuang Autonomous Region. IRI itself regarded this conference as opening "a new chapter in IRI's electoral reform program." In December 2002, 50,000 copies of *The National Measures on Villager Committee Elections* were printed with sponsorship from the Carter Center. MCA has distributed 40,000 copies (10,000 per province) of the book to Fujian, Shanxi, Hunan and Jilin provinces.[30] There are reasons to believe that this book will be instrumental in further standardizing and institutionalizing village elections at the national level.

Concluding remarks

After looking in detail the external dimension of rural democratization in China, with the focus on NGOs' support for village elections, some insights can be drawn.

First, it is obvious that foreign NGOs have unquestionably played an important role in promoting village elections in China, and the Carter Center and IRI are exceptional actors among the external promoters of rural democracy in China.

Second, it is also obvious that these foreign NGOs need good domestic partners to help them manage their projects effectively and successfully. Indeed, the establishment of networks is critical to the success of any NGO activities, and NGOs are better off cooperating with the country's governmental than non-governmental agencies. That the Carter Center has been rather effective in the promotion of village elections in China derives, in part, to its maintaining a friendly relationship with the Chinese government, a feat unmatched by any other foreign NGO. IRI and the Carter Center found excellent partners in the MCA and then the NPC. Both were obvious partners for foreign NGOs, given MCA's responsibility in the implementation affairs of village elections and NPC's legislative power.

Third, NGOs should focus on certain non-sensitive areas to promote democracy. Activities run by IRI and the Carter Center show that their assistance was prudently restricted to technically sound but non-controversial areas; such an approach has won the approval of the Chinese government and ensured a continuing welcome for their other programs in the country.

In brief, under the current political system, Chinese democracy will have to be built by internal actors; in other words, the responsibility for democratic development lies with the Chinese people. However, as shown by IRI and the Carter Center, village elections need and will continue to require the support of external actors, even though foreign NGOs are limited in their approach. Moreover, in the age of globalization, the so-called distinction between the internal and the external will become more and more blurred. The interaction, and negotiation, between foreign NGOs and their Chinese partners, in particular the Chinese government, in conducting China's village elections has shown the outworking of the dialectic law governing internal and external factors.

Notes

1 The author wishes to thank Dr He Baogang of University of Deakin of Australia for his comments and suggestions, Mr Wang Zhenyao of Ministry of Civil Affairs and Mr Zhang Xiaogan of the Fujian Bureau of Civil Affairs for their help in the surveys he conducted in Beijing and Fujian in December 2001, respectively.
2 Armin K. Nolting, "External Actors in the Processes of Democratic Consolidation: The European Union and Malawi," in *Democracy and Political Change in the "Third World"*, ed. Jeff Haynes (London: Routledge, 2001), p. 99.
3 Di Palma, *To Craft Democracy: An Essay on Democratic Transition* (Berkeley: University of California, 1990), pp. 14–15.
4 Daniel Kelliher, "The Chinese Debate Over Village Self-Government," *The China Journal*, no. 37 (January 1997), p. 63.
5 Shi Tianjian, "Village Committee Elections in China: Institutionalist Tactics for Democracy," *World Politics*, Vol. 51, no. 3 (April 1999), p. 395.
6 Kevin J. O'Brein and Lianjiang Li, "Accommodating 'Democracy' in a One-Party State: Introducing Village Elections in China," *China Quarterly*, no. 162 (June 2000), pp. 483–484.
7 He Baogang, "The Making of a Nascent Civil Society in Contemporary China" (conference paper presented in February 2002 at Griffith University, Australia).
8 Becky Shelley, "Political Globalization and the Politics of International Non-governmental Organizations: The Case of Village Democracy in China," *Australian Journal of Political Science*, Vol. 35, no. 2 (July 2000), p. 225.
9 Ibid., pp. 226–229.

10 Di Palma, *To Craft Democracy: An Essay on Democratic Transition*, pp. 182–183.
11 Robert A. Pastor, "Democratization and the International Community," in *The Democratic Invention*, eds Marc F. Plattner and Joao Carlos Espada (Baltimore and London: The Johns Hopkins University Press, 2000), p. 108.
12 Ibid., p. 110.
13 Uganda's case seems to give proof to this theory. Susan Dicklitch noted that the relationship between NGOs and the regime in Uganda was not competitive, but complementary. She then pointed out, "It remains complementary only as long as the NGO remains within behavioral parameters accepted by the regime, and linked to the national development plan in Uganda." Susan Dicklitch, "NGOs and Democratization in Transitional Societies: Lessons from Uganda," *International Politics*, Vol. 38, no. 1 (March 2001), p. 36.
14 Paul C. Grove, "The Roles of Foreign Non-Governmental Organizations in Development and Promotion of Village Elections in China," *American Asian Review*, Vol. XVIII, no. 3 (Fall 2000), pp. 114–117.
15 Amy Epstein Gadsden and Anne F. Thurston, "Village Elections in China: Progress, Problems and Prospects" (IRI's report, January 2001).
16 Susan Dicklitch, "NGOs and Democratization in Transitional Societies: Lessons from Uganda," *International Politics*, Vol. 38, no. 1 (March 2001), p. 28.
17 The Carter Center, *What is Our Mission?* URL: www.cartercenter.org/aboutus.html, accessed on October 10, 2006.
18 International Republic Institute, *What is IRI? What type of Work Does IRI Do?* www.iri.org/FAQ.asp, accessed on October 10, 2006.
19 International Republic Institute, *IRI in Asia and the Middle East.* www.iri.org/countries.asp, accessed on October 10, 2006.
20 Claude E. Welch, Jr, "Conclusion," in *NGOs and Human Rights: Promise and Performance*, ed. Claude E. Welch, Jr (Philadelphia: University of Pennsylvania Press, 2001), p. 268.
21 The Carter Center, "The Mission of President Jimmy Carter to the People's Republic of China," September 2–6, 2001. www.cartercenter.org/CHINA/dox/reports, accessed on October 10, 2006.
22 Amy Epstein Gadsden and Anne F. Thurston, *Village Elections in China: Progress, Problems and Prospects* (International Republican Institute, 2001). www.iri.org/asia/china/pdfs/chinaFinalReport.pdf, accessed on October 10, 2006.
23 Anne F. Thurston, *Muddling Toward Democracy: Political Change in Grassroots China* (Washington, DC: United States Institute of Peace), p. 42.
24 Interview with Mr Zhang Xiaogan of Fujian Bureau of Civil Affairs in December 2001.
25 See Robert A. Pastor and Quingshan, Tan, "The Meaning of China's Village Elections," *China Quarterly*, no. 162 (June 2000), p. 492.
26 Interview with Mr Zhang Xiaogan of Fujian Bureau of Civil Affairs in December 2001.
27 See Liu Xitang, *San sheng jiu xian cun min wei yuan hui xuan ju shu ju fen xi ji xiang mu ping gu zhuan jia yi jian* (*Analysis of the Village Elections Data from Nine Counties of Three Provinces and the Experts' Assessment*) (MCA's report, 1999).
28 The Carter Center, "Memorandum of Understanding Between the Ministry of Civil Affairs People's Republic of China and the Carter Center," March 14, 1998. www.cartercenter.org/CHINA/dox/reports/mou.html, accessed on October 10, 2006.
29 The Carter Center, "Training Seminars on Villager Committee Elections," December 23–26, 2000, March 3–6, 2001, in Beijing. www.cartercenter.org/CHINA/dox/seminar.html, accessed on October 10, 2006.
30 The Ministry of Civil Affairs, "The Most Recent News on Village Self-government," December 26, 2001. www.chinarural.org, accessed on October 10, 2006.

Index

For Product Safety Concerns and Information please contact our EU
representative GPSR@taylorandfrancis.com
Taylor & Francis Verlag GmbH, Kaufingerstraße 24, 80331 München, Germany

www.ingramcontent.com/pod-product-compliance
Lightning Source LLC
Chambersburg PA
CBHW070357270326
41926CB00014B/2592